A River
Swift and Deadly

Lee Carraway Smith

Maj. Gen. Fred L. Walker, commander, 36th Division.

A River Swift and Deadly

The 36th "Texas" Infantry Division
at the Rapido River

Lee Carraway Smith

EAKIN PRESS ☆ Austin, Texas

FIRST EDITION

Published in the United States of America
By Eakin Press
A Division of Sunbelt Media, Inc.
P.O. Box 90159
Austin, TX 78709
email: eakinpub@sig.net

2 3 4 5 6 7 8 9

ISBN 1-57168-222-8

To the men of the
36th Infantry Division.
Their courage is the heart of this book.

American forces, on the east side of the Rapido River, can hardly be concealed. Liri River is in foreground. — US Army photo

Contents

The 143rd advances to the edge of the river under smoke screen, January 22, 1944.
— US Army photo

Preface

In the infantry, dying is a necessary cost of doing business. If the infantryman survives his first battle, he comes to expect losses because it is the infantry that moves the arrows forward on the map and advancement has its price. It is the job of the generals to see that the most is gained with the least loss. If the strategy is sound and the operation goes well, the losses are accepted and the process begins again. There are those times, however infrequent, when everything goes wrong, nothing is gained, and even the most veteran officers and men must search deep within themselves to reconcile the terrible losses. This is the story of such a time and of the men in the 36th "Texas" Infantry Division who fought in the Rapido River battle but refused to accept the official explanation for why so many were called to such great sacrifice.

In interviews of over one hundred men from the 36th Division who fought at the Rapido, two emotions stand out. First is the loyalty and love that the men have for one another. Theirs is a close bond forged in the cold and mud of the Italian winter, when supplies were short and replacements for heavy losses of men were slow to arrive. One man stated that he was closer to the men in his company than to any of his brothers. This closeness is at the heart of the Rapido story.

The second is the bravery of the men who went forward in a battle where victory was less likely than death. This is not a story of just the few whose deeds of heroism stand out but, rather, of the average soldier who was called upon to go about the business of war day after day. They did not flinch from their responsibility, and they often did not stand out for special recognition.

Thus, the emphasis of this book is not upon the politics and personalities within the command structure. Instead, it is a view from the foxhole, with a broad overview of the politics and the commanders.

I would like to thank the men of the 36th Division who shared their experiences with me. Special thanks goes to Col. Oran C. Stovall, Maj. Gen. Albert B. Crowther, Maj. Gen. Robert Ives, Carl Strom, Jim C. Maddox, Richard Manton, Rudolph M. Trevino, Julian M. Quarles, James D. Sumner, and Billy E. Kirby. Photos without credits were generously provided by the individuals in those photos. I want to thank my husband and family for their support, patience, and encouragement. I also want to thank Steve Brown and Derek Davis for their assistance in proofreading and for their comments.

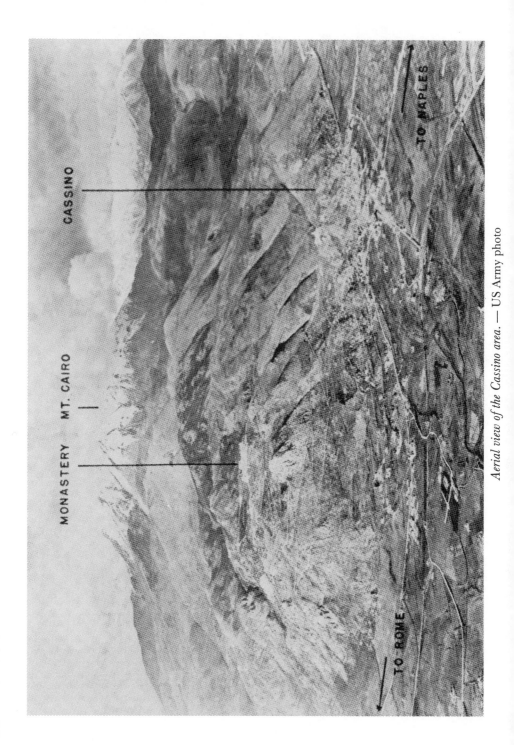

Aerial view of the Cassino area. — US Army photo

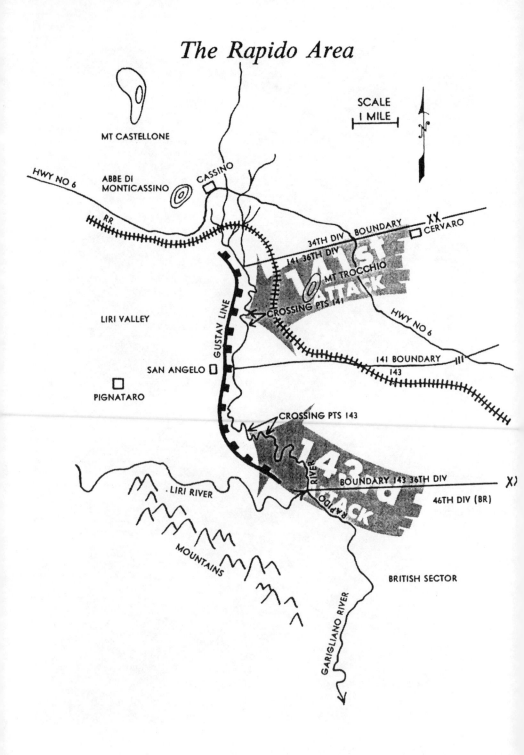

The Rapido Area

SCALE
1 MILE

MT CASTELLONE

HWY NO 6

ABBE DI
MONTICASSINO

CASSINO

RR

34TH DIV BOUNDARY
141 36TH DIV

CERVARO

141 ST ATTACK

MT TROCCHIO

LIRI VALLEY

GUSTAV LINE

CROSSING PTS 141

HWY NO 6

141 BOUNDARY
143

SAN ANGELO

PIGNATARO

CROSSING PTS 143

143RD ATTACK

LIRI RIVER

RAPIDO RIVER

BOUNDARY 143 36TH DIV

46TH DIV (BR)

MOUNTAINS

BRITISH SECTOR

GARIGLIANO RIVER

CHAPTER ONE:

Setting the Stage

The combined factors of an inexperienced and ambitious army commander, political pressure, unheeded tactical advice, constraints of time and materiel, the weather, and an excellent blend of the natural terrain and German ingenuity all merged with deadly force and greeted the courageous men of the 36th "Texas" [1] Infantry Division as they attempted to cross the Rapido River in Italy on January 20, 1944. Almost two full regiments of infantrymen were lost. The Allies planned to advance on Rome after the 36th Division crossed the Rapido River, broke the Gustav Line, and linked up with other Fifth Army forces at Anzio. The failure at the Rapido, along with a snail-paced breakout from the beaches at Anzio, delayed the Allied liberation of Rome for four months. The men of the 36th carried the memory of the Rapido tragedy with them as they fought through Europe, then vented their anger and frustration in a 1946 resolution in which the 36th Division Association called for a congressional investigation of their former Fifth Army commander, Gen. Mark Wayne Clark.

This National Guard division's involvement in WWII began in late 1940, after Hitler's continued aggression in Europe, as well as Japan's alignment with Germany and Italy, broadened the prospects for global war. Congress, pessimistic of avoiding armed conflict in either Europe or the Pacific, passed legislation which al-

1

lowed the National Guard and reserves to be called to federal
service and instituted a draft.[2]

There were eighteen National Guard divisions in 1940 which
were mobilized in a gradual manner from the fall of 1940 through
1941. All eighteen National Guard divisions were "shot through
with state-level politics. Almost without exception, the senior commanders — the generals and colonels — were political appointees
who were militarily incompetent."[3] Gen. George C. Marshall,
army chief of staff, chose Brig. Gen. Lesley J. McNair to fill the position as his chief of staff.[4] McNair, responsible for training the now
former National Guard troops, "had to fire almost every officer in
the Guard from major general through colonel, and a large percentage of the lower-ranking officers."[5]

However, Marshall was "sensitive to national guard politics."
He determined that "there would be no wholesale substitution of
regular army officers for guard officers on the staff level. Even if
there had been enough available regulars, a wholesale substitution
would have caused a counterproductive public furor in the home
state, destroyed the 'state' character of the division and unfairly
blocked the promotion of qualified guardsmen to higher rank."
Regular army commanding generals were to find "the qualified
men in the Guard division and promote them into positions of responsibility."[6]

When President Franklin D. Roosevelt federalized the 36th Infantry Division of the Texas National Guard on November 25,
1940, at Camp Bowie, Texas, he had no way to foresee that these
men would one day be involved in one of the most controversial
battles fought during World War II. At the time of its mobilization,
the 36th Division was under the command of sixty-two-year-old
Maj. Gen. Claude V. Birkhead. Birkhead had served in the 36th
Division for over twenty years, but he was not to be the one to lead
them into battle.[7]

Ten months later, on September 13, 1941, Brig. Gen. Fred L.
Walker was selected to command the 36th Division. Walker was
nine years younger than Birkhead and had been an officer in the
regular army for thirty years. He was well-qualified for the job at
hand.

Fred L. Walker was born in Ohio on June 11, 1887. He served
in the Ohio Cavalry for four years while he attended Ohio State
University. Upon his graduation from Ohio State with a degree of

engineer of mines in 1911, he entered the regular army. Prior to World War I, he served in infantry regiments in both the Philippines and Mexico. In the autumn of 1917, he was promoted to captain and assigned to the 30th Infantry in the 3rd Division, where he was given command of the 1st Battalion. While serving overseas in this capacity, he was awarded the Distinguished Service Cross for the "outstanding leadership" he displayed as the battalion commander during the Second Battle of the Marne, fought July 15–18, 1918. He was also awarded the Purple Heart for wounds he received during the battle. While still overseas he was promoted to the rank of lieutenant colonel and served as the division inspector.

After the war he held various peacetime military assignments, among which was a three-year stint as an instructor in the infantry school at Fort Benning, Georgia. He was a student at the command and general staff school as well as the Army War College, and served a tour of duty in China. On April 19, 1941, he "was appointed" a brigadier general and assigned to the 2nd Division in San Antonio, where he served as assistant division commander until he was given command of the 36th Division.[8] General Walker's selection as commander of the 36th Division was due in large part to the recommendation of General McNair's deputy chief of staff, Brig. Gen. Mark Wayne Clark. Clark told McNair, "I believed Walker was the man for the job." [9]

On September 13, 1941, while on maneuvers in Louisiana, Brigadier General Walker was notified that he had been placed in command of the 36th Division, relieving Major General Birkhead. Since the 36th Division was also participating in the Louisiana maneuvers, Walker was able to assume his post quickly and immediately began to evaluate the officers in his command and the morale and readiness of the division. Fifteen days later the Louisiana maneuvers concluded, and the 36th returned to Camp Bowie. On October 2, Walker recorded in his journal, "Although I had some misgivings when I was assigned to the 36th, I have become devoted to its personnel during the past two weeks because of their wholehearted cooperation and enthusiastic desire to comply with all of my directives." [10] With the declaration of war following Pearl Harbor, Walker was promoted to major general on January 13, 1942.[11]

The 36th Division was reduced from a square division to a triangle division in February 1942. This meant that one of the four regiments, the 144th, was removed from the division and assigned elsewhere, thus reducing the division's strength from 22,000 men to 16,000 men. The three remaining infantry regiments, the 141st, 142nd, and 143rd, were made up of 3,600 men each. Other units within the division were reduced in size accordingly. The War Department deemed the new triangular division alignment to be more maneuverable and economical in manpower and materiel than the prewar square configuration.[12]

Rapid growth of the army necessitated the removal of many key personnel and cadre from the 36th to other army units. Some of these vacated positions were filled with new men from states other than Texas, but due to the War Department's slowness in sending officer replacements, many junior-grade officer slots were filled by promoting outstanding NCOs and enlisted men already in the division. Thus, while the division did begin to lose some of its "all Texan" character during early training, many Texans were retained in key positions.[13]

The 36th Division moved to Camp Blanding, Florida, in February 1942 and continued to train.[14] On April 17, Brig. Gen. Mark Wayne Clark, now chief of staff of McNair's Army Ground Forces, visited the 36th Division. Major General Walker noted in his journal, "Wayne has come up fast within a year from major to brigadier." [15] The two men's paths first crossed in the 1930s, when Walker was Clark's instructor at the Army War College. They crossed again in 1938 at Fort Lewis, Washington, when Walker was the executive officer of the infantry regiment in which Clark was a major. Walker noted, "We were there for some 18 months and became very good friends, although he is much younger than I." General Walker also noted, "Wayne said that I am on General McNair's list to be a corps commander. I told him I was pleased, but knowing his predilection for such 'carrots' I do not take it too seriously." [16]

A month later, on June 21, 1942, Walker noted that Wayne Clark had been promoted to major general and assigned to command II Corps. "Clark, who is many years my junior, is now in command over me," Walker wrote. "This is in line with the policy of General Marshall and the War Department of putting youth in command in the theater of operations. I think this policy is a mistake. To replace experience with inexperience means a slowing down in battle efficiency until the youngsters acquire the knowledge they lack. Many of us, who served in combat units in World

War I, have a lot of practical experience that should be used now." [17]

The 36th Division spent from July 19 until August 14, 1942, in the Carolinas on maneuvers.[18] By August 21 they were in Camp Edwards, Massachusetts, for various types of special training and remained there until they were shipped overseas.[19]

By the time the division ended training in the States, the enlisted ranks were down to about sixty percent Texans, but it would be mainly Texan officers and NCOs that would lead the men of the 36th overseas and into combat.

CHAPTER TWO:

Baptism of Fire

In April 1943 the 36th Division was ordered to North Africa as an element of Lt. Gen. Mark Clark's newly formed Fifth Army. There they continued to train, but five months would pass before the 36th would see combat. During this time they received training in mountain and amphibious operations.[1]

Fifth Army was trained and ready for combat, but their first combat assignment would have to wait for the Allied forces to finish the campaign in Sicily. After Sicily, the Allies turned their attention to the Italian mainland. Clark would send his Fifth Army ashore at Salerno. Two of his divisions, the 34th and the 36th, were available for the Salerno landing in September 1943. The 34th Division had experience in battle in North Africa as part of Patton's II Corps[2] but Clark said, "I selected the 36th for the initial attack because I felt it had good leadership and high caliber personnel." [3]

When the men of the 36th waded ashore at Salerno on September 9, 1943, they became the first American unit that fought on the mainland of Europe in World War II.[4] That they fought only the Germans surprised the men because they had prepared to fight both Germans and Italians. While on the ships to Salerno, the men of the 36th heard Gen. Dwight D. Eisenhower, supreme commander of Allied forces in the Mediterranean, announce via radio that "hostilities between the United Nations and Italy have terminated, effective at once." The armistice between the United Nations and Italy was completed on September 3, when the Italian government accepted terms of unconditional surrender. The Italian government agreed to transfer its naval and air units to the Allies and to withdraw its army from occupied territory and the front line in Italy. However, the announcement of Italy's capitulation "was delayed until the last minute to permit the Italian army to stop fighting and still not allow the Germans time to occupy the coastal defenses. The commanding officers, however, believed that even with such short notice the Germans might have been able to take over the entire defense and that resistance to the invasion would stiffen." [5]

The troops of the 36th reacted to news of the Italian surrender with mixed feelings. Some were angry that the war, for which they had trained so long, was practically over because they felt the Germans would withdraw from Italy after Germany lost her Italian ally. Others felt relief that the surrender would lessen the enemy they faced that day. From the moment they landed on the Salerno beaches, the men of the 36th found that the Germans were a motivated and disciplined enemy who would not easily yield Italy despite the Italian surrender.[6]

Despite German resistance, the Allies secured the beachhead at Salerno and then moved on with their assault of southern Italy.[7] The men of the 36th entered Naples by the end of September, after which General Clark cabled his wife: "in the grand manner of conquerors: 'I give you Naples for your birthday.' " [8] With their foothold in Italy firmly established, the Allies gained a vital harbor at Naples which allowed resupply of Fifth Army units as they pushed northward.[9] Clark was pleased that they gained the air bases that the Allies needed, "principally Foggia." [10] These airfields allowed "two-way" bombing of Germany from the south.[11] The Allies were in command of the entire southern tip of Italy after they secured the south bank of the Volturno River on October 6.[12]

At the same time in early October, Adolf Hitler, against the advice of one of his most brilliant tacticians, changed his strategy in Italy. Originally planning to withdraw his forces behind Rome and to hold only northern Italy,[13] he now desired a counter-offensive to retake "southern Italy and perhaps even Sicily." He consulted his two top commanders in Italy, Field Marshal Erwin Rommel and Field Marshal Albert Kesselring. Rommel felt Hitler's plan would not work, fearing that the Allies "would tie down frontally the mass of the German forces engaged in southern Italy and then make a surprise landing . . . in the Po Valley in order to cut off the German forces and thus collapse the entire front of the 'Fortress of Europe.' " Kesselring felt Hitler was correct in opting to fight in southern Italy.[14] Hitler was unsure which of his commanders to agree with; however, he did not want to lose Rome to the Allies because he felt control of Rome was necessary for Mussolini to establish his "puppet regime." [15] In November 1943, Hitler's decision was to appoint Kesselring chief of the southwest command.

Fifty-eight-year-old Field Marshal Kesselring had a long and distinguished military record that began when he joined the 2nd Bavarian Foot Artillery Regiment in 1904. He served in the German army in both the field and on the staff during World War I. From 1930 to 1931, he commanded the 4th Artillery Regiment in Dresden. On October 1, 1933, he was discharged from the army and took up the position of head of the administration office of the Luftwaffe. Kesselring, long fascinated with air power, had learned to fly in his late forties. He commanded the 1st Air Fleet in the Polish war and was awarded the Knight's Cross of the Iron Cross at the end of the Polish campaign. Later he commanded the 2nd Air Fleet, which took part in the Battle of Britain, as well as the invasion of Russia. Early in 1942, Kesselring and his air fleet were transferred to Italy. Hitler's appointment of commander-in-chief-south gave Kesselring authority over all German forces in the Mediterranean.[16]

The Germans lost no time in strengthening the "Winterstellung" [17] winter line, which was a series of three different lines known to the Allies as the Barbara Line, the Bernhard Line, and the Gustav Line.[18] At the forward was the Barbara Line, an "ill-defined and hastily constructed position resembling a strong outpost line of resistance; it ran from Monte Massico located near the west coast through the villages of Teano and Presenzano and into the Maltese Mountains." [19] The Bernhard Line formed a "wide belt of defensive positions anchored on the mouth of the Garigliano River, on the forbidding masses of Monte Camino, Monte la Difensa, Monte Maggiore and on the bulking height of Mont Sammucro." [20] The Gustav Line, the strongest of the three, was "based securely on the Garigliano and Rapido Rivers and the natural fortress of Monte Cassino. The Gustav Line ran along the Matese range and into the Sangro River in the Adriatic sector." [21] Control of the mountainous area south of Rome now was critical to both sides in the Italian campaign.

In mid-November 1943, the 36th Division relieved Maj. Gen. Lucien Truscott's 3rd Division and began a series of mountain fights as they inched their way up the Italian boot.[22] A horrible winter fell upon them, and "mud became the only alternative to the mountains. Transportation became virtually useless in the forward area." [23] Cold, rain-soaked, and muddy, the men of the 36th carried all supplies by hand up steep mountain trails to the front line. The 36th continued to fight under these conditions and captured San Pietro, Mount Lungo, and Mount Maggiore. Finally, the 34th Division relieved the "Texas" division from the front line on December 29.[24]

The 36th Division suffered heavy losses during the winter battles. In addition to the loss of men from death and battle injuries, many of the men began to experience trench foot. This painful and often debilitating disorder was caused by the lack of circulation in wet, cold feet. The men were supposed to take their shoes off once a day and rub their feet, but this was not always possible when they were engaged in combat.[25] When the division was pulled off the front lines in late December, the regiments had been severely depleted of infantrymen. It was hoped the rest period would be long enough for the regiments to rebuild, with sufficient time for all of the men to rest and for those less seriously wounded and ill to recover and return to the division before they had to go back to the front.

CHAPTER THREE:

The Allies Plan While the Germans Prepare

Hitler's decision to hold and defend the Bernhard Line caused grave concern among the Allied commanders and "set the stage for the bloody battles of the Rapido River, Monte Cassino, and Anzio." [1] On October 24, Gen. Harold Alexander, commander of the 15th Army Group,[2] informed Winston Churchill and Gen. Dwight Eisenhower of his concern that the Allies might find themselves involved in a "slogging match" that would leave the troops exhausted and unable to hold their position when they reached the northern side of Rome. General Eisenhower cabled Alexander's warning to President Franklin D. Roosevelt. Two days later, Roosevelt received a cable from Churchill which stated he felt they were "sinking in Italy" and that "at all costs we must win Rome and the airfields north of it." The Italian campaign was designed "to draw the Germans into southern Italy and to keep them there when they should have been thinking of reenforcing the eastern front where the Russians were breaking through and getting ready on the western front where the Western Allies were just about to land." Thus, Churchill felt the Italian campaign had helped "Russia advance in the only way in which it could have been helped at the time." [3] He felt Alexander and Eisenhower should have whatever they needed to win the battle in Italy, "no matter what effect is produced on subsequent operations." [4]

10

During late November and early December, Churchill took advantage of the time he spent with President Roosevelt and Marshal Joseph Stalin at the Tehran Conference to express his desire to invigorate the campaign in Italy and present his plan for Operation Shingle, an amphibious landing at Anzio. Churchill regarded war as a "romantic calling, a gentleman's game," and Italy was one game he did not intend to lose.[5] In early November, Churchill told Alexander to draw up a plan for an amphibious assault on Italy for early 1944. General Alexander decided Anzio would be the best location for an amphibious landing, with the goal of advancing to Rome and eventually into the Po Valley. Churchill introduced his plans for the Anzio assault, code-named Shingle, during the Tehran Conference. Shingle would require 88 landing-ship tanks (LSTs) to be retained in Italy.[6] There were 104 LSTs in Italy, but Eisenhower had scheduled 68 of them to be sent to England where the Allies planned to store supplies they would need for Operation Overlord, to be staged in June 1944. By Christmas, Churchill convinced Eisenhower to recommend to Roosevelt that the LSTs needed for Anzio remain in Italy until February. Four days later, Roosevelt gave his approval with the understanding that Shingle was not to delay either Overlord or Anvil.[7] Anvil, an attack across the Mediterranean on southern France, was to take place shortly after the troops in Overlord crossed the English Channel. "The southern attack . . . was designed to split the enemy defense in France and facilitate" the main attack.[8] On December 27, 1943, Mark Clark wrote, "The Prime had once again demonstrated his ability to force decisions, and it was a decision with which I fully agreed." [9]

Churchill had provided the opportunity, Alexander had provided the site, and it was up to the inexperienced Clark[10] to provide the attack plan. Salerno was the first battle in which he commanded an army.[11]

Mark Wayne Clark began his military career after he graduated from West Point in April 1917, 110th out of a class of 139, and received his commission as a second lieutenant. Almost immediately he became ill and was on sick leave for six months. He worried that the loss of time would affect his career.[12]

However, in December 1917, the army assigned him the command of Company K of the 11th Infantry, 5th Division, stationed in Georgia. His new command put him in charge of 200 men. He made a good impression on his commander, Maj. R. W. Kingman, and less than a year later he attained a temporary wartime rank of captain. Thirteen months after graduation, Clark was in France.

Clark hoped to advance his rank and position of authority while he served in World War I, but his dream of advancement in the infantry was short-lived. One month after he arrived in France, Major Kingman became ill and he recommended Clark take over his position as commander of the 3rd Battalion as it prepared for battle. Three days later, Clark found himself in his first and only battle of World War I. Clark and his men spent the first two days marching so they could "get into position to relieve the French." The next day they rested until dark, at which time they were able to move forward. "Americans shuffled and stumbled in the darkness to replace French soldiers who walked to the rear." [13] The Germans shelled the area and killed one private and wounded Clark.[14] Six weeks later, army doctors judged Clark unfit for infantry duty. The decision of the army doctors not only removed Clark from the infantry career he so desired, but also placed him in positions where promotions would come slower. Biographer Martin Blumenson felt that Clark's "motivation to excel probably stemmed from his desire to emulate, then redeem his father. Col. Charles Carr Clark had an ordinary career." [15] Clark had no choice but to accept an assignment to the position of staff officer with the Army Supply Section.[16]

Although Clark had hoped for an infantry assignment, he was instead given a series of peacetime staff positions for which he proved well-suited. Clark remained a captain in the regular army from November 1919 until January 1933, when he rose to the rank of major. Seven years later, he attained the rank of lieutenant colonel and served as deputy chief of staff and later as chief of staff to Lt. Gen. Lesley J. McNair in Washington, D.C. By that time it was necessary to integrate the many draftees into the ranks, and Lieutenant Colonel Clark used this assignment to showcase his skills as an astute organizer and planner.[17] Once again, the impression Clark made on his superiors paid off. A good impression was important to him because he saw it as the only way he could move up in the military structure during peacetime. When he transferred from Fort Lewis to Washington, D.C. in 1940, he took with him "[ten] boxes of professional books." [18] However, Clark was not one to spend much time reading. As the rank in his graduation class indicated, Clark was "no intellectual," and friends guessed that "his yearly ration of books amounts to two at the most." [19]

The onset of World War II gave Lieutenant Colonel Clark another chance to rise rapidly in the ranks. He did an excellent job for McNair and a year later, in 1941, he skipped over the rank of colonel and became a brigadier general. Clark received a promotion to major general in April 1942, and a month later he and General Eisenhower flew to England to prepare for the buildup of American forces in the European theater.[20] "As chief of the American ground officers in England he was also, probably, General Eisenhower's closest intimate in the story-book development of the North Africa Campaign." [21] Seven months after his promotion to major general, Clark rose in rank again on November 11, 1942,[22] when he received his third star and was the "youngest lieutenant general in the history of the United States Army." [23] Less than two months later he was given command of the Fifth Army.[24] Clark's meteoric rise in rank and influence exceeded even his expectations: "Among his fellow officers only his friend Dwight D. Eisenhower had risen faster than he." [25]

Initially, Eisenhower's opportunity for advancement was made possible by Clark. "Eisenhower became chief of staff of the Third Army, stationed in San Antonio, in June 1941, under the veteran Gen. Walter Kruger. Apparently he was first called to Kruger's attention by Mark Clark." [26] Later, Clark recommended Eisenhower to Gen. George C. Marshall, the U.S. Army chief of staff, when Marshall needed to replace the chief of his war plans section after Pearl Harbor. "Many years later Eisenhower told Clark, 'You are more responsible than anybody in this country for giving me my opportunity.' No doubt he was referring to Clark's kindness at Fort Lewis as well as bringing Eisenhower to Marshall's attention." [27] In an opportune twist of fate, Clark's friendship with Eisenhower also helped Clark gain the prominence he had attained.

When Alexander assigned Clark to plan the Anzio invasion, "Mark Clark had reached the supreme moment in his career." [28] He had longed for an opportunity such as this all of his adult life. "Ambition was a good thing, Clark felt, because it forced a man to drive himself. And now he would drive himself ruthlessly." [29] In his book *Calculated Risk*, Clark recorded his goal: "I was determined that the Fifth Army was going to capture Rome and I probably was overly sensitive to indications that practically everybody else was trying to get into the act." [30] The closer Clark got to Rome, "the more he resented playing second fiddle to a British general. Certainly in his view, he deserved to be recognized as the real commander in Italy." [31] The risk was great. If he succeeded he would be the hero, but if he failed he could ruin his chances for further advancement, not to mention harm the Allied movement in Europe.

General Alexander's "formal instructions" to Clark concerning the Anzio-Rapido attack were that "the Fifth Army was . . . directed to make as strong a thrust as possible towards Cassino and Fronione . . . prior to the [Anzio] assault landing to draw . . . enemy reserves which might be employed against the landing forces, and . . . create a breach in his front through which . . . to link up rapidly with the seaborne operation." [32] General Clark decided to "assist the amphibious landing at Anzio" by launching a "massive attack against the Gustav Line, particularly those stationed in the Rome area; and to break through the Gustav Line then speed up the Liri Valley to a quick juncture with the Anzio forces." [33] He planned the assault on the Gustav Line to occur in four phases, the first of which would begin on January 12, when the French Expeditionary Force, 2nd Moroccan and 3rd Algerian Divisions, were to attack and seize the high ground to the north and northwest of Cassino. Three days later, the 36th Division and the 1st Armored Division were "to secure" Mount Trocchio.[34] The British 46th Division was to make two crossings of the Garigliano River on January 17. They were to make one crossing not far from the coast and another just to the left of the juncture with the Rapido on the left flank of the 36th Division. Finally, on January 20, Gen. Fred L. Walker and his 36th Division were to make the main thrust across the Gustav Line by crossing the Rapido River and breaking into the Liri Valley. Then the 36th was to join up with armor and proceed through the Liri Valley to a link-up with the rest of the Fifth Army that was to land in Anzio on January 22.[35] General Alexander offered to transfer troops to Clark. Winter weather hampered the New Zealand Corps, part of the Eighth Army, and they were available to Clark if he wanted them. Clark declined Alexander's offer because he felt it would take too much time to move them into battle positions. Clark was on a tight schedule due to the limited time the LSTs would remain at his disposal before the priorities of Overlord and Anvil claimed them.[36]

Meanwhile, the Germans busied themselves with their plans

to strengthen the Gustav Line after they chose the area of Cassino as the "hard core" of their main defense.[37] They could not have made a better choice. For generations, the Italian Military College had used Cassino as a classic example of an impregnable natural defense barrier.[38] Although any senior Italian officer could have told the Allied commanders that the Germans would likely make a defensive stand there, apparently the Allies never consulted them. The speculation is that there was "no awareness among the higher Allied echelons that Cassino might prove any more difficult than what had gone before." [39]

One reason this area was so valuable to the Germans was the observation it afforded. In World War II, observation was the key to success in a land battle. Gunnery techniques and wireless sets of the times could "direct the guns of an entire army within a few minutes on any target" visible.[40]

Although the Germans would try to defend the Barbara and Bernhard lines "stubbornly," they were determined to hold the Gustav Line.[41] The Gustav Line covered "about 100 miles" through the middle of Italy.[42] It stretched from the port of Minturno at the Tyrrhenian Sea and followed the Garigliano and Rapido rivers to the Liri Valley, where it crossed the valley to the town of Cassino "along the [five]-mile promontory of Monte Cassino" and then went up into the "wild Abruzzi mountains." [43]

The monastery of Monte Cassino, founded by St. Benedict in the sixteenth century, dominated the area which encompassed the Gustav Line.[44] The Benedictine Abbey loomed 1,700 feet above the towns, rivers, and valleys. It was "a vast breath-taking flying buttress of cream coloured travertine stone, at one point 220 yards long, its bronzed roof gleaming under the winter sun." [45] The mere sight of it was awesome, and the threat of its use as a defensive position was an effective deterrent to attack.

As the war slogged on through the muddy winter of 1943, increasingly this brilliant structure became a menacing symbol of an omniscient enemy that the Allies sensed was within its walls. Cpl. Stewart T. Stanuell, Battery C, 155th Field Artillery of the 36th Division, said, "The monastery was the first thing you saw in the morning and the last thing you saw at night." [46] T/Sgt. Owen Arnold, 1st Platoon, C Company, 141st Infantry Regiment of the 36th, said, "You could look up there and see this thing and knew . . . those people were up there . . . To me it was a horrible thing be-

cause they could see everything we would do. That's the reason . . .
we hid during the day in camouflage, where they couldn't see us.
But you could always look back up and see that rascal — it could
control the whole valley. There were not any enemy troops in there
but they were dug around there — they had to be because any time
some of our people would make a move . . . *kerwham* — they'd hit
us. And we didn't see them." [47]

The Americans thought Germans were inside the Abbey,[48] but
Field Marshal Kesselring had "given express orders" that no Ger-
mans were to enter the Abbey. Kesselring posted a guard at the en-
trance of the Abbey to make sure that his men obeyed the order.
Kesselring did this to preserve the Abbey from Allied bombs.[49]
Gen. Frido von Senger und Etterlin was commander of the 14th
Panzer Corps which would oppose the 36th Division at the Rapido.
The former Rhodes Scholar at Oxford, a devout Catholic and lay-
member of the Benedictine order, noted, "I was only too pleased to
agree that the principal abbey should be spared from military operations. Nobody would want to sponsor the destruction of a cul-
tural monument of this kind merely to gain a tactical advantage.
But even under normal conditions Monte Cassino would never
have been occupied by artillery spotters. True, it commanded a
view of the entire district, the town and the Via Cassilina. But on
our side it was the considered tactical opinion that so conspicuous
a landmark would be quite unsuitable as an observation post, since
we could expect it to be put out of action by heavy fire very soon
after the big battle had started. It was the German practice to place
the artillery observers halfway up the hills in a concealed position
with a camouflaged background." One exception to Kesselring's
order occurred when General von Senger attended mass at the
Abbey on Christmas, 1943, "to confirm that no German soldiers
were visiting the place." [50] He continued, "When entering the gate
I saw the barrage-fire of several hundred guns of both belligerents
at my feet, but I did not study the view from any of the windows of
the convent." [51] From the German positions on Monte Cassino an
observer could watch every move in either the Liri or the Rapido
valleys. Even in the moonlight it was possible from this vantage
point to pick out the shapes of hills four miles or more away.[52]

The natural terrain of the area along the Gustav Line was excellent for defense, and General von Senger was determined to
make it even better. With the help of his 14th Panzer Corps and a

large detachment from the Todt Labor Organization, General von Senger transformed the Gustav Line into an infantryman's nightmare. He blasted the mountainsides to prepare gun emplacements, enlarged natural caves, and created new caves that could house men and weapons. He covered these with materials from the mountain to hide them from aerial reconnaissance. Then he positioned machine-gun nests on the mountainsides in such a fashion that any attacker would face interlocking machine-gun fire. Both sides of the Rapido River were laced with barbed wire, mines with trip wires, and different devices to make noise to alert the defenders. He located cement pillboxes on both the mountainside and in the valley farmhouses. The general found the mountain gullies were the perfect places to set up mortars because the gullies not only provided the angle needed to fire the weapons but also provided protection from Allied artillery. Three months after he had begun, General von Senger and the Germans were prepared to defend the Gustav Line.[53]

About the same time, around January 7, 1944, though General Walker had not received orders to cross the Rapido River, his instincts told him that it would be a likely crossing site at some future date. Walker called his division staff engineer, Maj. Oran C. Stovall, and asked him to make an engineer estimate of the situation for planning purposes.[54] Stovall knew that the first job of the division engineer was to make an estimate of the situation before any river crossing or forward movement was made.[55] He flew in a Cub plane and went as "far forward" as he could because they did not "own" the river at the time.[56] He also interviewed civilians and prisoners of war. He checked and made map studies of the topography as well as the width of the river, with possible approach locations in mind. The crossing sites had to be within a certain sector. II Corps determined the sector boundaries. After looking over the area and gathering the information, he picked the crossing sites.[57] Stovall stated, "And then my plans of my observations were used by the original commanders who made the crossing and they approved my crossing sites, as did the commanding general and the general staff." [58] Due to the conditions Major Stovall observed in his reconnaissance work, he estimated "first that it would be impossible for us to get to the river. Secondly, that we couldn't cross it, and third, if we got across the river there was no place to go." [59]

Major Stovall submitted his engineer estimate to the corps en-

gineer, Col. Leonard B. Gallagher, and the 19th regimental commander from II Corps, Col. Joseph O. Killian, who was going to
support the 111th Engineers, for their approval. Both men approved the plan and agreed with Major Stovall's findings.[60] Colonel Killian was surprised that he would be assisting the 36th Division. He said originally the 3rd Division was going to be the
division that would cross at the Rapido River. Then plans changed
and the 3rd Division was diverted to Anzio.[61] General Walker
noted in his journal that Colonel Gallagher and the assistant corps
engineer, Colonel Wilson, agreed with Major Stovall that "any attack north of Cassino will be blocked by mountains. They looked
upon the Liri Valley as a muddy bottleneck, guarded by an organized defense behind an unfordable river, without suitable approach routes or exits." Stovall had stated that "any attack made
north or south of Highway 6 would create an impassable situation
and end in failure and result in the loss of a great many lives. Gallagher and Wilson were not opposed to his views." [62]

General Walker worried that the Rapido presented a mirror
image of a situation he experienced in World War I at the Marne
River. He was in command of the 30th Infantry Regiment in the
3rd Division. On July 15, 1918, he helped the division achieve the
name "The Rock on the Marne." He recorded that on that day ". . .
a German division of about 10,000 men made an attack across the
river. In good defensive positions along the Marne, my battalion of
1,200 soldiers turned the Germans back, disorganized, confused,
and slaughtered them. That experience taught me the great advantage . . . the defenders of an unfordable river have over the attack-
ers. I was particularly impressed because my men were fighting
their first battle against veteran German soldiers." [63] General
Walker was well aware that in 1944 the situation was reversed.

On January 12 the 36th Division moved a step closer to their
destiny at the Rapido when Clark ordered them to move into the
"Mt. Porchia–Lungo–Rotondo area" as they replaced the 6th
Motorized Infantry, which was part of the 1st Armored Division,
just east of the Rapido River.[64] The next day orders came to move
forward to the Rapido. Walker noted in his journal, "As yet, no official word that we are to cross it. However, I strongly suspect we
will have to cross it and in my conversation with Clark and Keyes I
have mentioned the difficulties involved. They do not want to talk
about them."[65] General Walker silently "wrestled with his doubts

and fears without daring to reveal his feelings to his subordinates. He even considered asking to be relieved from his command in protest." However, he could not leave his men to fight the battle with a new commander. "In retrospect, the general's decision was the only possible one. He had to lead the Division into this attack, knowing that none of his officers or men could refuse to partake in the forthcoming battles. For the soldiers, from the General down to the GI, there was no alternative." [66]

On January 15 the 36th Division attacked, took Mount Trocchio, and was in control of five miles along the Rapido River. The next day, January 16, General Clark met in conference with his senior commanders and "outlined his plans for the next phase of the Fifth Army's northward drive." His proposal called for an "immediate thrust across the Rapido River by an infantry division" to secure a beachhead. The First Armored Division would "pour" across the Rapido beachhead and would "pound" up Highway 6 (the Via Roma) through the Liri Valley toward Rome which was ninety miles away.[67]

General Harmon, commander of the First Armored Division, was present at the meeting. He recalled that every commander at the meeting promptly rejected Clark's plan: "With an unaccustomed unanimity, [they] all pointed out that such a tactic was impossible because the enemy controlled both of the ridges overlooking the valley." Unless the Allies controlled at least one of the ridges, it would be unreasonable to expect success.[68]

Clark overruled the counsel of his senior commanders and confirmed Walker's worst fears. Clark firmly stated, "The 36th Infantry Division would cross the Rapido and establish a beachhead; then the First Armored would throw a bridge across the river and bring up its tanks." [69] At last, after weeks of speculation, Walker knew that the Rapido River lay in wait for the 36th Division. Four days later, Walker's men would face the Germans there. Walker doubted four days was enough time to prepare for the crossing.

CHAPTER FOUR:

Final Preparations for the River Crossing

Immediately after General Clark confirmed that the 36th Division would be ordered to cross the Rapido River, General Walker began to make the final necessary preparations. It would be up to the 141st and 143rd Infantry Regiments to get the job done. A few weeks before, the 142nd and 143rd had practiced launching boats on the Volturno River, but Walker did not think the practice would help much because, unlike the Rapido, the Volturno was a very placid river. The 142nd Infantry Regiment was not available to the 36th Division for the Rapido because it was held in corps reserve during the attack.[1]

As G-2, Lt. Col. Albert B. Crowther was responsible for information concerning the strength and placement of the enemy the 36th Division would face at the Rapido River. He began to gather information about the German strength as soon as the division arrived in the area, around January 12. Crowther stated "I was always very careful — I had to be because General Walker, whom I served, was a man who wanted factual information . . . not theory . . . I had a lot of respect for him . . . he was a fine person and . . . I was going to be sure that every bit of information was as correct as I could possibly verify and we had the time to do that at this Rapido River action." During the daylight hours, he was able to gather information from reports that came in from divisional obser-

20

vation posts. He sent out patrols at night and was responsible for coordination of all patrols from all the regiments and battalions. The information gathered by these two means helped him to know what was going on in the regions close to the river.

In order to gather information on the area farther back from the river, Crowther studied aerial photographs that revealed some artillery positions. However, artillery strength and position were primarily "estimated" by observed counter-battery fire and patrol reports. On the basis of such intelligence, Crowther concluded that "their depth was outstanding."

Crowther also received information from OSS agents who landed with the 36th at Salerno and infiltrated behind German lines dressed "in native clothing." These agents sent intelligence information back to "higher headquarters" which would "filter it down" to the division level.

Crowther recalled he had "a fine group of interrogators who, interestingly enough, were young German Jews who had come to this country before the European war started and they were university graduates. It wasn't easy to get prisoners . . . who could give you some valuable information . . . Capturing an officer was very difficult . . . The officers were usually . . . very arrogant and you couldn't get much out of them." He said the enlisted men were more willing to talk. "They had a lot of Austrians in those units — they hated the Nazis but they were afraid of their [officers and NCOs] because if there ever was any indication that a man was going to surrender when they shouldn't, they wouldn't hesitate to shoot him."

As far as the Rapido River action was concerned, Crowther had reliable information about the enemy and their disposition. "The whole position in that area . . . was strongly organized. They had organized anti-tank weapons in depth . . . to repulse any kind of an armored attack — for seven . . . to ten miles. In back of that they had reserve units that were complete divisions — motorized divisions and others that could have reached our front . . . within a twenty-four-hour period. We established . . . a main line of resistance where they had trenches and concrete pillboxes where they had their strong points — their automatic weapons and heavy machine guns."

Crowther said he was involved in a number of conferences with the planning staff, which included General Walker and Walker's son, Lt. Col. Fred L. Walker, Jr., who was the G-3 (operations officer). Crowther said there were also conferences with their counterparts at the corps level and at the army level. General Gruenther, chief of staff for the Fifth Army under General Clark, was always present at those meetings. The men discussed alternative plans of attacking, Crowther recalled, and "time and time again . . . everybody would say it was impossible at this time and [at] this strongest point [with] limited roadway access to use armor — all the negative things about it." When orders to make the attack were received, he thought it "unbelievable." The first Crowther had heard that the decision had been made was early one afternoon shortly after lunch. "General Walker had just returned from a meeting and he told me, 'I'm going to have a conference tonight . . . of all the regimental commanders because we've been ordered to attack across the Rapido River.' "

Walker told Crowther that he wanted him to brief the commanders about the situation. Crowther said, "We talked a few minutes about it and I told him, 'General, it's going to be awfully hard for me to keep from sounding so pessimistic about this.' " Crowther told Walker that it might influence how some of the regimental infantry — the regimental commanders — felt about the plan. "General Walker said, 'Well, you must be very careful . . . You just give them the enemy situations — don't make any comments other than that.' But they could see it of course — they knew what they were going against." [2]

Major Stovall, after submitting his engineer estimate to division and corps, had been gathering the supplies needed to prepare for the crossing. He went to the Fifth Army supply officer and the Fifth Army "didn't have anything," so he went to the Fifth Army engineer, Gen. Frank O. Bowman, for the supplies he needed. It was General Bowman's responsibility to get the necessary supplies for the crossing and, according to Stovall, "he must have known there would be such a crossing for two or three months." Major Stovall knew he would need reconnaissance boats and footbridges for the crossing, but there was not a footbridge in Italy like he needed. General Bowman's second in command asked Stovall if he had an appointment. Stovall said, "Well, certainly not — I'm the only fighting engineer unit in the line and I came for help." The officer told Stovall that he had to have an appointment to see the general. Stovall commented, "It was the only time they even suggested such a thing." Major Stovall left Bowman's office and went to Naples "to see what [he] could scrounge up." He located pneumatic boats that could hold three men and M-2 plywood boats that could carry eleven or twelve men as well as two engineer operators. The design of the wooden boats better suited a river that was wider than the Rapido, but they were the best Stovall could find at the time. He also found some Bailey bridge walkways, which he thought he could modify into makeshift footbridges.[3]

Using the Bailey bridge walkways, Stovall did fashion the footbridges. He recalled, "I put 2x12s across . . . and lashed them to [pneumatic boats]." Then he lashed the Bailey bridge walkways to the 2x12s. "It was just a Rube Goldberg thing . . . it wasn't any good, but I couldn't get anything any better." [4]

After the 36th took the area which faced the Rapido, Stovall was able to verify some of the information he had acquired earlier in January. The regimental commanders approved Stovall's selection of crossing sites, just as General Walker and the general staff had. Two battalions of the 19th Engineer Combat Regiment from Fifth Army, under the command of Col. Joseph O. Killian, were assigned to assist the 111th Engineers. As division engineer, it was Major Stovall's responsibility to coordinate all of the engineers' tasks. With the addition of the two battalions, the work could be divided. The 111th Engineers would prepare the area and get the necessary boat and bridge equipment into the area, and the 19th Engineers would assist in the actual crossing. The 111th Engineers would immediately resume their support of the infantry on the other side of the river after the area was in the hands of the 36th Division. Major Stovall said Killian was a "splendid gentleman. One of the finest men I ever knew and a very capable engineer."

If it had not been for Major Stovall's ingenuity, the men of the 36th would have faced a river crossing with no bridges. In addition to eight of the improvised "Bailey bridge" footbridges, he had his shop construct a bridge using three-quarter-inch pipe.[5]

Capt. Clifton "Jack" Bellamy of the 111th Engineers, Stovall's operations officer, drew up the general plan for the employment of all engineer troops — "all subject to Major Stovall's approval." Bellamy stated, "On almost any operation you have enough of what you need." But the situation was "worse at this battle." Bellamy came up with the design for a three-quarter-inch pipe bridge.[6] Stovall needed four pipe bridges. The engineers were able to build one pipe bridge, but they ran out of time before they could make the other three.[7]

It was also up to the engineers to remove the mines from the Allied side of the river. Many of the men had trained while blindfolded so they could defuse mines in the dark.[8] Companies A and C of the 111th Engineers and two other companies from the 19th Engineers worked on removing the mines. The engineers worked at night under the cover of darkness because the Germans on the other side of the river could see every movement on the 36th's side, and they had a constant aim trained on the Americans. Major Stovall used six men on their hands and knees to get the mines out. They used bayonets to probe the area in front of them as they inched their way down to the river. Although it had not rained in the area for about ten days, mud "shoe mouth deep" covered the entire area.[9] The engineers were able to get many of the mines out but, even if they had been able to work in daylight, it would have been impossible to find all of the mines the Germans had planted in the Italian blackland soil. Darkness, mud, and the limitation of time made the mine-clearing operation hazardous and difficult, and often incomplete.[10]

The engineers used tape to mark the "clear" lanes that led to the river. The troops would travel down these paths on their way to the river the night of January 20. Unfortunately, the Germans could see the white tape as easily as could the Americans, so the engineers switched the lane markers from white tape to brown marline cord. Because the brown cord was less visible at night, the soldiers could follow it only by holding it in their hands. This method was safer because the white tape would have been covered in mud very shortly after the troops began walking to the river and would have been lost in the mud and darkness. By using the brown cord, it was harder for the Germans to preset their guns on the lane markers.[11]

"Buck" Sgt. Donald Barnett, A Company, 111th Engineers, was a squad leader at the time of the Rapido. He and his squad were among the groups of men who worked on clearing the minefields in the 141st sector. Barnett recalled that night when seven or eight of the men were close together, down on their knees. "This fellow is right here and another guy here. And you're probing. And he comes this way and you go that way, probing with a probing instrument . . . You can't get way ahead of the others. You had to go pretty close together and when you got all across it just scoot up a little bit and go again for 100 or 200 yards." He continued, "They had these little personnel mines . . . box mines . . . just enough to blow your hand off if you hit one . . . or if [you] stepped on it, blow [your] leg off." [12]

On January 17, Maj. Luther H. Wolff, a physician in the Eleventh Field Hospital, noted, "The infantry of the Thirty-sixth Division is now on the left bank of the Rapido River, and we are getting an epidemic of horrible mine wounds with traumatic amputations of one or both legs. The Germans are using a new type of nonmetallic mine called 'shue mines,' which cannot be detected except by probing. 'Tellar' and 'Bouncing Betty' mines are bad enough but these little shue mines are worse. One lad with a leg off told me he stepped on the first mine while putting a rubber raft in the river for a patrol. Litter bearers came up; one of them stepped on another mine, and another leg was lost. A doctor came up, stepped on still another mine, and was killed." [13]

Barnett stated, "They had S mines [shrapnel mines] . . . if you stepped on them there was a prong sticking out and if you stepped on that" the ball bearings inside would "shoot out . . . jump, and burst just over your head . . . Personally I never did get in contact with those." These mines were also referred to as Bouncing Bettys.

The Germans also had Tellar mines. Barnett described these as "big, round mines filled with TNT. Tellar mines are mostly anti-tank mines." These mines were often booby-trapped with a hidden wire tied to the detonator that would set the mine off as the men walked past. Barnett said, "You just feel around and try to dig under them and see if that detonator is on under there and hope there isn't. If there is . . . you need to be awful careful to try to get it out. Well — more likely you could tie onto it and pull it . . . You had to be awful careful about disarming that thing because they're real easy to go off . . . you would have to have . . . something that could disarm it by putting a pin in a hole . . . to keep that thing from jumping and setting it off." [14]

Barnett's squad didn't find any mines that night. The Germans would toss the mines out in a random fashion and then bury them where they landed. Barnett concluded, "There might have been some mines over there twenty feet from us, but we didn't get any in that group." As the men cleared each little section forward, they would lay down white tape to show the area was clear. They cleared a wide path to the river for the men to walk down to the river. When they got to the edge of the river, they "could hear the Germans on the other side talking and digging." [15]

Capt. Ernest L. Petree was the commander of C Company, 111th Engineers, in support of the 143rd Infantry Regiment. He and his men were also on their hands and knees as they probed for mines with bayonets while they cleared a path for the 143rd Infantry to walk down. When they found a mine they "would find the edge of it and uncover it by hand." Then they would "take the fuse out and stack them up." They worked on the minefield at night and spent their days getting equipment ready for the crossing.[16]

Capt. O. Wayne Crisman commanded B Company, 111th Engineers. Normally, B Company supported the 142nd Infantry Regiment. With the 142nd Regiment held in corps reserve during the Rapido battle, the engineers in B Company were freed up to assist in other ways. During the Rapido action it was B Company's responsibility to maintain the roads that led to the river.[17]

The roads of rural Italy that served donkeys and carts well for centuries now became quagmires under the weight of tanks and trucks. The muddy Italian roads were barely suitable for foot traffic, much less heavy vehicles. B Company had to work at night. Crisman said, "We'd work on the roads as far forward as we could, but we had to wait until they were ready to cross until we could move forward because they wanted to maintain secrecy."

Crisman continued, "We didn't have much gravel but we would use mainly bulldozers on them to build them up as high as we could. Some places we'd use logs to support the vehicles . . . Whenever we could get timber we would build the roads up so they would drain and then if possible board them — use board roads." They were only able to get one road prepared and they also opened "up some trails in other areas." Crisman recalled, "I don't think any of them got all the way to the river." [18]

The men of the 36th would have had to carry the boats and bridge equipment from the supply area behind Mount Trocchio to the river by hand, even if the roads had been in better condition. The Germans were close enough they could have heard the noise of the trucks as the men drove toward the river.

Platoon Sgt. Alfred Dietrick, B Company, 141st Infantry, recalled a daytime reconnaissance patrol to the river on January 17 that had somewhat dubious results. Led by Lt. Martin J. Tully, the patrol made their way toward the river but en route they encountered an Italian farmhouse still occupied by a family. The family offered the six men some *vino* and, as any infantryman would do in the interest of goodwill, they accepted the offer several times over. After leaving the farmhouse they found themselves in an open area with the lieutenant up ahead. As they proceeded through the clearing, Lieutenant Tully told his men, "Hey, you guys watch these wires here." Dietrick then realized the lieutenant had led them into a minefield. As Dietrick remembered, "He walked right through it! We all walked right through [the minefield]." [19]

Lt. Gabriel Navarette, E Company, 141st Infantry, the former first sergeant of E Company who had recently received a battlefield promotion, went on two patrols of the Rapido River. The first patrol went well and he returned safely to his company area. During the afternoon of January 17, Lieutenant Navarette was on Mount Trocchio looking at the far side of the river through some "very powerful field glasses" when he noticed "consertina barbed wire on the other side of the river." Navarette mentioned the barbed wire to his captain a short while later, and told him, "Look, this is not in this report." The captain agreed and later that evening he sent Navarette's platoon on their second patrol across the Rapido. Navarette looked around for the best approach to the river, and once he found it, he had to figure out the safest way to get his men down there through the minefields. Navarette took the lead and instructed the men to only step in his footprints. One of his sergeants told him that he would go out in front because the lieutenant would be more valuable to the men once they got to the Rapido. The sergeant, also a very strong swimmer, tied a rope around his waist and swam across the river. Once across the river, he secured the rope and Navarette and the rest of his men grabbed the rope and pulled themselves across the river in a rubber reconnaissance boat.

When Navarette's patrol neared the consertina wire he called for one of his soldiers. "I told him, 'You go straight through here and you will find that consertina wire. You cut the wire . . . make two or three cuts there so we can go through.'" Navarette gave him some wire cutters and sent him on his way. Navarette continued, "But . . . that was not my intent . . . in other words I was using him for a decoy . . . Sometimes you have to do things like that in . . . war . . . once he [got] to the wire . . . I [knew] they would fire on him

. . . and we would be able to see where the fire was coming from . . .
and then . . . maybe we could make a flanking movement.

"While he was cutting the barbed wire [the Germans] tried to
shoot him . . . firing at him with machine guns . . . he was hit in the
back . . . not bad — just a scratch. Then I saw where the machine
guns were . . . so we made a flanking movement and then we got
the machine guns . . . they had some infantry there too . . . they
started to go back . . . We kept following them . . . to their main
body and then, of course, since we were only a platoon we had to
retreat."

By that time, Navarette was wounded. He saw the Germans
coming closer and he sent his men ahead of him back to the river
bank. Navarette said, "There was a German there that I could kill
. . . [I] got my hunting knife and I opened him up to get a lot of
blood. Then I put the blood on my face and when the Germans
came over . . . they saw me there and they just kicked me aside . . .
I acted . . . like I was dead . . . Finally, when the Germans left . . .
I started to see which was the best way to go back . . ." By this
time, the morning of January 18, Navarette knew he couldn't do
anything in the daytime, so he waited there until dark. Navarette
recalled when he reached his men in hiding by the river "there was
a tree by the river and . . . the Germans way back saw us and they
started firing mortars at the tree."

Capt. John L. Chapin was across the river in radio contact
with Navarette and he was instructing Navarette to get on the boat,
but Navarette kept telling his men to get in the boat and go across.
Captain Chapin radioed Navarette once more and told him that
this time he meant for him to get in the boat. Navarette got in the
boat, and when they were halfway across the river a mortar shell
hit right in the middle of the boat. The shell didn't injure the men
because it exploded under the water. The men swam back to the
German side of the river and waited until they could send another
boat over.[20]

Captain Chapin sent 2nd Lt. Richard M. Manton and his platoon to assist Navarette and his men. Manton stated, "We carried
a rubber assault boat and some rope. One of my brave men . . . vol-
unteered to swim across the river with a rope tied around his waist.
We tied the other end of the rope to the rubber boat. He was a
strong swimmer and he made it to the opposite shore and then
pulled the boat across. A few men at a time got into the rubber boat

and we pulled them back across the stream. While we were doing this the enemy began shelling us with mortar fire. We had no alternative but to hang onto the rope and continue to pull the boat back and forth until everyone was across the river safely. God must have been with us, and watching over us, because none of us was hit by the mortar fire. Navarette's patrol was quite badly shot up, but once on our side they were all able to get back to the company." [21]

On the afternoon of January 18 or 19, Maj. Armin F. Puck, provost marshal, spent some time with General Walker discussing plans for two traffic sections that Puck would establish after the bridges were installed for vehicles. He was to have one assembly area in the 141st sector and another assembly area in the 143rd sector. The men were having this discussion in Walker's truck, and as Puck took his exit he glanced at the war tent and saw General Clark, General Keyes, and several other men leaving. Clark and Keyes made their way over to the truck. Puck saluted the men and told them that General Walker was in this truck. He asked if they would like to call for the general or just go in. Puck continued, "So they went in — the two of them — and I stuck around. For some reason the door was open and I heard Clark specifically say, 'Now Fred, I want you to make every effort to get troops across that Rapido River and if we have a break through and join up with Anzio — My God — what we' — words to that effect." [22]

Capt. Richard M. Burrage, commander of headquarters, 1st Battalion, 143rd Infantry, attended a meeting "with about twenty officers" at the 143rd Regimental headquarters on the afternoon of January 19. The regimental commander, Col. William H. Martin, told the men, "We had a hard time at Salerno, we'd had a hard time coming on up through . . . but this was one battle we had a chance to . . . prove ourselves." Burrage stated, "He was trying to boost the morale . . . He was a very dedicated person. I don't think he was overly concerned about his men as opposed to his mission." Burrage continued, "General Martin did his best . . . the division told us down to the exact company what the formation would be — who would go — and there was no latitude for [Colonel] Martin or my commander — then Major Frazior — to exercise any independent judgment." [23]

On January 19, as work continued to prepare the crossing site, commanders sent out final reconnaissance patrols to gather the latest information available. Night listening patrols were also used to reconnoiter the Germans' positions. Platoon Sgt. Alfred Dietrick, B Company, 141st Infantry, recalled such a patrol on the night of January 19 that ended his "career" with the 36th. "If you listen at night at the front you can hear a pin drop . . . any slight movement . . . anybody [that] takes a step [or] a voice . . . will carry through [to you]." While on patrol Dietrick's leg slipped into a crevice and he tore all the ligaments in his knee. His knee began to swell and eventually locked into place. Reluctantly, he went to the aid station and was sent back to the hospital. He would miss the Rapido battle by one day.[24]

On the morning of January 20, despite unprotected flanks, the crossing areas lay ready for the men of the 36th to use that night. The engineers had cleared the mines as best they could and they had marked the lanes the men were to use. There was little or nothing the men of the 36th could do about the lack of protection on their flanks. Earlier attempts by the French and British on each flank had failed.

On January 12 the French had succeeded in gaining a small dent of about four miles in the Gustav Line. By January 15 the French troops were exhausted and had to rest. They had had a rough three days due to the Germans, the weather, and the terrain.[25] Though they had breached the Gustav Line, they had failed to take the high ground north and west of Cassino as Clark had outlined in Phase One of his plan.

On January 17, as Clark had planned, the British Tenth Corps crossed the Garigliano River and, with the aid of naval artillery support, established an initial small beachhead. German defense of the area was light and a heavy fog concealed the British troops as they moved into the area. The British were able to establish a small beachhead of four miles within the Gustav Line.[26]

Kesselring immediately reinforced the area with two Panzer-Grenadier divisions. Kesselring stated, "That made the Allies' task more difficult."[27] Ernst-Georg von Heyking, with the 3rd Panzer-Grenadiers in Italy during the time, recalled, "When the British 10th Corps break [sic] through at the southern Garigliano my division was reserved along the coast. We were brought here very rapidly to stop the British because General von Senger was afraid that a breaking in could become a breaking through." [28]

To the disappointment of the 36th Division, on January 19, a day later than expected, the British Tenth Corps made another unsuccessful attempt to cross the Garigliano River. The British 46th Division was supposed to cross the river just to the left flank of the 36th. Their mission was to break the Gustav Line and provide protection for the American unit as it crossed the river the next night. The British made one or two brief attempts to cross the Garigliano but soon withdrew. They did not make much of an effort toward crossing because they felt it would be impossible to accomplish a river crossing there. The 36th would have to cross the Rapido the next night with no protection on either flank.[29]

CHAPTER FIVE:

The First Attack

General Walker felt the failure of the British to cross the Garigliano and provide protection on the left flank was "an omen of the future." To best insure a successful crossing, he would need the cover of darkness. He had scheduled the crossing for 8:00 P.M. General Clark called General Walker on the phone that evening, Walker recorded in his journal, "and sent his best wishes; said he was worried about our success. I think he is worried over the fact he made an unwise tactical decision when he ordered troops to cross the Rapido River under these adverse conditions." Walker noted, "However, if we get some breaks we may succeed. But they will have to be in the nature of miracles." [1]

General Walker wanted to be out with his men that night, but he knew it would be best if he remained at his command post where he "could be better informed" and where he "could better influence the course of the battle." Walker continued, "Actually, I will have little influence on the battle because everything is committed; I have no reserves; use of artillery ammunition is restricted; and I have no freedom of maneuver." General Walker sent his assistant division commander, Brig. Gen. William H. Wilbur, to the 141st Command Post where he could keep a close eye on the proceedings.[2]

Nine days before his fifty-fifth birthday, General Wilbur re-

placed Brig. Gen. Otto F. Lange as assistant division commander
on September 15, 1943.[3] Wilbur, who graduated from West Point,
twenty-fifth in the class of 1912,[4] was awarded the Medal of Honor
while still a colonel, for a mission he undertook in North Africa in
1942. Shortly after that, he was promoted to the rank of brigadier
general.[5] General Wilbur, a member of Gen. George S. Patton's
staff, requested that Capt. James D. Sumner, Jr., serve as his aide-
de-camp. Sumner recalled, "I had known him back in the States
. . . He was entitled to an aide-de-camp but the highest ranking officer that a brigadier general could have for an aide-de-camp [was]
a first lieutenant. And at that point I was a captain . . . This man
was living with General Patton and . . . General Patton told him he
would have me transferred to General Patton's headquarters and
put into the Intelligence Section but that I would be his [Wilbur's]
unofficial aide." [6]

Sumner described Wilbur: "He was a very, very disciplined,
dogmatic, intelligent, highly educated man. He was probably one
of the best informed and educated men in the military . . . He
didn't exactly have what you would call a very pleasing personality. He was a very blunt . . . outspoken individual and he just
pulled no punches at all. He was a very, very tough man and de-
manded absolute discipline and so forth . . . I think that's the reason he made a lot of enemies among his officers." [7] A number of the
36th Division officers nicknamed their assistant division commander "22 Dash Wilbur," because the infantry field manual was
22-5[8] and they viewed Wilbur as strictly by the book. Sumner continued, "Probably without a doubt . . . Wilbur was one of the greatest tacticians that the army had . . . the only thing wrong with him
was that he was many years ahead of the time . . . in addition to
that he had a crass personality."

Sumner later became the executive officer of the 3rd Battalion,
143rd Infantry Regiment in the 36th Division. General Wilbur visited with Sumner in the battalion headquarters and of the visit
Sumner remembered, "I know he . . . thought it [the Rapido at-
tack] was a tremendous tactical blunder." [9]

General Walker's desperate hope for a few breaks would go
unanswered, and there were no miracles evident for the men of the
36th on that cold night of January 20, 1944. At 7:30 P.M. the 36th
began a heavy artillery barrage directed at targets on the German

side. Thirty minutes later, the artillery stopped and the 141st and 143rd infantry regiments began their trek across the river.[10]

The 141st and 143rd regiments made the initial crossing, with the 142nd Regiment in reserve. The 1st Battalion of the 142nd was stationed east of Mount Trocchio, temporarily under the control of the 36th Division. If the 1st Battalion was not committed by the 36th, it would revert back into corps reserve. The 2nd and 3rd Battalions of the 142nd Infantry Regiment remained in corps reserve and were ordered to assemble east of Mount Trocchio. They possessed corps orders for attack should the 141st and 143rd regiments be successful in their crossings.[11]

The area between Mount Trocchio and the Rapido River was flat, cleared, and muddy. The Germans had removed any trees or brush native to the area so that the men had to cross between 500 to 1,000 feet of open land. Some of the paths were sunken below ground level.

Swollen by winter rains, the Rapido River ran cold and swift in front of its cleared approaches. It resembled an oversized mountain stream as it flowed a fast four to five miles per hour. Though only thirty yards wide, its swift flow and steep banks, which rose three to four feet above the water, made it a difficult crossing site even under ideal conditions.[12] 1st Lt. Julian H. Philips, G Company, 143rd Infantry Regiment, recalled, "The river was a bad affair. The first time I saw it, I thought I could jump it." [13] However, he said, it would have been easier to carry out such an operation over a wider river, as the launching sites would have been less vulnerable "out further from the enemy." A wider river would have allowed the 36th Artillery "to plaster the enemy bank during the launching and even for a part of the journey across." The Germans would have been less informed about what the Americans were doing and where they were doing it.[14]

Although Major Stovall picked four crossing sites in his engineer estimate, he suggested to Walker that both infantry regiments should use the two available points at the "S" bend of the river because the area was not as marshy and afforded better protection for the men.[15] Walker ordered the 141st Regiment, under the command of Lt. Col. Aaron W. Wyatt, to cross at the "S" bend of the river north of the village of Sant' Angelo. He ordered the 143rd Regiment, under the command of Col. William H. Martin, to cross south of there not far from the site of the abortive British attempt the night before.[16] Lieutenant Colonel Wyatt had been in command of the 141st since the middle of December, when he replaced Col. Richard Werner, who had been wounded during the battle for San Pietro.[17] Colonel Martin had been in command of the 143rd since before the 36th left the States.[18]

★ ★ ★

The 2nd Battalion of the 141st Infantry Regiment was held in regimental reserve on January 20. Maj. Milton J. Landry, commander of the 2nd Battalion, was ordered to "make a demonstration" that would indicate a crossing was being made south of the designated crossing area. Major Landry maneuvered his battalion into position by infiltrating a few men at a time "through German lines" over a period of three or four days. Landry stated, "We were promised that if we could take this river line then we wouldn't have to cross it — they'd send a replacement outfit up to take our place." [19]

The 1st Battalion, 141st Infantry Regiment, was commanded by Capt. Erman W. Newman. Companies A, B, and C from this battalion were ordered to cross the river at 8:00 P.M. on January 20. They were to capture and occupy their primary objectives on the other side of the Rapido River and be prepared before daylight on the 21st to attack Sant' Angelo from the north and capture it in conjunction with the 143rd Regiment.[20]

Companies I, K, and L in the 3rd Battalion, 141st Infantry Regiment, were ordered to cross the Rapido an hour later, at 9:00 P.M. on footbridges the engineers were to install after the attack began. They were ordered to capture certain objectives and be prepared before daylight to attack Sant' Angelo from the west. They were to assist the 1st Battalion with the capture of Sant' Angelo.[21]

During the afternoon of January 20, Captain Newman, 1st Battalion commander, issued his orders for the crossing that night. Lt. Col. John C. L. Adams, who was assigned as an observer with the battalion, was impressed with Captain Newman. Adams noted that Newman "clearly and briefly passed his instructions." Adams continued, "His past battle experience was very evident in his careful attention to . . . checking on details . . ."

Shortly after the meeting, the 1st Battalion received a message that a "lucky (?) hit destroyed 29" of the battalion's rubber boats. Adams accompanied Newman as he "investigated to see if it was merely lucky." The officers discovered the boats were apparently

hit by one volley. Adams noted, "[Our] investigation left us still
doubtful . . . The dump area and the road approach (along which
jeeps, T.D., Infantry, and Engineers) had been going for days . . .
was under observation from Monte Cassino and other high ground
near San Angelo. (La Pietra defilladed the dump from view only
from the direction of San Angelo.)" Captain Newman made
"prompt and effective change of plans to meet the situation." [22] He
left the dump at 7:00 P.M. "with a wire party to establish the 1st
Battalion forward command post at the river." [23]

Capt. Selsar R. Harmanson, B Company commander, 141st
Infantry, "called a critique for all [his] NCOs at a farmhouse just
before the attack." T/Sgt. C. P. "Buddy" Autrey and the others
were well aware of the dangers that faced them. Autrey said, "We'd
been up there and seen what the river was — we had been on patrols." Autrey continued, "Captain Harmanson passed out cigars
to all the NCOs in the room. We all lit up. It's a wonder all of that
smoke in the room didn't kill all of us." One of the things Captain
Harmanson said at the meeting was, "This is going to be a surprise
attack and I don't want you saying anything. I don't care if you're
drowning I don't want you to say anything." Years later Autrey
mused, "I've often thought about all the preparatory shelling, etc.
It always amuses me how meticulous he was." [24]

Companies A, B, and C cleared the final assembly area by
6:00 P.M. and proceeded to the engineer boat dump to pick up their
boats and their 19th Engineer guides.[25] The night was dark with all
traces of the moon and stars obscured by a cold, thick fog. The 19th
Engineer guides with B Company turned at the wrong place; instead of guiding the men to the "S" bend of the river, they guided
them into the vicinity of the forward battalion command post. The
column of men had to be turned around and "a great deal of confusion resulted during which an enemy artillery barrage was laid
into the area." [26] Technical Sergeant Autrey, B Company, stated,
"The big mistake of the operation was carrying the boats and
bridge equipment. We were exposed for too long a time in those
roadways while we were going down the lanes. [In] certain places
it was necessary to get off the roadway. We got into a minefield and
a number of men were killed. All [of] that time that we were exposed . . . they knew we were coming and we paid dearly in the
flood plain on the way to the river." [27]

2nd Lt. Carl Strom's Third Platoon, B Company, 141st In-

fantry, was selected "by the luck of the draw of the cards" to lead B
Company's attack across the river. This was Strom's first battle,
but he had observed the area across the river earlier in the day and
he knew the crossing would be difficult.

His men struggled down a muddy, sunken road as they carried
the heavy plywood boats on their shoulders in sixteen-man teams.
The darkness, mud, and a full complement of combat gear made
the burden of the 400-pound boats even greater. "You could hardly
see your hand in front of your face and they were struggling down
this sunken road . . . they were tripping on the sides of the banks
and so forth," Strom recalled.

As Lieutenant Strom, with his runner and an engineer guide,
waited at the river for his men, he perceived that the river would be
difficult. But Strom would soon know just how terrible a task his
men faced. His men were 200 to 300 feet from him when two "German shells came in and . . . landed either on the boats or between
the boats and . . . wiped out my whole platoon except for me and
my runner who was with me." The shells killed the company commander, Captain Selsar R. Harmanson, and severely wounded the
company executive officer, Lt. Martin J. Tully. Chaos erupted.
They had to clear the bodies, the wounded, and the area, and at
the same time continue to help other platoons as they came down
the path to press the attack.[28] Lt. Martin Tully was wounded in
the leg during the barrage, but he continued to guide men to the
river and helped clear debris until he collapsed, after which he was
evacuated from the area.[29]

"Although it was his first night of combat, Lieutenant Taylor,
now the senior officer, became the company commander and had
to reorganize his men," Strom said. "I don't know what happened
to Arnold, but Taylor was the company commander and he'd been
in combat just exactly as long as I had. Around midnight, Lieutenant Taylor got them to the river." [30] T/Sgt. C. P. "Buddy" Autrey
recalled, "We had so many casualties that we had to drag the boats
the last several hundred yards because we didn't have enough men
to carry them." [31] Strom recalled, "The poor guy [Taylor] . . . got
us down to the river and I was bringing up the rear with some of
the fellows and we . . . tried to launch the boats — the ones that
were left. Some of them had holes in them, which we were not
aware of because you couldn't see [them]. Each boat held twelve to
fifteen men. We loaded up a couple of boats, pushed them out in

the stream, and they sank because they had holes in them. The men carried forty to fifty pounds of equipment and between fifteen and twenty of them drowned. The men that could, swam to either shore." [32]

The men of the 36th continued to try to launch the boats across the Rapido. Autrey remembered, "At the river they slid the first boat down the bank, which had a forty- to fifty-degree slope, and put it into the water tip first. It sank immediately. I tried to tell them to put the boats into the water sideways because of the slope and the current." The engineers had attached ropes to the boats and the men were supposed to paddle across the river. Men on the opposite shore would drag the empty boats back across the river so they could be used again. Autrey recalled, "The guys were paddling but the current was washing us downstream. I reached over the side of the boat and tried to fill my canteen with water and a guy in the rear of the boat hollered, 'Water is coming over the stern.' We had reached the end of the rope." The engineers had estimated the boats would drift fifty to one hundred yards, but the current was so swift it carried the men much farther down the river. Autrey said they were "suspended in the middle of the river." [33] The engineers cut the rope, and the boat, now quite full of water, sank. The men in the boat were thrown into the river.

Autrey was wearing his newly issued combat uniform, which consisted of "roomy pants with a lot of pockets." The pants had a twill exterior and a double lining made of wool. The jacket was also twill with a double wool lining. He also had on a wool overcoat. In addition to his clothing he had a sniper's rifle, grenades, a field phone, and a map case. Despite all this, he grabbed hold of Pvt. Carl W. Buckley, who was having difficulty swimming, and tried to drag Buckley with him as he swam to the German side. "Our gear got wet and pulled us under. I had to let go of the young man and he drowned . . . Eight of twelve of us drowned and four swam to the German side." [34]

The current had moved the four men 500 to 600 yards downstream from where they were supposed to be. Autrey removed his heavy, soaking wet combat uniform after he got to the German side of the river. He stated, "We didn't know about the booby traps and land mines on the German side." He told the men to put their feet where he put his and they moved slowly back down the river bank. "When we got to the place where we were supposed to be, we shouted across the river but no one could hear us. We couldn't use the field phone because we didn't have any wires up." Wet, cold, and without weapons, the four men remained on the German side of the river until mid-morning the next day.[35]

The Germans began shelling the 36th sector after the first American artillery barrage, and they continued to cover the area with artillery fire, interlocking machine-gun fire and mortars. Neither the darkness nor the fog hindered the German fire because their guns were locked on the area. "Crack German troops raked them with every weapon of warfare, when they plunged into the swiftly moving waters of the Rapido." [36]

The engineers were able to get a footbridge across the river around 4:00 A.M., and the men began to trickle across the river into the teeth of withering German fire.

Once the men crossed the Rapido, they encountered barbed wire, mines, and booby traps. The Germans lost no time in turning artillery and machine guns on the Americans and the shelling was so intense "the ground shook like jelly." [37] The men in B Company sought cover where they could. The lucky ones crawled into ditches and shell holes filled with water. They could not raise their heads without drawing intense German fire. The Americans could not seek advice from their commanders because German fire destroyed all communication lines that led to the other side of the river.[38]

The men of Company B realized they had no hope of meeting their objectives without communication, armor, and reinforcements. Their only hope of survival was to make their way back across the river as soon as possible. Some were able to recross just before dawn on January 21, others had to wait until that night.

Fog subdued the light of dawn on the 21st. Autrey and the three other men with him located a footbridge which had been erected after they had crossed the river. "The bridge lacked meeting the opposite bank by twelve to fifteen feet," Autrey recalled. "We waded out to the footbridge and came back [across the river] and we were looking for our unit — it didn't exist except for the few men still pinned down on the other side." [39]

After Second Lieutenant Strom's platoon was destroyed by the incoming German shell, he no longer had a command. He attached himself to another platoon and eventually crossed the river on a footbridge shortly after 4:00 A.M. They spent the day unable to raise their heads out of the water-filled holes and ditches in which they sought a semblance of cover. Strom recalled, "Periodically during the day the Germans would drop . . . heavy shells in there and if you stuck your head up you'd automatically draw machine-gun fire." A machine-gun bullet grazed his helmet but he was not hurt. "Men were being killed and wounded all around." They stayed there all day without a working radio. No support troops arrived. Strom threw a smoke bomb toward the house that had been their primary objective in an effort to draw American artillery fire — no artillery support came. "A little observer plane came over a couple of times but nothing happened." The pilot "didn't call any fire in or anything . . . there was no fire from our side of the river ahead of us. The only thing that was coming through was German."

Shortly after dusk, as dark descended, Strom said, "Okay let's go back. There's not enough of us left to do anything here." The remnants of B Company made their way back to the river and located the bridge on which they had crossed the night before. According to Strom, "both ends of the bridge were blown out but the ropes were still in the center part of the bridge over the deepest part of the water." They were able to get their wounded on the bridge and crossed the river. Strom noted when he finally got back to Mount Trocchio "there were fourteen men and two officers left in the company." [40]

On the night of January 20, the 19th Engineers who led A Company to the river wandered into a minefield. The men in A Company found themselves stranded in the minefield with their company commander, Lt. Warren G. Beasley, severely wounded. Beasley could no longer function, and Lt. Clarence M. Artymovich assumed his command.

Lieutenant Artymovich was unable to make contact with the 1st Battalion command post, so he attached A Company to "3rd Battalion elements which had come up, to await the installation of the footbridges." [41] Much of A Company was able to cross the river at about 4:00 A.M. on the footbridges in the 3rd Battalion sector.

By daylight, Lieutenants Roscoe and Artymovich, with the men of A Company, were as far as the barbed wire which surrounded one of the German strongpoints. Artymovich, CO of A Company, and most of his men were killed there. "Roscoe and two men were not hit and swam back across the river." [42]

On the 20th, C Company, 141st Infantry, commanded by Capt. John McCain, didn't fare much better than A Company.

They, too, went through a minefield, but they were able to extricate themselves from it without much delay and then made their way to the river. 2nd Lt. William E. Everett, 4th Platoon, C Company, recalled, "We supposedly had guides to take us through the minefields and all [of] that went to hell with the confusion of the German artillery, *nebelwefers*, mines, . . . dark and fog. The Germans were intersecting the lines . . . [they would] fire a burst, move two clicks right and fire another burst. They just kept searching like that . . . When you got in close enough . . . they laid down . . . final protective lines — which [were] bands of fire that interlock.

"It was just mass confusion . . . you couldn't tell what the hell was going on. Between the darkness, the rifle fire, the fire of machine guns and mortars . . . and the river fog . . . it was like fighting an octopus in a crooked sack. It was just confusion. Control was impossible and you didn't know what the hell was going on and trying to keep quiet — it's pretty hard when you're dying to keep quiet." [43]

T/Sgt. Mac Acosta, C Company, "finally got down to the . . . [river] bank." He recalled that they crawled on their bellies like snakes. Acosta slithered down the bank into "a furrow some farmer had dug long before . . . and we had to wait and I don't know why . . . being a sergeant you don't know what the hell is going on. You've got to wait for the officers to tell you . . . So you wait and you wait and you wait. And you say 'What the hell is going on?' Everybody is asking each other and you say, 'Hell, I don't know.' And all the time the Germans were firing . . . machine-gun crossfire . . . down the river. You could see the tracers just bouncing off the water."

Acosta continued, "I remember laying on that bank and looking toward Cassino, toward the foot of the mountain where the monastery is, and you could see the *nebelwefer* fire — you could actually see it fire . . . You could hear *zoop, zoop, zoop, zoop, zoop* and they were screaming meamies . . . you could see the fire leave the barrel . . . Oh boy, here they come. And then there's five shells up in the air and they're screaming — oh, it's loud; it's a terrible noise . . . And it scares the hell out of you and you don't know where they're going to hit because they sound like they're going to hit right on top of you . . . they go way up and then they start coming down." [44] Lieutenant Everett said it sounded like a "streetcar coming down a hill sideways with its brakes on." [45]

Finally, Acosta received word that C Company had gotten one platoon across.[46] It was time to inch forward and get into the boats. The boats were full of holes, Lieutenant Everett recalled: "We tried to launch our boats, . . . quite a few of them looked like colanders . . . full of holes." [47]

C Company was not able to get any more men across the Rapido that night. Captain McCain "kept the men together." Everett continued, "And we heard about the bridge and began to move around to get into position to cross the bridge, which was down below us and to our left. The light started to break and Mac [Captain McCain] very wisely got us the hell out of there." The men were pretty well scattered by that time as they made their way across the open field in front of the river back to their original positions. The men in C Company helped evacuate some of the wounded, and Everett saw some men in ditches and he "yelled at them." He thought they had taken "defensive positions" and he was angry because they were not helping. Lieutenant Everett felt "pretty bad" he had yelled at the men because he soon discovered the men were not hiding at all — "they were dead." [48]

★   ★   ★

Meanwhile, on January 20, the 3rd Battalion of the 141st Infantry Regiment also encountered numerous problems which delayed their crossing. The men from the 19th Engineers who led I Company to the river lost track of the white tape which marked the lanes cleared of mines. German fire had torn the tape to such an extent that the engineers strayed into the minefield. Pvt. George Purcell, I Company, recalled the men walked down a sunken road. "And we came into a meadow and we could no longer see the tapes by this time. The artillery had knocked the tapes down . . . and of course, we were scattered and people were being killed and wounded. We . . . [stepped] over people to get down there . . . I remember one time the mortars came in and I was down and then they kind of stopped and I put my rifle down to push myself up and when I did I tripped a mine. And I just fell forward and then stuck to the man on either side of me . . ." The mine explosion "took a chunk out of the Browning Automatic . . . stock" but it did not injure Purcell. Purcell continued, "But the concussion . . . gets you."[49] The men in I Company proceeded to make their way down to the river.

When I Company arrived at the river, they found that all the bridges but one which had been designated for the 141st sector were destroyed. "Of the four bridges which were to be installed [in the 141st Regimental sector] one was defective and never taken from the engineer dump. Another had been destroyed in a mine-field en route to the river." Artillery fire destroyed the "third . . . in the vicinity of the crossing . . . Hence only one serviceable foot-bridge was available at the crossing site." The men in the 3rd Battalion had to delay their crossing because the men in the 1st Battalion "were given priority" and were "rushed across" the single bridge "first." The 2nd Battalion of the 19th Engineers also experienced extreme difficulty as they attempted to install an "eight ton infantry support bridge." By 4:00 A.M. it was "obvious that the support bridge couldn't be installed that night. Anti-tank and vehicular elements that had been scheduled to cross were notified to remain in their former positions."[50]

The 3rd Battalion commander, Maj. Robert E. Mehaffey, and his S-3, Capt. Edgar Ford, both crossed the Rapido River on the night of January 20. Major Mehaffey had previously served as the battalion executive officer. He became the battalion commander about a week earlier when the former battalion commander, Colonel Richardson, was wounded. Captain Ford assisted as he and Mehaffey got as many men across the Rapido as possible and stabilized "the situation on the German side" of the river.[51]

Eighteen-year-old Pvt. George Purcell, I Company, was one of the men from the 3rd Battalion who was able to cross the river that night. He recalled either Major Mehaffey or Captain Ford "was there [at the bridge] and as each one of us came down he said, 'God be with you' or something to that effect and we went across the bridge."[52] Mehaffey said, "It could have been either one of us because one of us was there at the bridge all the time. We relieved each other when we could. Ford was my right hand."[53]

Once across the river, Purcell and the men in his crossing party turned to the left and proceeded to advance parallel to the river. They approached a German machine-gun nest that was firing in their direction. I Company had been ordered to cross the river with their weapons unloaded and their bayonets fixed, but Purcell had left the magazine in his BAR without a round in the chamber. Purcell recalled, "I was the lead man at that point and I was laying there figuring out what we were gonna do about the machine gun." Purcell felt his sergeant tug at his boot; he turned and the sergeant informed Purcell it was time to withdraw. Purcell continued, "We had been under constant . . . murderous fire since . . . the evening before" and it was then "somewhere around five o'clock in the morning." They had only been able to move a little more than a mile since they began their attack the night before, and as Purcell recalled, they had still not fired a round. Purcell stated, "So we went back to the bridge—there were four men from I Company and they had us cover the withdrawal . . . while the other people pulled back across . . . And then we came back . . . the bridge was so badly shot up by the Germans that it just was hanging by each end. There was no more flotation and the water was . . . running over it . . . nevertheless, we walked back across on that." [54]

When they went back to the American side of the river they had "one officer" and their sergeant with them. Enemy fire hit the sergeant as he crossed the bridge. Once across the bridge, the men began to retrace their steps back to their company area when an artillery shell came in and the men all hit the ground. A piece of the shell hit the officer and killed him. Purcell said, "We went back to our organized positions and by this time we were all just dazed." [55]

★   ★   ★

The men of the 143rd Infantry Regiment, under the command of Col. William H. Martin, had as difficult a time crossing the Rapido River on the night of January 20 as did the men of the 141st. The area where they crossed was a very marshy wheatfield, which added to their problems. "You could dig down six or eight inches and water would fill the hole," [56] recalled Maj. David M. Frazior.

Frazior, 1st Battalion commander, 143rd Infantry Regiment, led a battalion in which seventy-five percent of his officers were replacements. His executive officer, Capt. Milton H. Steffan, was transferred from the 2nd Battalion to the 1st Battalion after San Pietro. His S-3 joined the battalion on January 18, two days before the first crossing.[57]

At 8:00 P.M. the leading elements of the 1st Battalion, 143rd Infantry, arrived at their crossing point on the Rapido River. The men carried pneumatic reconnaissance boats as the 19th Engineers guided them to the river. A dense fog caused extremely low visibility. Intermittent artillery and mortar fire was falling in the vicinity, but there was no small-arms fire "at that time." [58] Companies A and B crossed the river first and were "fairly successful." C Company crossed the river at 11:00 P.M. Major Frazior stated, "All were basically across by 1:00 A.M." [59]

2nd Lt. Raymond Nunez, 3rd Platoon, A Company, had recently received a battlefield commission and was transferred from C Company to A Company, 143rd Infantry.[60] Lieutenant Nunez "was the first to cross" the Rapido River from the 1st Battalion of the 143rd Regiment. He "immediately" encountered both small-arms and mortar fire.[61]

Cpl. Zeb Sunday, B Company, 143rd Infantry, attempted to cross the river on the night of the 20th. As Corporal Sunday's boat was being loaded to cross the river "somebody hit S/Sgt. Jack F. O'Neal's Thompson sub-machine gun . . . and it went off." O'Neal was hit in the leg and the boat sank. All of the men were thrown into the water and were swept downstream. Sunday and the others grabbed anything they could to get out of the river. Sunday recalled, "It was dark . . . you couldn't see . . . and they were firing on us." [62]

Pfc Riley Tidwell, B Company, had joined the 36th Division when he was sixteen years old, and he was the youngest man in B Company when he crossed the river on January 20. Tidwell was a radio operator and he and his commanding officer, Lt. Richard W. Dasher, and others were in an irrigation ditch on the German side of the river. Tidwell had his earphones in place and "was listening to all of the chatter" when he looked around and found the others "had all left." Tidwell couldn't determine what had happened or where they had gone and elected to make his way back to the river. Tidwell thought he would be captured before he got back to the American side so he "pulled the tube out of his radio," which rendered the radio useless to the Germans. Then he swam across the Rapido back to the American side.[63]

Pfc Ervald "Wimpy" Wethington, B Company, 143rd Infantry, crossed the river the first night in a boat. When Wethington and his group reached the far side of the river, they found the murderous German fire made it difficult to even get out of the boat. He said, "[The Germans] knew we were coming across there and they had machine gun fire all along the [bank]. They were just firing a pattern . . . I don't think they were seeing us." Wethington continued, "I believe that was about the worst thing I ever [saw] us try. We didn't get very far the first night." [64]

While on the German side of the river, Frazior's executive officer, Capt. Milton H. Steffan, took a patrol in about 200 to 300 yards to a high bluff where the Germans had laced the area with barbed wire. Enemy machine guns fired just across the top of the wheat. Steffan and his patrol took out two machine guns and a third German machine gun "got him and his patrol." Steffan was severely wounded. The Germans took him prisoner and he died at a German aid station. The following "October or November" Frazior was with a group of men that learned that Captain Steffan was buried in a German cemetery about a mile north of Cassino near the site of the aid station. However, these facts were not known at the time, and the only information Major Frazior could discern was that Captain Steffan was last seen charging a machine gun. He was listed as missing in action. Major Frazior recalled, "The papers came in for Steffan's promotion to major while he was on the river." [65]

By daylight on the 21st, the 1st Battalion on the German side of the river "had been unable to make any progress against the German-prepared positions, and were under heavy machine gun, mortar, and artillery fire. They had been forced into a pocket, with the river to their backs, and were receiving fire from German tanks or self propelled guns in hull-down positions west of the road." [66]

Major Frazior had a "511 radio that could sometimes get back to regiment." He requested orders to pull back across the river "because we were just out in the open and smoke was all that was protecting" his men. Gen. Fred L. Walker denied Frazior's request.[67] Walker's orders to Frazior were to "dig in and stay there." [68] However, before Major Frazior could receive these orders he brought his battalion back across the river[69] because "fire had become so intense as to make his position untenable, and his battalion was threatened with being wiped out completely." [70] Major Frazior and his men were able to bring their wounded back with them as they returned across the footbridge.[71]

★   ★   ★

The 3rd Battalion of the 143rd Infantry Regiment, commanded by Maj. Louis H. Ressijac, was unable to get anyone across the Rapido River on January 20.

Capt. Henry C. Bragaw, commander of K Company, 143rd

Infantry, and his men spent hours stranded in a minefield on the night of January 20, unable to get to the river. Pvt. Robert L. Mallory, K Company, recalled, "Bragaw had us down there the first night and he brought us back . . . he was . . . well respected. Everybody liked him. [Bragaw] was standing there as we went back to the company area and everybody was happy, and he said, 'It won't do no good — you'll have to go tomorrow.' So we knew we were going back the next day." [72]

S/Sgt. Billy E. Kirby, K Company, recalled that was not the first minefield K Company had encountered in the area. Kirby said, "We had been doing all these patrols right there at the river . . . For many days there they . . . [shelled] our company bivouac area. Then someone tripped a mine and we discovered we'd dug in [in] a minefield. And how we did it without blowing half of us, I don't know." [73]

The 19th Engineer guides also led L Company into a minefield as they made their way down to the river. 1st Sgt. Manuel L. "Mexican" Jones, L Company, was injured while in the minefield when one of the men in front of him tripped a mine. The mine killed two people in front of Jones, two people behind him, two people behind them, skipped two people, and then killed four more. Jones suffered concussion from the explosion and was knocked unconscious. He lay in the minefield several hours before he could be evacuated.[74]

Pfc Jack E. Bridge, medical detachment, L Company, was also wounded that January 20. Bridge was the company aide man and he was in the process of assisting the injured men near the river when a piece of shrapnel hit him at 10:30 P.M. Bridge said, "I was fortunate in a sense . . . there were some communication wires [that] had been laid . . . One of the aide men was heading on back up . . . it was kind of a busy area there and I remember . . . him hollering . . . He said, 'If you can crawl follow those wires and start back.' " Bridge crawled on the ground and followed the wires about a hundred yards, then some men on their way back to the river with litters stopped and picked him up. The litter bearers carried him another hundred yards back to a jeep, which carried three litters at a time to the field hospital. Bridge arrived at the field hospital between 2:30 and 3:00 A.M.[75]

Capt. Guy Rogers was commander of M Company, 143rd Regiment, a support company armed with machine guns and mortars. "Two machine gun platoons were attached to two separate companies . . . Mortars support the whole battalion. The mortars never got across," Rogers recalled. "We moved into position [January 17 or 18] and we came under artillery fire as we moved up. We set up a defense on the east bank of the Rapido two or three days before the crossing. The morning of the river crossing everything proceeded . . . well." They used pneumatic boats, and when the Germans opened fire most of the boats were destroyed. "The engineers got a bridge up and it was being used mainly for the evacuation of the wounded. Just before daylight they decided the crossing was a failure and we pulled back." [76]

Col. William H. Martin, 143rd regimental commander, went to the river the night of the 20th to oversee the crossing. Capt. Bert D. Carlton, 143rd Headquarters, was at the river with Colonel Martin. Carlton said, "When we realized that daylight was going to catch us and we weren't going to get the people across . . . Martin ordered them out." [77] Carlton continued, "We went back up to the CP about 4:30 A.M. and reviewed what had happened and . . . started working on plans to reorganize what we had left for the next morning." [78]

At 5:15 A.M. on January 21, the assistant division commander, Gen. William H. Wilbur, gave orders "that all the elements on this side [the American side] of the river be withdrawn to the assembly area before daybreak, and that the men who had succeeded in getting across the river be instructed to dig in at their present positions and hold." [79]

General Walker noted in his journal that the 143rd crossing sector had one damaged bridge left on the morning of January 21. S/Sgt. Robert "Buck" Glover, C Company, 141st Regiment, summed up the difficulties incurred by all the men that night when he later stated, "The whole Fifth Army couldn't have crossed — in waves." [80]

CHAPTER SIX:

The Second Attack

During the early morning hours of January 21, the battalion commanders told the men who were not across the river to cease the attack. Their ordeal would have ended there had General Keyes, the II Corps commander, not pressed for a renewed effort, At 10:00 A.M., Keyes went to Walker's command post and ordered him to make the second attack before noon because "the sun shining in the eyes of the German defenders would make it more difficult for them to observe" the 36th's operations. Walker noted Keyes's chief of staff, Col. Francis M. Willems, "carried a clip board upon which a number of lines and arrows had been drawn to indicate what we were to do. Anybody can draw lines on a map; that doesn't require brains nor tactical ability. But it does require knowledge, skill, discipline, and many other good qualities to figure out, in detail, with reasonable accuracy, the difficulties that lie in the way, and just how and when and with what the difficulties are to be overcome so that success will result." Walker "realized that nether Keyes, nor those with him, understood the situation nor the problems." He told Keyes "that no real gains" had been made in the first attack and that it would require more time than Keyes had allowed to prepare for another attack. "But he [Keyes] was impatient, in a determined mood, and insisted upon the attack by noon." Walker recorded in his diary, "I felt like saying that battles are not won by wishing, while ignoring the facts, but this was no place to court insubordination."[1]

Walker stated he would carry out the orders as soon as he could "confer with the 19th Engineers" whose job it was to replace the lost boats and to construct the footbridges at the river.[2] The attack was set for 2:00 P.M. but was postponed twice until 4:00 P.M.[3] "All contact with the men across the river was lost by the morning of January 21, and their whereabouts on the western side of the river were never accurately determined . . . All attempts to establish communications with them was ineffectual. The sound of American small arms fire heard during the morning and day, however, indicated that the men had moved substantially inland from the river toward the West."[4] Several wounded men were able to get back to the American side of the river during the daylight hours of the 21st and they "indicated that the units across the river . . . had suffered heavily." The men further stated that "constant shelling of their positions prevented an effectual reorganization of the men or any further progress toward objectives." It was also apparent that "all communication was hopelessly beyond repair."[5]

The original plan was for the 141st Infantry Regiment to cross the Rapido at noon "with the 2nd and 3rd Battalions as assault elements."[6] General Walker later advised the 141st that the attack hour had been set back to 3:00 P.M. and ultimately the crossing time was delayed until 9:00 P.M. "due to failure of crossing equipment to arrive on time and mechanical difficulties."[7]

A smoke screen concealed the movement of the men as they made their way to the river on the afternoon of January 21. The Germans began firing at 4:00 P.M. and the men of the 36th had a repeat of the events of the night before. "The assault boats . . . again proved totally inadequate for the task. Many capsized in the swift current, and others were rendered useless by enemy mortar and artillery fires . . . The majority of men who crossed did so by means of improvised footbridges. Mines along the approaches to the crossing sites created additional serious hazards." In spite of the difficulties nearly all of the troops in the 2nd and 3rd battalions of the 141st were able to get across the river on the night of January 21. Lieutenant Colonel Wyatt left his command post and went to the forward regimental command post at 8:00 P.M. in order to be in "close contact with the proceedings."[8]

Maj. Milton J. Landry, commander of the 2nd Battalion,

141st Regiment, received several hundred replacements and about fifteen officers to bolster the strength of his battalion after dark. Landry recalled, "They came up and we had to . . . call the companies and have them bring runners up there and pick up the men and the officers that were assigned to their organizations . . . This was at night and pitch black so you couldn't have any lights whatsoever. All of these men had to be assigned to an outfit and then a few minutes later we [got] orders to make the crossing."[9] Col. Joseph O. Killian, the commander of two battalions of the 19th Regimental Engineers Combat Corps, was "up to the front line of the infantry units" and "he saw new men coming in."[10]

It is very difficult for an infantry unit to receive replacements under such conditions. S/Sgt. Billy E. Kirby best described the difficulties involved when he said, "You don't stop to think — you react. This is the reason that you go through [training] . . . the best way to describe it is athletics. Football — how you do drills over and over and over . . . That's what you do in an infantry outfit. You train as a squad . . . and you do it over and over . . . When it's all over with you probably don't remember what you did or how you did it. You just get through it. It's kind of like if you were ever in an emergency — in an automobile accident or fire . . . You do these things and it's very confused. And you do it and you look back and you say well how did you even do it . . . You don't know how you did it . . . in battle it's no different. I suppose you have a plan, but when the firing starts, your plans kind of go astray . . . it's usually just total confusion . . . the thing that keeps you going is that you develop . . . a great pride in your outfit.

"You develop a great feeling toward the guys you're with. And even though you're scared to death and you'd like to say the hell with this . . . you know that everybody's depending on you . . . We were together for two years before we went to war. Even though we lost a lot of the guys, there was still . . . a nucleus of the same guys we went overseas with . . . Everybody [had] a job and if somebody [didn't] do his job then you [were] in trouble . . . And you train together and I don't think you ever get to a point that you realize, well we're finally gelled and we're a good group. It's . . . something . . . that you just find out . . . Certain people you can kind of depend on more [than the ones] you kind of carry . . . One battle does it . . . you either depend on him or you don't after that one battle."[11]

Landry recalled, "We had to jump off about nine o'clock that night . . . We got the guys — they picked up their boats — but when . . . you'd run into an officer or an enlisted man and you'd ask him what his name [was] because it was so dark and . . . they'd tell you what their name was and you'd ask them what organization they were from and some of them didn't even know. They had just joined the outfit that night and they hadn't found their company yet . . . and we were making a river crossing . . . Over half of our battalion strength had never seen their people . . . most of the officers had never seen the troops that they were commanding."[12]

Landry had set up a command post on the edge of the river bank on the American side of the river and he had "put another one on the other side of the river" so there would be just a short distance between the two command posts. Landry "finally" got his battalion through the minefield and across the river. He recalled that "the Germans could hear them coming and they kept dropping artillery shells in there." He continued, "We didn't have people wounded from the artillery and mortar fires as much that night as we did from the minefield." After Landry got his battalion across on one footbridge, they tried to spread out.[13] By 12:55 A.M., January 22, E Company was across the river and G Company immediately followed. F Company encountered great difficulty and was only able to get a few men across. H Company was able to get some men across the river after the rifle companies crossed, as did the men from the Battalion and Headquarters Company.[14]

Once across the river, the men were under constant German machine-gun fire as they tried to progress. The Germans had looped barbed wire all around the area and the Americans found themselves in pockets of the wire. Major Landry was on the German side of the river when he radioed General Wilbur "and explained to him what the situation was." General Wilbur told Landry to "see if you can break out of there" because "we have just made a landing up the coast [Anzio] and they will probably cut the route off for the Germans to withdraw [on] Route 6." Wilbur advised Landry to get ready to move forward. Landry told Wilbur, "Well, you'd better get on the horn and notify the Germans because there ain't a damned thing we're doing — there's nothing we can do that would cause them to withdraw . . . We can't even shoot at them. We're down here and as you go through the valley . . .

they're shooting at us and we can't figure out where the hell they are."[15]

Capt. John L. Chapin, E Company commander, got his men across the Rapido and inland 500 yards to the barbed wire. Aside from a few officers, E Company was composed entirely of Hispanic troops. Captain Chapin had been raised in El Paso, Texas, and he spoke fluent Spanish. One of his former officers recalled, "Chapin was a very . . . brilliant man . . . an unusually good officer. Probably the best company commander in the business . . . And I loved John — I really did. He was so good to me. He knew my shortcomings and accepted them and made me a pretty damn good officer." Chapin talked to that officer every night until he was properly prepared and well qualified to lead troops in combat. Chapin loved the men in his company and their love for him and loyalty to him was an integral part of the excellent fighting unit that E Company proved to be.[16]

The men in E Company crossed the river with fixed bayonets and were moving forward in company formation when a German machine gun opened up fire on their right flank and pinned the company down. Pfc Rudolph M. Trevino, E Company, had just returned to the company the night before after a stay in the hospital at Naples.[17] Captain Chapin ordered Trevino, along with Sgt. Roque Segura and Pfc Julio De Hoyas, to destroy the machine-gun nest. Trevino recalled, "We moved very carefully to the right flank. It was pitch dark, we came upon a small rise in the terrain for better observation. We took out our hand grenades and each one of us counted to three and we threw the hand grenades at the machine-gun nest and put it out of commission. I think we killed all of the machine-gun crew because we heard no more firing. About the time we had thrown the hand grenades we received small rifle fire from the Germans on our left flank, and since we were on top of that rise . . . we made good targets for the enemy because of the silhouettes we three men caused. We got the hell down from that small rise and started to head back to rejoin our company."

Trevino continued, "As we were running, I heard Sgt. Roque Segura holler, 'I'm hit,' but I could see him still running behind me and Julio De Hoyas, and about that time Julio was hit and fell to the ground. I rushed to him and could see where the rifle shot glazed the back of his neck at an angle upwards to his steel helmet." The bullet burned his skin and went up and made a hole in

the top of his helmet. "There was a hole in the back of his steel helmet. Otherwise he was not hurt badly, but that was close enough."
Trevino said, "I was lucky I did not receive a scratch."[18] He did not
see Sgt. Roque Segura again. He did not know until he returned to
the States after the war that Segura had been captured later the
same night.

Trevino recalled they reached the barbed wire and the main
group of men in their company and as daylight approached "the
Germans really opened up." Captain Chapin had some of his men
trying to cut through the barbed wire so they could advance. He
gave the order for the men to dig in and "fire foolhardily men, fire
foolhardily." Captain Chapin was just to the left and behind Private First Class Trevino when German machine-gun fire hit him.
Trevino looked around and his captain was dead.

A short while later, Trevino heard someone shout, "Cease fire
— pass it on." Trevino responded, "Who said cease fire?" and
someone answered, "That lieutenant over there." His eyes
searched through the smoke and fog. He saw a lieutenant he didn't
recognize. "He was one of . . . the replacements. I don't know when
he joined us." The lieutenant had taken his shirt off and removed
the shirt to his white long johns, then wrapped the sleeves around
his carbine rifle and waved it in the air as he shouted his orders to
cease fire.[19]

Such behavior by a junior officer, while not common, occurred
with sufficient frequency to cause Gen. Omar Bradley to express
his concern about the unrealistic training maneuvers in the United
States. In a letter to Army Chief of Staff George Marshall, Bradley
noted, "In maneuvers, when two forces meet, the umpires invaria-
bly decide that the smaller force must withdraw, or if greatly out-
numbered it must surrender."[20] Rather than showing a reluctance
to continue the fight, this officer may have just been doing as he
was trained.

When Trevino passed the word, T/Sgt. Eduardo Romo raised
his rifle to shoot the man that had given the orders to cease fire.
Trevino asked him what he was doing and Romo replied, "I'm
going to kill that SOB." Trevino later explained, "Our captain . . .
had said to fire foolhardily. I know Romo took that [to mean] . . .
fight to the last man." Trevino told Romo an officer had given the
order, and Romo lowered his rifle.[21]

In a matter of seconds, German soldiers who had been surrounding the area came forward. When the Americans raised their hands in the air, the firing stopped. "There were two or three Germans on top of each GI," Trevino remembered. One of the Germans was at Trevino's foxhole and he leaned forward with his bayonet on Trevino's throat. All he said to Trevino was, "Zip-zip." Trevino recalled, "I didn't know what he meant . . . But I put two and two together. I guess if I didn't come out I was going to hear zip-zip with the bullets." Trevino continued, "I had my arms up and I pointed. I said, 'I'm not touching my rifle,' because if I had grabbed my rifle he would have had a right to blow my brains out." Trevino's foxhole was so deep that his head was level with the ground. He had to turn around to work himself out and he thought, "He's going to jab that bayonet on my shoulder blade back here . . . I just hope he pulls the trigger and it will be over with soon . . . you won't feel anything." The German soldier stood there as Trevino got out and then he told Trevino, "Come comrade." The Germans took the men in E Company back to the rear area. Trevino was held in transit camp for a month before he was moved to a work camp in Austria.[22]

2nd Lt. Richard M. Manton was a weapons platoon leader in E Company. His platoon handled light weapons, 30-caliber air-cooled machine guns, and 60mm mortars. The men in his platoon had machine guns, base plates for mortars, mortars, and ammunition strapped to their backs when they crossed the Rapido River on the pontoon bridge. They advanced forward about 200 yards until they hit a pocket of barbed wire. The enemy "was shooting from right and left." Manton and his men were immediately pinned down. Manton "radioed in and asked permission to withdraw." He was told to stay where he was and to hold what area he had. They dug in and tried to fight as best they could, all the while under a constant artillery attack. Manton said, "We ran out of ammunition and were still pinned down . . . we had nothing to fight back with and and we still couldn't get permission to withdraw."

On the morning of the 22nd, Manton continued, "We took a terrific shelling — the ground just trembled. The enemy artillery came in in waves. As the artillery drew back, the German infantry came in." Manton looked up and a German soldier was holding a rifle pointed at him. Manton had studied German in high school and when the German said, *"Rous,"* Manton knew that he wanted him to get out of the foxhole. Manton turned to get his Musette bag which contained his cigarettes and other personal items. The German soldier would not let him and Manton had to crawl out of his foxhole with nothing. Manton said, "I climbed out of the hole and he indicated where we were to go. They moved us back to their rear area. They herded us together in a group."

While they were in this area, an American private walked up to Manton and said, "What can I do with this?" He had a hand grenade. Manton told him to put the pin back in it and the private said he couldn't because the pin was gone. Manton knew if the grenade went off it would cause the Germans to start firing at the men. He called a German officer to come over and he was able to explain that the pin was gone. The German showed him where to throw the grenade and it went off without further incident.

The Germans separated the officers from the enlisted men. Manton spent most of his time as a prisoner of war at Offizer Lager 64 (Oflag 64) in Schubin, Poland.[23]

January 22 was also the end of E Company's distinction of being the Hispanic company. With almost every man in the company either killed, wounded, or captured, the company had been deprived of its ethnic distinction as well as its well-established reputation as a company of fierce and determined fighters.

Maj. Armin F. Puck, division provost marshal, and Lt. Col. Robert L. Cox, the division signal officer, crossed the river late in the afternoon on January 21. Around 8:00 the next morning, Puck decided to return to the American side of the river after he saw "our side just had nothing left."[24] Just after he made his decision to leave, he looked around and he saw "sixty or seventy men [from E Company, 141st Regiment] in hastily dug positions." Puck observed the Germans as they moved in and began to capture the men.[25] Puck recalled, "When I took out I went from one tree stump to another and every time I'd hear something come in — about three or four times — I hit the ground . . . [then] I got up and I ran again. I knew about where the bridge was and I made it all right . . . I slipped and slid and got on top of it." Puck was crossing the bridge when he was hit by enemy fire. "The bridge was grimy and muddy — maybe bloody," Puck said. "I was half crawling and half holding on to one of the ropes . . . I slipped and I fell down." The top half of Puck's body landed on the American river bank, and his waist and legs were in the river. As he was falling from the bridge Puck thought, "Oh my God, I'm going to hit a shue mine because [the Germans] had mined the whole area." Puck hit the bank "and nothing happened." He recalled, "I laid there a few minutes — I didn't know whether to move — I didn't know what to do for a couple of minutes." A few minutes later two engineers walked across the bridge and saw Puck lying there. Puck said, "Thank goodness . . . I didn't have to make a decision . . . I'd of crawled out of that thing somehow, I guess."[26] The two men "grabbed [Puck's] . . . pistol belt . . . and pulled [him] out and took [him] to the 141st aide tent."[27] Puck heard the two engineers say, "I didn't know that son of a bitch was a major," when they saw him riding off in a jeep.[28]

T/Sgt. Sammie D. Petty, 1st Platoon, F Company, 141st Regiment, had twenty new men in his platoon at the time of the Rapido battle. Petty stated F Company spent thirty-five days on the line around San Pietro "and when we pulled off we didn't have but . . . twenty-six men left in our company." During the first attack across the Rapido, F Company had been in reserve. Petty recalled seeing General Wilbur in the company area where he observed the action below during the first attack. It was the first time Petty had seen a general.

Around 1:00 on the afternoon of January 21, the F Company commander, 1st Lt. John R. Potts, sent a runner to Petty's platoon to tell him to "get the 1st Platoon ready to go — that we were going to attack the river at 3:00 o'clock [P.M.]" Petty recalled, "And you talk about a funny feeling running across you — it was like a sentence to death. And I just didn't figure anybody would be stupid enough to try to cross that river at two or three o'clock in the evening. Because the Germans . . . [were] at Cassino . . . that monastery. It just stood out like a sore thumb. You could see it for miles and miles . . . It was just standing there and everybody said . . . that's an observation point — they were watching right down our throats." Years later Petty recalled, "I think that was the only time during the war that I really [gave] up . . . when twilight turned to darkness I was thinking this is my last old day on earth . . . I know I always thought I might get killed but I never did think I was going to get killed at that particular time. I always thought I might get killed tomorrow . . . That was one time I thought — this is it, there's no way I'm going to get back out of this operation."

Petty got his platoon ready to go. He said, "We stripped down to what we called combat readiness. We dropped our packs and everything — just put extra rations and extra ammunition and hand grenades and got everything ready to go." Then Petty went to the company command post and talked to the company commander. Petty said, "I never will forget it. Lieutenant Potts said, 'Damn . . . I wish I'd just been born and a girl baby at that.' "

Petty did not know what caused the delay in time but the 1st Platoon did not attempt to cross the river until 8:00 P.M. that night, although that was two hours ahead of any other platoon in F Company. Petty continued, "We started down to the river and our orders [were] to cross the river with unloaded rifles . . . that never was quite clear whether that meant no ammunition in your rifle at all or no round in the chamber of your rifle but it could have been either one. [General Walker] . . . later . . . denied that he ever put out an order like that but [our orders were] to cross the river with unloaded rifles and to infiltrate — there wasn't supposed to be . . . shooting 1,500 yards in that general direction."

Petty and his platoon spent about thirty minutes getting down to the river. He said, "We were lucky there wasn't artillery fire or anything on us as we were going down there." Most of the men were to cross in one of the large wooden boats and then the others would cross on the rubber rafts. The bank was about three feet higher than the water and the men were trying to be as quiet as possible because a German machine gun was shooting harassing fire in their direction. It seemed to Petty that "they were firing right in your face but it was a little further back" and the men did not want to draw the fire upon themselves. There was considerable noise from the wooden boat as they eased it over the gravel bank and into the river.

Petty and the two other men in his rubber boat made it across the river and started walking upriver to contact the other men in the platoon who had crossed the river. Petty recalled, "We . . . got to where they put one of these bridges across the night before and I heard somebody hollering 'help' and I walked down to the water and there was one of the guys . . . in my platoon . . . his pack got caught . . . and he was about to drown." Petty pulled the man out of the water and asked him what had happened. The big wooden boat had turned over and thrown the men into the water. Two of the twenty men in the boat drowned.

Another man was shouting from across the river, and Petty went back over the deflated pontoon bridge to the American side to check on his other men. Petty does not recall how the men he had crossed the river with got back, but they returned the next morning along with the rest of his platoon, except for the two men who drowned the night before. Once again across the river, Petty recalled, "there were all these guys up on the river bank that had gotten out. Of course they were wringing wet . . . and cold and nobody had any rifles or anything. They had . . . lost all of their equipment so we stood around a little bit and then we decided to go back to the company area."

After they arrived at the company area, they sent word to supply to bring up more rifles and ammunition. Around 10:00 P.M., while the 1st Platoon was waiting to be resupplied, the rest of F Company tried to cross the river. Petty said he still doesn't know why the 1st Platoon was sent out so far ahead of the rest of the company.[29]

2nd Lt. Bill McFadden, F Company, recalled that it was quite hard to cross the river in the boats because "none of us had ever seen one of those boats before. And we didn't know how to coordinate our actions together and to work them into the upstream to keep them from swamping . . . Most of them swamped because of the rapidity of the water. And . . . as a unit . . . none of us had ever done this as a team before." He successfully crossed the river by boat and got "just on the bank" of the German side of the river. McFadden said, "When we found out our company did not get over intact . . . we were told to get back to the other side and reorganize the people."[30] Lieutenant Potts as well as a number of men were wounded and others were killed.[31] "By the next morning . . . what was left of the company was back in the company area again." The men in F Company remained in their observation positions for over a week expecting to make another attack on the Rapido River.[32]

Nineteen-year-old 2nd Lt. Kenneth Saul, Weapons Platoon, G Company, 141st Regiment, experienced his first combat at the Rapido as the 36th Division made a second attempt to cross the river. Saul said that usually the mortar section crossed behind the rifle companies. Saul recalled, "We walked down to the river. It was a foggy night and you couldn't see two feet in front of you. We had to stay on the road. Tape marked the roads. Shells blew the tapes up. The engineer that was going to take us down to the river lost his way and the Germans were shelling us and we dropped our [wooden boat]. We never got where we were supposed to get as soon as we were supposed to get there."

The men finally got to the river and put three mortars in the boat. When they tipped the boat to get it into the water, the mortars fell forward and knocked the front of the boat out. The men had to get another boat and when they got into it the engineers were putting up a pontoon bridge nearby. Saul and the men in his boat used the bridge to pull themselves along until they were half-way out in the water at which time they began to paddle. Saul said, "We paddled, and paddled, and paddled and got to a shore — unfortunately, we didn't know it was our shore. We saw a silhouette — it was our first sergeant. He said, 'Saul, what in the hell are you doing here?'"

Saul's company commander told him that since the Germans were shelling the area so heavily he should set up his mortars on the American side of the river. After daylight Saul's platoon pulled out and went to their original positions. There were "21 men out of 180" left. Saul observed, "I was the only officer left." He thought to himself, "If this is what combat is going to be, I don't want any part of it."[33]

Saul continued, "The next day we sat there and waited and the battalion commander said to take a patrol out to see where we don't have the drop off [on the river bank]." On the patrol some of the men got lost, and the rest of them got within 200 yards of the river. Saul said, "We couldn't accomplish our mission. One man in our squad was killed by a sniper, but we were not aware of it until we got back. We sent a sergeant and another man out, but he was dead when they found him. The next night we tried the same thing . . . German shells came in and as soon as they came in you dropped by the side of the road. While I was laying there waiting for the shells to stop I felt something underneath me. As I brought my hand to my head I felt arms and a head — I was on top of a dead man. They'd shelled us unmercifully [during the crossing attempts]. I'd say there was a dead man every ten yards, just like they were in formation . . . We reassembled in our area and they said, 'We're not going to try it again.' They said we had too many dead and wounded. We went on to the assembly area in the rear . . . we got our mail and a hot meal."[34]

Major Landry, 2nd Battalion commander, was wounded four times on January 22. While Captain Chapin was trying to get a hole in the barbed wire, Major Landry had gone back to see what progress they were making. Landry said, "We were getting a lot of artillery fire . . . earlier I was laying there beside [Chapin] talking to him . . . and this machine gun kept firing right over so I knew when I left him I had to crawl so far and then I could get up and kind of scoot and run back to where I was . . . I got to where I'd run and I'd kind of hit that mud and slide underneath there."

Landry went out again to check on Chapin's progress. He ran and slid and thought he hit a rock and bruised his chest. Landry recalled, "So when I got through talking to him . . . I eased around and I crawled back . . . and one of the aid men looked at me and he said, 'Did that shell hit you?'" Landry told him he didn't know. The aid man continued, "When you hit the ground over there, there was a mortar shell that hit right beside you." Landry told him that he thought he had hit a rock. The aid man told Landry that he had a hole in his jacket and he thought he'd better take a look at it. Landry said, "So he opened up my jacket and he opened up my shirt . . . and my undershirt had a hole in it and there was a hole in my chest and the blood was just kind of oozing out of it. And they put a patch on it and made me take a bunch of little damned pills. But my fountain pen and pencil was a Parker Lifetime . . . and a shell fragment went between the two and cut the clip off of the pencil — it almost lasted a lifetime."[35]

By 2:33 A.M. it was evident that "all attempts to install a support bridge were unsuccessful . . . and were abandoned." The engineers were "ordered to bring up and install a Bailey bridge instead. The project was carried forward, preparations began on the approaches, and the equipment [was] gathered in the vicinity of the 'S' bend" of the river by 4:30 A.M. on the 22nd. Enemy fire was too intense to allow for the complete installation of the Bailey bridge, and at 6:30 A.M. "Division Headquarters notified Lieutenant Colonel Wyatt that General Walker wanted work on the bridge continued in spite of enemy fire. This was complied with, but the attempts were ineffectual."[36]

The 141st Infantry Regiment Operations Report further described the scene: "In order to obscure enemy observation units across the river, arrangements had been made to place smoke pots along the Rapido and on Mount Trocchio, before dawn on January 22. This work was detailed to the elements of the 1st Battalion which hadn't succeeded in crossing the night of January 20–21.

Over 300 pots were placed and ignited before dawn, and additional ones set out during the day to maintain the screen. The pots were placed well upwind, so as not to reveal any specific location or activities."[37]

At 9:00 A.M. on January 22, Lt. Col. Andrew F. Price, executive officer, 141st Infantry Regiment, "visited the forward Regimental Command Post and the 2nd and 3rd Battalion forward Command Post on the eastern side of the river to check the situation and expedite any possible reorganization" in an effort to continue the attack toward the regimental objectives.[38]

Between 9:30 and 10:00 A.M. the Germans fired "some old 170mm artillery pieces," which they had captured from the Italians, into the 2nd Battalion sector. Landry noted, "Six rounds of that 170mm stuff fell in there right underneath me . . . the first one knocked me in the air . . . and the boys said it looked like when . . . I was getting ready to fall another one would hit and it would carry me further . . . I went through the air about seventy feet down the embankment before I hit the ground. The first round . . . hit so close to me that I didn't get much fragmentation from it — just a slab of shell exploded and hit me in the hip . . . and blistered my hip and knocked the hip out of joint . . . a few long fragments did go into my leg . . . I used two boat oars that were on the bank [as crutches]." Landry continued, "So they patched the holes in me where those shell fragments went in and, of course, my legs were awful sore and I used those boat oars."[39]

At 11:00 A.M. Lieutenant Colonel Wyatt "sent a message to each of the Battalion commanding officers, directing them that no one must withdraw across the river, and that continued attempts had to be made to organize, dig in, and bring fire power against the enemy."[40]

By noon, Major Landry had been bleeding heavily since the artillery shell wounded him and he started toward E Company "to see if Chapin had ever gotten the hole cut through the barbed wire . . . and to tell Chapin that he might have to take over command of the battalion" if he passed out from the loss of blood. Landry was unaware that Chapin had been killed just a short time before.

Landry reached the spot where the German machine gun had been hitting and he started to drop to the ground, but the machine gun had been moved and the fire hit him in the legs before he reached the ground. Landry thought his leg was cut off at the knee.

His knee stung but he could not feel the lower part of his leg. He recalled, "One of the aid men crawled out there, and I told him I thought my leg was cut off at the knee. It felt just like you'd use a dull saber and just whack it off at the knee. And he turned me over and messed around and said, 'Oh you've got a boot on the end of something out here — I guess it's your leg. You've got both your legs.' But I was paralyzed and couldn't move my legs, so they put a rope around me and they drug me back out from under that fire and on over to the embankment . . . The aid man said, 'Major, I hate to tell you this, but there's not enough bandage on this side of the river to [plug] all the holes through you.'"

Two of the men tied ropes around Major Landry and around themselves and they dragged him across the river by pulling themselves along the ropes that had supported the pontoon bridge and by swimming. Once they reached the American side, they laid Landry on the bank so the aid men could put him on a stretcher. The men who had assisted Landry across the river then returned to the German side of the river to rejoin their unit and resume their fight.[41]

Landry recalled, "When I got over there and they started to pick me up, we had so many casualties they had asked coast artillerymen from Naples to come up and act as litter bearers to carry the wounded off the battlefield . . . Those four boys had never been around anything like that — they were carrying me off but before they did, I saw this stack of people laying over there and the very bottom person was my executive officer, Capt. Richard E. "Red" Lehman. On the top was my artillery forward observer . . . he had the whole side of his head blown away . . . I figured he was dead . . . I had them take all of the others off. Some of them were dead, and they got Lehman and took him out and he wouldn't go back to the hospital from the aid station until he was sure they got me out of there. While I was on the stretcher, they got me across the minefield and we were getting right to the edge of that old railroad embankment." Landry heard *nebelwefers* coming in and he told the litter bearers, "Now y'all don't know what this is, but just in a few minutes they're going to hit right here so set me down in the ditch and y'all hit the ditch and lay down." The litter bearers put him down in the middle of the road and hit the ditch. The *nebelwefers* landed next to Landry, and a rock went into the side of his throat and hit his voice box. They finally got him to the hospital the next

morning. Major Landry had been wounded four times that day —
his thirtieth birthday.[42]

Landry recalled, "Two years later when I was at O'Riley General Hospital in Springfield, Missouri, I saw the artillery forward
observer. He was there to get a glass eye. They had rebuilt his
head. I was very happy."[43]

1st Lt. Sidney E. Lurie, adjutant, 2nd Battalion, 141st Infantry Regiment, recalled that after Captain Lehman was hit, Lehman
said, "I didn't want any cheese — I just wanted out of the trap."[44]

★   ★   ★

Maj. Robert E. Mehaffey, commander of the 3rd Battalion,
got his orders for the battalion to cross the river on the 21st from
the 141st Regimental executive officer, Col. Andrew F. Price.
Major Mehaffey spoke to Col. Carl Phinney at division headquarters and Phinney said, "The whole division staff had been talking
about the corps and had gotten a consideration." Mehaffey said
Phinney "asked if he could [get me through] if I wanted to be put
through to corps myself, and I certainly did." Mehaffey discussed
the situation with Keyes and told him that he did not feel the tactics involved in this operation were sound. As the II Corps commander, it was General Keyes's job to outline the attack because he
was the plans officer. Years later, Mehaffey said, "The tactics were
not sound at all. I didn't have a corporal that didn't have better
tactical knowledge than what was used there. Certainly, there were
reasons for this being ordered in this manner, but those reasons
didn't justify what happened there." Mehaffey "toyed with the idea
of refusing the order, which would have been a court-martial" and
he knew "somebody else would have to carry it out." He followed
orders and got most of his men across the river.

Major Mehaffey and his S-3, Capt. Edgar Ford, both crossed
the Rapido several times again on January 22. Mehaffey said,
"This was my position — where I needed to be if [I was] . . . to
have any influence in what [happened] there."[45]

Pvt. George Purcell, Company I, 141st Regiment, and the men
with whom he had crossed the river during the first attack, went
back out the evening of the 21st and "tried to do it again." He recalled, "We didn't even get across the river that evening. We came
back and did some patrols. I went on those patrols and by this time
there were so few people they appointed me an acting non-commissioned officer." By around 2:00 P.M. on the 22nd the men returned

to the company area "and approximately nine infantrymen held the company front." Purcell continued, "We were along the front that the company originally occupied and we took turns, two to a hole. One would stay awake a couple of hours, then the other one would relieve him — this type of thing all through the night. Finally later that day they pulled us back. But we had lost effectively 80% of the company."[46]

Early on the morning of the 22nd, Captain Ford "was going back and forth across the Rapido trying to stabilize everything." While he stood on the American side of the river, a shell fragment hit and broke his thigh. Major Mehaffey crossed the river and was walking with his S-2, Lt. Shona K. Aldridge, when they found Ford wounded. The two men carried him toward the nearest aid station.[47]

Major Mehaffey crossed the Rapido for a second time on the 22nd and remained there until he "was hit around mid-morning."[48] Mehaffey "was standing near some entrenched troops . . . While trying to get a better view of the enemy defenses, a German tank appeared and Mehaffey saw a muzzle flash as it fired. The exploding shell hit the sand beneath the bank and tossed him into the air, and a large piece of shrapnel tore through his chest, emerging at his back."[49] He immediately turned over the command of the battalion to Lieutenant Aldridge.[50] Mehaffey recalled, "When I was hit I managed to get back to the footbridge, but I had lost so much blood that I was woozy by that time. So I got down and crawled on my hands and knees with my hands on the outside of this walkway. One of the pontoons had been blown up or shot and lost the air and the little old thing dipped down in the water. I just kept crawling, and that cold water went into my clothing and just brought me alert quick." As soon as he got on the American side of the river, "the medics were right there." The medics immediately started plasma on Mehaffey and put him on a litter, then placed him on a jeep which took him to the field hospital. Mehaffey "passed out and . . . didn't regain consciousness for nine days." Mehaffey said, "A young chest surgeon . . . caught me back there. He was a very innovative person and in my case he realized he didn't have a whole lot to lose so he did some different things. For instance, he rigged up a flier's mask — oxygen mask — and a hose and a bellows and a bottle of oxygen out of the shop. And the ward boy breathed for me with this bellows and when he got tired they

would relieve him . . . So many interesting things came out of this.
Those automatic Bennett [respirators] are in every hospital in the
world today."[51]

Lieutenant Aldridge served as the battalion commander for
about an hour until "Lt. Col. Henry A. Goss, an officer recently assigned to the division . . . assumed command of the 3rd Battalion.
By 2:15 P.M. Goss and Lt. Shona K. Aldridge had also been criti-
cally wounded; thirty minutes later both were dead."[52]

Reports began coming into the 141st Regimental Command
around 4:00 P.M. that the enemy had begun a series of counterattacks against units located on the German side of the river. "The
only information available on these attacks consisted of individual
accounts of the survivors, and at best reflect incomplete views. The
smoke haze, laid down to screen reorganization activities and protect our men, obscured any over-all picture, and greatly aided the
enemy in his counterattack."[53] Around the same time, Pvt. Savino
Manella, one of the medical aid men from A Company, 1st Battalion, 141st Infantry Regiment, arrived at the Regimental Command
Post with a note from the German commanding officer, who asked
"for a cessation of artillery fire for several hours to enable the Germans to evacuate the German and 'English' wounded." The Germans had captured Private Manella on the morning of the 21st
after the initial attempt to cross the river. He "had been attending
the American wounded in a room of a farmhouse within the German positions." Manella reported "that several large groups of
fresh German replacements had reported into the area during the
day of January 22. He had been released about noon of the 22nd
with the note, and had made his way back to" the American side.
The Operations Report noted that "because of the informal nature
of the note and the circumstances surrounding the transaction, the
note was interpreted as having been designed only as a ruse to secure relief from" American artillery fire.[54]

The report continued: "These pieced together accounts indicate that at about [4:00 P.M.], January 22, the Germans began a series of counterattacks by first feeling out the exact location and
strength of our units, with about two companies of men. This continued until [5:00 P.M.], when a counterattack of major proportions
was brought to bear in the form of an encirclement. Hard bitter
fighting repulsed this and several subsequent attempts by the Germans to overrun the regimental positions. The enemy was able,

however, to gain a well-defined concept of our relatively confined positions, and subsequently saturate the entire position with repeated concentrations of artillery, mortar and automatic weapon fire."[55]

By 5:00 P.M. "the commanding officers and executive officers of both the 2nd and 3rd Battalions, together with all the company commanders . . . had either been killed or wounded. Telephone communications, which had been maintained with great difficulties from time to time during the day, had been irretrievably lost. Efforts to resupply ammunition, water, and rations were equally unavailing, since enemy fire completely commanded the river line and the approaches to the east."[56]

"The severe losses suffered caused an entire revision of plans for operations for the night of January 22. Lieutenant Colonel Wyatt had given orders for continued attempts to install a Bailey bridge across the river, and a covering force from Company 'C' had proceeded to the crossing site to protect the engineer personnel. The urgency was dictated by the need to get armored elements across as soon as possible. At . . . [10:40 P.M.], January 22, . . . the engineers were directed to abandon the bridge attempt and the covering force was withdrawn."[57] The report stated that "surviving elements of the 2nd and 3rd Battalions, supplemented by the men who had been able to work their way back across the Rapido, effected what organization they could on the east [American] bank of the river."[58]

★   ★   ★

The 143rd Infantry Regiment began an attack between 2:30 and 4:00 P.M.[59] "Heavy smoke from pots, chemical mortars, and artillery was placed along the far and near side of the river."[60] After the first crossing attempt, Major Frazior, 1st Battalion commander, got back to his CP around 11:00 A.M. on the 21st. Shortly after that Colonel Martin called and told Frazior to be ready to cross the river again at 2:00 P.M. Frazior had to get ammunition, food, and regroup for the attack. Headquarters moved the time up several times, and the 1st Battalion began its second attempt to cross the Rapido at 4:00 P.M.[61]

As the first troops reached the river, enemy artillery and mortar fire began falling. A Company met heavy machine-gun fire when it sent the first wave across. Despite the heavy, continuous fire, A Company completed its crossing and B Company immediately followed. Both A and B companies were across the Rapido by 6:35 P.M. Major Frazior crossed the river with B Company "and reported no progress against heavy resistance."[62]

An hour later, C Company still had not been able to cross the river. At 8:33 P.M. the commanding officer, 1st Battalion, 19th Engineers, reported that all of the 1st Battalion was across the river. He also reported one footbridge was completed and the installation of a second bridge was in progress. However, at 11:17 P.M., the 1st Battalion got word back to regiment that C Company was still unable to cross the river. Major Frazior "was directed to speed the crossing" of C Company. Heavy machine-gun fire and mortar fire prevented the 1st Battalion from advancing very far, and the men were unable to relay much information.[63]

1st Lt. Russell J. Darkes, 143rd Infantry Regiment, and his men spent ten hours in icy water as they lay on the sunken road and waited to cross the Rapido. The icy water and long wait increased the pain Darkes was suffering from wounds he had received the night before. At long last, he received orders to attack. Lieutenant Darkes "organized his company and crossed the river on an ice covered footbridge. In the face of intense enemy artillery and machine-gun fire from the front and both flanks, he led his men forward" until they received orders to cease the attack.[64]

2nd Lt. John Burtucco, 143rd Infantry Regiment, had returned to the river "to lead the remainder of his platoon into the fight." Two of his men fell into the icy, rapidly flowing water. Lieutenant Burtucco jumped into the river and pulled them to safety. Once he reached the shore, he reorganized his platoon and proceeded across the river back into the fight.[65]

Three men from B Company, 143rd Regiment, recalled their very different experiences during the second crossing. Pfc Riley M. Tidwell, B Company, was hit by enemy fire as he began to cross the river. He said, "I was hit and then I crossed the river on a pontoon boat. We stayed on the German side that night." He was able to get back across the river the next day and was sent to the hospital.[66]

Cpl. Zeb Sunday, B Company, was in a pontoon boat with seven other men. Sunday recalled, "The second time we [were] going to cross, we thought we [were] across the river . . . there was a little sandbar out there . . . and we got stranded . . . about halfway or maybe a little bit further across [the river]. We thought we

[were] across but we [weren't] . . . Some of us dug in and some swam back . . . Some of us couldn't get back because the river was swift, and with their packs . . . and rifles . . . we lost quite a few men there." Sunday was fortunate that he was one of the men who managed to swim back to the American side.[67]

Pfc Ervald "Wimpy" Wethington, B Company, his company commander, and eight other men were able to get across the river and through the barbed wire on the German side during the second crossing. The men came within sight of a "German battalion headquarters." Wethington felt they could have gone on from there had they been able to get some reinforcement from other troops.

As it was, the men observed the headquarters "looked like it was almost in solid rock where they'd dug in. They had these rocket guns *[nebelwerfers]* . . . and we [were] watching them loading that thing . . . and . . . they had a wire on it . . . and they'd take that wire all the way around" behind the rock in which they were dug in "and they'd fire that thing by remote control." Wethington continued, "We should have tried to knock it out but we knew we didn't have enough to do anything. Even if we'd knocked it out they'd have killed all the rest of us. They did kill most of us or capture us . . . [and] our artillery was putting shells in on us." The men had gotten further back than had been anticipated and Wethington said, "That's the reason we were getting all that shell fire from the Americans . . . they were really laying shell fire on them."[68]

The men began to make their way back to the river and "it was just as hard to get back . . . through the barbed wire. We were knocking [into] booby traps and hollering and wanting to know who [was hit]. And then they [were] opening machine-gun fire right down there on the barbed wire." Only four of the men were able to get back to the river. Wethington said, "Coming back, it had [been] daylight a long time. But it was lucky for us they still laid that smoke screen. There's no way in the world we could have gotten back to the river if it hadn't been for that smoke screen."[69]

1st Sgt. Ovil Gallet, C Company, 143rd Regiment, and his men waited, ready to cross the river, for most of the night of January 21. The cold dampness of the night "aggravated an old foot wound but despite his intense pain, Gallet continually moved among his men" to both encourage them and maintain control for the upcoming assault. Gallet realized, hobbled as he was by the old injury, his presence would "impede the progress of his men" so he appointed another man to lead the men into combat across the Rapido. Once he received word that his men were successfully across the river, he found a "partially inflated boat and made his way to the [German side] . . . With resolute fortitude he limped forward through mine fields and barbed wire entanglements" and continuous enemy fire. He regained contact with his company and once again assumed his command and led his men forward.[70]

Early on the morning of the 22nd, Major Frazior had "recrossed the river" to the American side "and was at the sunken road." His "radio man, runner, reserve company commander, weapons company commander, and several others were in the same location." Three 50mm mortar rounds came in and one hit in front of them, one hit behind them, and one hit right on them. The mortar blew off part of one of Major Frazior's hands. He was the only man in the group who was injured.[71]

Major Frazior went to his CP and a doctor "put a tourniquet on it."[72] At 1:35 A.M. Frazior called Colonel Martin and reported he had been wounded and was on the American side of the river. He also told Martin "that his battalion was making no progress," and that C Company still had not completely crossed the river.[73]

Colonel Martin ordered "Lt. Col. Michael A. Meath . . . to the 1st Battalion to take over the command." Martin sent his assistant S-3 and liaison officer, Capt. Joel W. Westbrook, to guide Lieutenant Colonel Meath to the 1st Battalion Headquarters.[74] Westbrook and Meath were not able to reach the 1st Battalion command post until 5:00 A.M. "Major Frazior still awaited them, having refused to leave his post until he could acquaint the relieving officer with the situation."[75]

Westbrook said, "I was there at regiment and regiment asked me to take him down to the 1st Battalion and to be the executive officer and S-3. It was in the night — very difficult to get down there. In fact, I had to crawl on my hands and knees sometimes. In any event, we got to Colonel Frazior. He was wounded and he gave us the situation as he saw it, and it was very grave. All the rifle companies were casualties [as were] the S-3 and executive officer and S-2. They were all casualties."[76] At last Frazior was able to go to the hospital.[77]

Westbrook continued, "Then I took the battalion commander down to the river and started" a reorganization.[78] By this time, most of the 1st Battalion had been driven back to the American side of the river. "The bridge and boats had all been destroyed. The big job was to reorganize, as Companies 'A', 'B' and 'C' had lost their commanders and the battalion was in the open flat ground with little or no protection from artillery fire. Meath was ordered to improve his positions by moving to the high ground further back, reorganize and await instructions."[79]

Westbrook said, "One of the main problems behind the crossing was that the regiments had suffered very heavy casualties previously at the battle of San Pietro. And we had, therefore, a very large infusion of new people. It was understood in the military that you don't learn how to fight in battle — you learn in training. In small units they don't have formal SOPs [standard operating procedures] the way they do at regiment and division and so on. But it works out in training. You get to know how this sergeant behaves and this BAR man behaves . . . But these troops had not had that experience together. So when I started reorganizing, it didn't make so much difference which company I put these people in. I'd grab a lieutenant and say 'You're in Company B' and I'd send him some men over . . . The Germans began shelling us while we were doing this, and the new battalion commander said he had something to do at the command post and he went back."[80]

★   ★   ★

The 3rd Battalion of the 143rd Infantry Regiment was under mortar and artillery fire when it reached the river at 2:30 P.M. on January 21.[81] Companies K, I, and L crossed the river in pontoon boats "after which the first footbridge was put in the water."[82] The entire 3rd Battalion, now under the command of Lt. Col. Paul D. Carter[83] was across the Rapido by 6:30 P.M.[84] They were under constant heavy machine-gun fire "from the time the first wave hit the water."[85]

The men in K Company crossed the Rapido around 3:00 P.M. on January 21. Pvt. Gerald L. "Mac" McAfee, BAR man, K Company, 143rd Regiment, and four other men were carrying a pontoon boat to the river on the 21st when a German shell came in and hit right in the middle of the pontoon boat. McAfee was wounded and never made it across the river.[86]

S/Sgt. Wilbur Crawford, K Company, recalled, "At three o'clock on the 21st of January we crossed the river. We were told to use fixed bayonets — not to fire. Our weapons were loaded. I crossed the river in a rubber pontoon boat." Once he was across the Rapido, Crawford advanced "about 100 to 150 yards" before he was wounded. He "pulled out at daylight the next day." Crawford recalled, "Medics had set up rubber boats that had ropes on them and pulled us across the river. Five minutes after we got back to our side some GI came up and put his arm around my shoulder to help me. There was a general there and he asked the guy who was helping me where he was wounded and when he found out he wasn't wounded, he made him go back. I don't know who the general was, but he was a tough old dude."

He continued, "They operated on me in a field hospital. I had a spinal block and the doctor stopped in the middle of the operation to smoke a cigarette and he gave me one too." Crawford was sent from the field hospital to the hospital in Naples and from there he was sent home. Crawford recalled, "I was in the middle of the ocean on my way home when they announced Normandy."[87]

S/Sgt. Lewis "Dude" Evans was in charge of the Weapons Platoon, K Company, on January 21. Evans recalled, "The regular sergeant, Tack Walker, was in the hospital and I was filling in for him . . . but I was really a staff sergeant in charge of machine guns. But due to the fact that the other fellow was in this hospital I was in charge of the machine guns and mortars. I didn't even know my own men's names. I had a paper in my pocket and I'd say what's your name. And I'd take it out and look at my paper to see if he belonged to me."[88]

S/Sgt. Billy E. Kirby, in a machine-gun section with K Company, got through the barbed wire entanglements that the Germans had so effectively installed. Kirby recalled, "Some riflemen cut the hole in the wire. They cut it or blew it, I don't know how, but they cut a hole in the wire. We were crawling and machine-gun fire was just ringing in our ears. There were little irrigation ditches [and you tried] to crawl up in those ditches and [tried] to keep as low as you [could] . . . I was with our company commander and the firing had just about stopped." Kirby remembered that Capt. Henry C. Bragaw, K Company commander, "stopped everybody" in order to find out "who we had and where they were" before the company advanced any further. Kirby said, "We were so close to the Germans" that American artillery fire "was really hitting in." Captain Bragaw "was trying to get communications back to our artillery to lift . . . the artillery. They were hindering us more than they were the Germans." Bragaw sent Kirby to the right to see who was there. Kirby did not know if Bragaw got through with the message to lift the artillery but he noted, "While I was over there looking, it was quiet." Shortly after Kirby left to locate the other men, Captain Bragaw was killed and his runner, Pvt. Stanley J. Saarloos, was wounded.[89] 2nd Lt. Alvin Amelunke, M Company, 143rd Regiment, was beside Captain Bragaw when he was killed. Amelunke later said, "It is a coincidence that two days before, the captain had sent a letter to his wife and family, and he must have had some intuition that something was going to happen to him, because later we got the information that he was predicting his time had come."[90]

Meanwhile, Kirby was searching for people. He recalled, "You couldn't see anything. So I was just crawling and trying to find our guys . . . I found three guys in my machine-gun section. I couldn't find anyone else. I think most of them had already been killed or wounded. These three guys were in a shell hole. I was laying there talking to them and I heard this explosion." A German sniper shot Kirby through the shoulder. Kirby said the bullet severed all the nerves in his arm. "I thought my arm was blown off because it was dark and I couldn't see whether I had it." K Company's first sergeant, Orville R. "Red" Jones, was also wounded. "He was strafed right down his back." Despite his own wounds, Jones helped Kirby "get back across the river." Kirby noted, "I guess because I was losing a lot of blood — you kind of get sleepy. And I'd want to stop. If it hadn't been for him I would have laid down there and died at that time. He just made me keep going. We got to that river and we found a boat. Those rubber boats were in compartments where one compartment could be punctured and the other compartments could still be up. So that one compartment was still good." Jones, Kirby, and another man got into the boat. Kirby doesn't remember having any oars, but somehow Jones and the other soldier got the boat across the river to the American side. Kirby said the trip back across the river "is real hazy but we got back across it then we found the aid station. It was in a cave." Kirby continued, "The men in the aid station sent us back because they didn't have any more supplies. They'd had so many wounded come through the aid station that they didn't have supplies. And sometime, hours and hours and hours [later], we got back to this other aid station where they were able to take care of us."[91]

Capt. Bert D. Carlton, 143rd Headquarters, recalled that Red

Jones stormed into the aid station saying, "Patch up these holes and give me a gun — I'm going to kill every son of a bitch in Germany." Carlton said, "Of course, he didn't. He never came back to the unit." Jones was transferred to the base section in Naples after his wounds healed. Carlton recalled that he and several other men were in Naples waiting to be rotated home after the war ended, and they heard someone behind them "running and hollering, whooping and hollering." Carlton continued, "We turned around and it was Red Jones. He was in the base section back there and he was just tickled to death to see someone he knew."[92]

S/Sgt. Lewis Evans had been talking to Captain Bragaw and he had "just walked away from him" when Bragaw was killed. Evans recalled, a while later, "Word got around that we were pulling back because it was just impossible and there wasn't hardly anyone left. I was going through one of [the] barbed wire entanglements . . . There was a kid, he hadn't been with us too long, had got one leg shot up pretty bad. He couldn't walk and he darn sure wasn't going to live long there. So I kind of drug him back to the river. When we got back there, there was a boat going across the river at the time. The last boat they told me. And it got sunk. The Germans could shoot down there with machine guns even in the dark . . . [The] guys started screaming and hollering that they were drowning." The Germans began to throw artillery shells into the area. Evans, the soldier with the injured leg, and Sgt. Gerald F. Zazzali were still on the river bank when the Germans began shelling the area. The young soldier and Sergeant Zazzali were both severely wounded by the shells. Evans dragged the young soldier "down in a ditch where he wouldn't get hit anymore." Evans recalled, "I said, 'Well, if one more shell hits I'm leaving.' One hit and I dove into the river and I swam it."[93]

T/Sgt. Charles R. Rummel, a platoon leader in K Company, crossed the river on the 21st.[94] On the 23rd he was listed on the 143rd casualty roster as missing in action.[95] Much later it was learned that both of his legs had received severe wounds while on the German side of the river. He was unable to make his way back to the American side, and during the periods of time that he drifted back into consciousness, he dragged himself to different water-filled foxholes and scrounged as many rations as he could. During the truce on January 25, he was not lucid enough to realize what was going on. Sometime later the Germans found him and took him prisoner. His injuries were so severe that German doctors had to remove both of his legs.[96]

Pfc Paul Blackmer was in Technical Sergeant Rummel's platoon. The Rapido crossing was his first experience in battle. Blackmer was a BAR man, and his assistant gunner was Pvt. Ray J. Bell. Blackmer said, "We were ordered to get into firing positions and the only thing we had for targets was machine-gun muzzle flashes. We did the best we could but we didn't have much to do it with." Blackmer and Bell "were side by side" and the Germans "were firing raking fire. They would point the muzzle down close to their position and then keep elevating that muzzle and [rake] the area. And while we were there we moved several times." Blackmer was uninjured, but Bell was wounded three times that night. Blackmer continued, "I heard people make reference to a bridge, but there was no bridge anywhere near where we were." A cable was stretched across the river "apparently by the engineers for us guys to use as hand over hand propulsion for the river rafts." When Bell was hit in one of his arms, he grabbed Blackmer and held on as Blackmer reached the cable and pulled both of them across the river. Blackmer recalled, "The current was very swift. We were at a thirty-degree angle and it was cold."

Once they were back across the river on the American side, Blackmer took Bell to the aid station. Bell was sent to the hospital and Blackmer returned to his company area. Upon his return there, he remembered, "I went to take a D-bar out of my haversack that I had right next to the powdered chocolate. They had shot that gator full of holes but fortunately I wasn't hit."[97]

T/Sgt. Jim C. "Bug Eyes" Maddox, 1st Platoon leader, K Company, was crossing the river in a pontoon boat with Cpl. O'-Dean T. Cox, Pvt. Robert Mallory, and Pvt. Riley Power. S/Sgt. Henry L. Dugan, from Sergeant Rummel's platoon, climbed into Maddox's boat after the boat in which he had been riding was blown up.[98]

Private Mallory had joined K Company after the battle of San Pietro. He was the first scout of the 1st Platoon. Mallory said of his position as a forward observer, "They just want you to die."[99]

The five men crossed the river and stayed together the entire time they were on the German side. Sgt. Maddox said, "It was so smoky, and we were crawling the biggest part of the time and then we'd run a little while. You don't know how far you got. I actually believe we got 700 to 800 yards in there." The men got through the barbed wire. Mallory knocked out two machine-gun nests; Maddox silenced one machine gun, and so did Dugan.[100]

Just prior to daybreak, the five men got back to the river. The only way they could get back across to the American side was to swim. Despite the swimming lessons they had taken while in the 36th Division, Maddox and Dugan could not swim, so the two men held on to a rope that Cox held while he swam across the river.[101]

When they arrived back at their company area, they found there were no officers left in the company. Bragaw's death hit the men hard. Years later, Maddox recalled, "At the time I thought he [Bragaw] was an old man but he probably wasn't over thirty. He was just like a daddy to us." Bragaw had spent a lot of time during which he had talked to, advised, and taught his men. Maddox served as the company commander for three days until Captain Bragaw's replacement arrived and took over the company command.[102]

Maddox sent Private First Class Blackmer and Private Mallory to man an outpost in front of the company area.[103] Blackmer recalled, "That was where I took up with the gentleman, Robert Mallory from Butler, Illinois. That's the first time I met old Robert — he was an eighteen-year-old blond-headed kid." The two men spent the next couple of days down there. Blackmer said, "We were there for the sole purpose of getting warning to our troops in case the German army decided to counterattack."[104]

Capt. Guy Rogers, company commander, M Company, 143rd Infantry Regiment, faced the river crossing with 120 men in his company, half of which were replacements who had arrived during the week of the Rapido attack. Rogers said, "The replacements had not received sufficient training with the organization to make them effective. Fact is, they had not been with us long enough for us to know their names — just cannon fodder — my casualties were among these men."[105]

On the afternoon of the 21st, Rogers recalled, "Once again the boats didn't get to the proper place at the proper time. Boats and men were destroyed. The chemical mortar company decided they would fire and silhouette the enemy. Short rounds fell in haystacks and silhouetted our people."[106]

Cpl. Carl McClendon, M Company, was just getting ready to

cross the river when he was hit by enemy fire. The medics were close by, and they took him to the 32nd Field Hospital.[107]

2nd Lt. Alvin Amelunke, M Company, received a battlefield commission at 11:00 P.M. on January 18. Amelunke's 30-caliber machine-gun platoon was attached to K Company for the Rapido crossing. On January 21 they started down to the river at about 4:00 P.M. under a heavy smoke screen and "a tremendous amount of [German] fire." The walls of the river bank "were so straight down," Amelunke recalled, "where we tried to get across, the Germans had put loose brush and limbs and trees into the sides of the river. If you got across in a pontoon [boat] and were trying to reach for something to hold on, or pull on to get on the other side, you'd reach into trees and limbs and brush that would just pull away — another obstacle. The engineers were having a terrible time trying to get a bridge across because of the heavy artillery and mortar fire. The Germans were looking down our throats. A lot of the pontoon [boats] were also hit and the men were lost — they were blown to pieces."[108]

Amelunke had between twenty-two and twenty-four men in his platoon. He said, "We did get across somewhere around 9:00 P.M. We were trying to go up the higher ground. We were on sloping ground and about 400 or 500 yards in front, the Germans had barbed wire entanglements all across and they were [in] back of those on high points looking right down on us. It was night, dark, and they couldn't see us but they knew what was out there and they had everything zeroed in — mortar fire and artillery fire." Amelunke was in the front with Captain Bragaw from K Company. Both men were on their knees "discussing and trying to decide what would be done, what should be done, and what was able to be done and about that time Bragaw caught a full blast from a German gun in his chest and he just grunted once and he was dead. That was probably around four in the morning and we tried to hold the positions until just around daylight and we realized that on each flank I Company had already failed. They had not come up abreast of us; they were not on our right flank. We realized they never made it as far as we did. L Company was put into action to our left. Temporarily they were in reserve as we made the attack."

L Company was almost wiped out in the attack. The company commander, 2nd Lt. Zerk Robertson, "wasn't hurt [but] he lost all of his other officers and most of his men." Robertson was not new to L Company, having served there as a platoon sergeant prior to being "one of the first three men in the 36th Division to receive a battlefield commission" not long before.[109] Amelunke continued, "L Company didn't come abreast of us on the right either, so we knew we were in a predicament. If daylight caught us, they'd kill all of us or take us prisoner. There was one walking bridge left and what was left of us managed to get back to the east side of the river just before daylight."[110]

Sgt. Edwin A. Nowacki, M Company, led a machine-gun section attached to K Company across the river "under intense mortar and artillery fire" after which they attacked the "enemy defensive positions . . . [despite] withering . . . small arms fire." Sergeant Nowacki "rallied his men and fearlessly led them forward. Upon making contact with the remaining elements of the company and finding that his superior officers were casualties, he assisted in reorganizing the rifle platoons as well as his own platoon by personally leading riflemen to positions of vantage."[111]

Sgt. Albert D. Smith, I Company, 143rd Regiment, assisted the engineers in getting men across the Rapido River. "During the . . . battle he organized a group and placed them in fighting positions. Then he directed a mortar squad where to fire and the men destroyed an . . . automatic weapon emplacement. When the enemy attacked his position in a bayonet charge he quickly secured an automatic rifle . . . and killed two [Germans] and dispersed the others."[112]

★ ★ ★

The 2nd Battalion had been held in reserve during the first Rapido River crossing on January 20. Lt. Col. Charles J. Denholm said his battalion "took terrible casualties" at San Pietro. "One company was 90 percent [destroyed] and the others were almost decimated. And then there was a rest period. But the difficulty with the rest period [was] that we were not given replacements." Denholm continued, "So at the time, I moved up onto the Rapido Line. I guess it was ten days ahead of the time we had to cross we finally got some replacements of men. We didn't get any officer replacements until three days ahead . . . So the unit was something like calling the farmers at Lexington to go do battle. Somebody higher up in the planning cycle wasn't taking account of the condition of the troops who were going to do this. At the time we made the crossing we were almost at full strength. Everybody came in, but they just came in too late to be any good."[113]

At 11:35 P.M. on January 21, the 2nd Battalion of the 143rd Infantry Regiment, under the command of Lt. Col. Charles J. Denholm, was taken out of regimental reserve and ordered to cross the river.[114] The 2nd Battalion was to cross at the 3rd Battalion site.[115] The 2nd Battalion arrived at the boat park at 2:00 A.M. From that point, engineers began to lead the 2nd Battalion to the river, but the guides got lost in the dense fog and were unable to locate the bridge on which the men were to cross. At some point between 2:00 and 2:30 A.M. "[b]attalion guides took over and guided the men to the bridge."[116] The company commander of 3rd Battalion Headquarters Company, "Capt. Herman H. Volheim . . . guided them to the bridge and across into enemy positions on the right of the 3rd Battalion." A short while later, Captain Volheim was reported missing in action.[117]

Records written by the 2nd Battalion at the time state, "[The] bridge found to be iced, well moored and all floats working, but no attempt was made to [extend] ramps to hit land satisfactorily. [The] ramp on enemy side rested at an angle of approximately 60 [degrees] from the ground, making it necessary for the troops to crawl up it on their hands and knees."[118]

At 2:30 A.M. E Company began to cross the bridge. They were followed by F Company, and at 4:30 A.M. both companies were across the river. A machine-gun platoon from H Company was attached to each company for the crossing.

As the two companies were crossing the river, Lieutenant Colonel Denholm met with the 3rd Battalion commander, Lieutenant Colonel Carter, shortly after 3:30 A.M. at the river bank to discuss the situation of the 3rd Battalion. Carter reported "he had no idea where his troops were." E Company reported by phone at 4:30 A.M. that they had found scattered groups of the 3rd Battalion at the barbed wire but that the men they had located did not know the location of the rest of the battalion. The men from E Company also reported they "found no breaks in [the] wire and concluded [the] wire had not yet been penetrated. This was erroneous as the 3rd [Battalion] had cut a hole in [the] wire 50 yards farther to the left. E Company was laying a white tape for troops, supplies, communications, and casualties to follow. Heavy wire line was continuously layed ahead of [the] weapons platoon."[119]

At 4:40 A.M. E Company was ordered to penetrate the barbed wire and push forward. F Company was ordered to follow E Company and come abreast of E Company on the right. Five minutes later, G Company was ordered to remain on the American side of the river near the bridge in order to protect it. The 2nd Battalion was ordered to set up its headquarters on the American side of the river.[120] "Lieutenant Colonel Denholm . . . did not move the battalion command post across the river because the troops had never penetrated far enough into the German defenses in order for the battalion CP to be moved. The battalion always maintained a forward CP and a rear CP, so that if one command post was destroyed the other command post could continue to have control of the situation. The forward command post of the battalion was under the direction of Capt. Carl R. Bayne, who was the operations officer or S-3 as it was known."[121]

T/Sgt. William S. Allen, E Company, said, "Everybody was to cross the river and none were to come back. We always thought we would succeed. We would be marching on Rome in a few days. We had so many replacements. I didn't have a man in my platoon I had known for more than a few days, much less a few weeks. The angle of the bridge was down and up and men would slide off. We lost a lot of men just crossing who had never done anything like that before." Allen recalled they were ordered "not to fire at will but they did have ammunition." Allen was captured while across the river and he was held as a prisoner of war until he was able to escape "the day Roosevelt died." Years later, Allen described the Rapido attack as a "suicide mission."[122]

T/Sgt. Robert M. Patterson, E Company, assumed command of his platoon after his platoon leader was wounded while they were across the Rapido in German territory. Patterson "found they had been cut off" and were surrounded "by a numerically superior enemy. With the lives of his [men] at stake, he cleverly distracted the [Germans] by allowing himself to be captured, while his men crawled away undetected." Sergeant Patterson "later escaped . . . and returned to his unit with valuable information."[123]

A mortar round seriously wounded the commanding officer of F Company, 2nd Lt. Robert F. Spencer, at 5:00 A.M. on the morning of January 22. Second Lieutenant Spencer refused to "leave the field till ordered to do so forty minutes later by Captain Bayne, S-

3." A short while later, Captain Bayne was "leading F Company through barbed wire when he was killed by machine gun fire."[124]

T/Sgt. Harry R. Moore, leader of the 2nd Platoon, F Company, remembered, "We took our first objective on my part of the attack and moved on to the [second] objective. They were counter attacking us from every direction and we fought until we ran out of ammo. And then we fought our way down to the river . . . I was hit in the left wrist and left leg by 6 Barrel mortars . . . We had to swim the river to get back to our side. Only [three] were left out of our platoon."[125]

S/Sgt. Thomas E. McCall, F Company, commanded a machine-gun section on the night of the 21st. McCall's section came under rifle and automatic weapons fire as they attempted to cross the bridge to the German side. Once across, heavy mortar and artillery shelling prevented McCall's section from setting up their weapons in positions that afforded cover. McCall managed to get his two machine guns set up, but the relentless German fire soon knocked out both guns.

One of McCall's gunners was still alive but severely wounded. McCall gave him first aid and remained with him until he died. By this time, the Rapido battle was over for most of McCall's men. For him it had just begun. McCall now found himself alone, with all of his men either killed or wounded. He grabbed one of the machine guns and fired it from the hip as he ran to within thirty yards of a German machine-gun position. He managed to silence that gun and continued to move forward firing as he advanced.

2nd Lt. Elmer Ward led his rifle platoon behind McCall's advance. Ward recalled, "[A]nother machine gun [sic] opened fire on him from a distance of 20 yards to his left." McCall silenced this position and immediately drew fire from still a third machine-gun nest about fifty yards behind him. Ward last saw McCall advancing on this position still firing his machine gun from his hip.

McCall was captured that night and was still a prisoner of war when, in April 1945, his father accepted the Congressional Medal of Honor on behalf of his son for his actions at the Rapido.[126]

Sgt. Joseph A. Cotropia, H Company in support of F Company, crossed the Rapido at 4:00 A.M. "with thirty-seven men." Cotropia said, "H Company got shelled from the time we started across. The fog was heavy and did not lift until 11:00 A.M. By that time our platoon officer was killed. We also had two sergeants killed." Cotropia was captured along with a number of other men in H Company and held as a prisoner of war for "about 500 days."[127]

S/Sgt. Frank T. Holland, Medical Detachment, 143rd Regiment, "established his aid point near the river bank." Throughout the morning of January 22, he treated the casualties despite continuous and intense enemy fire. "When he discovered several wounded men on the far bank of the river, he voluntarily formed a squad and led them under direct enemy observation and fire across the [river]. So intense was the enemy fire that it was necessary for him to wait several hours before he succeeded in moving boat loads of the wounded back across the river."[128]

At 9:15 A.M. Lieutenant Colonel Denholm went to the bridge and discovered two floats supporting the bridge had been punctured. He "immediately got the engineers on [the] phone to replace [the floats]. He was informed [the engineer] company was to be relieved in twenty minutes and a refusal to replace [the] floats was given until [the] new organization took over." Ten minutes later, Lieutenant Colonel Denholm crossed the bridge and found the weapons platoon of E and F companies "generally 100 to 175 yards in [the] rear of [the] companies prepared to assault enemy positions. Losses at [the] time were reported as heavy as the dead and wounded on the ground gave evidence." He returned to his CP on the American side of the river at 10:15 A.M. and once again requested that the bridge be repaired. He also requested smoke because the fog was beginning to thin out. Denholm recorded that the assault failed prior to 1:00 P.M., with all of his "officers killed or wounded except one reported captured (this included E, F, and two platoons [from] H Co., and [the] Battalion S-3)."[129]

1st Lt. Julian M. Quarles, who was serving as the commander of the 2nd Battalion's heavy weapons company, was assigned the job of S-3 that had been vacated by Captain Bayne's death. Quarles wrote, "After four months of combat, I had become accustomed to numerous casualties and the sights and sounds which you see and hear during a battle; but there are two sights at the Rapido which I will never forget. One was the sight of the body of a Company 'H' mortar section crewman which a shell had struck and the blast had removed the clothing from his body. The second one was seeing Captain Bayne, under whom I had served for almost a year, in a row of bodies returned from across the river who still had his helmet on, with one single bullet hole in his forehead between his eyes."[130] Captain Bayne and First Lieutenant Quarles "had been through a lot together." The two men had been captured at Salerno in September 1943. A week later they jumped from a train while in transport to a German prison camp. They worked their way through enemy territory for thirty-three days before they success-fully rejoined F Company, 143rd Infantry Regiment.[131]

At 9:00 A.M. the 3rd Battalion reported that they were running out of ammunition and they were "resupplied from forward dumps established on the river during the night. This ammunition had to be hand carried through terrific small arms and artillery fire. Nebelwefer fire came down on positions" from 9:00 to 10:00 A.M. By 11:17 A.M. the footbridge "had been almost . . . destroyed. Men were being driven back toward the river from both" the 2nd and 3rd battalions after "the position became untenable."[132]

At 12:40 P.M. on January 22, the 1st Battalion was reorganiz-ing on the American side of the river. The 2nd and 3rd battalions had been "savagely driven back" to the American side of the river and only had "a few isolated groups remaining" on the German side of the river still engaging the enemy. All three battalions were ordered to organize defensive positions on the high ground of the American side of the river "in the vicinity of their previously occu-pied assembly area."[133] "The Germans surrounded and eventually captured those still alive" across the river. By 10:00 P.M. on the night of January 22, "the sound of American weapons across the river had ceased."[134]

More men had been able to cross the river the second day but, once again, they were unable to advance on the other side. Walker recorded in his journal, "Because of the smoke[,] artillery support was ineffective. Signal communication with the east bank did not exist; hence there could be no coordination of our infantry and ar-tillery efforts. The need for ammunition, food and water could not be met. The wounded could not be evacuated."[135] Enemy fire had destroyed all of the boats and bridges. 2nd Lt. Carl Strom recalled, "We were trying to kill an elephant with a fly swatter."[136]

CHAPTER SEVEN

Again and Yet Again

By late afternoon of January 22, General Keyes knew the second attack had failed, yet he ordered a third attack, using the 142nd Regiment which was held in corps reserve at the time. He ordered the third attack for 2:30 A.M. on January 23. There were no boats and there were no bridges. Ammunition was short. Walker thought a third attack would be disastrous, but Keyes felt the third attack was justified because there were still men from the 36th across the river. Keyes said the Germans were "groggy" and that all they needed was another "blow" by a "fresh regiment to turn them out of their positions." He also felt German "morale" was low.[1]

Walker notified Col. George Lynch, the commander of the 142nd Infantry Regiment, and the other commanders who would be involved that the third attack was imminent. Since the time to prepare was so short, Walker sent General Wilbur to help the 142nd organize for its attack.[2]

After Keyes issued the order for the third attack, he talked to Clark and Clark canceled it. After the Keyes-Clark conversation, Keyes called Walker "and rescinded [the] order for the attack, adding, 'You are not going to do it anyway.' " Walker immediately canceled the order for the attack.[3]

Later that day Walker wrote in his journal, "Keyes's insulting

84

remark implies a charge of disloyalty and disobedience. Such a charge is baseless and untrue. I have done everything possible to comply with his orders."[4]

Meanwhile Clark's attempt to "stab a dagger into Kesselring's right flank at Anzio, with the blade directed at the Alban Hills" had already begun.[5] Earlier in the day, General Clark received word from General Lucas that 50,000 of the scheduled 110,000 men had successfully landed at Anzio. Lucas sent Clark the message, "No angels yet cutie Claudette." Lucas explained, "This, when properly decoded, meant 'No tanks yet but the 3rd Division and 1st Division [British] attacks are going well.' "[6] Lucas wrote, "We achieved what is certainly one of the most complete surprises in history . . . I could not believe my eyes when I stood on the bridge and saw no machine gun or other fire on the beach."[7]

Despite the excellent results of the surprise landing, Clark did not insist that Lucas push to Rome immediately. Instead he reminded Lucas, "Don't stick your neck out Johnny. I did at Salerno and got into trouble."[8]

"Clark distinctly altered the design" because he expected the Germans to react swiftly to the Anzio invasion. "Clark expected the troops to dig in and protect a small beachhead as at Salerno, and to advance some twenty miles inland to the Alban Hills only after defeating German counterattacks and building strength in the beachhead." The troops were not to advance rapidly to the Alban Hills unless the Germans "lightly opposed" the Allied landing at Anzio.[9]

General Lucas established a beachhead and it took the Americans four months to progress from the area.[10] "The German radio called Anzio 'a prison camp where the inmates feed themselves.' "[11] Churchill snorted, "I had hoped that we were hurling a wild cat onto the shore but all we got was a stranded whale."[12] "After the break-out in May, General Clark's Fifth Army headquarters issued a statement which broadly implied that Anzio was now fully justified — a statement many reporters refused to send to their papers."[13] Anzio stole most of the headlines during late January and early February, but the Rapido failures were far from forgotten at Fifth Army.

The day after Keyes issued the orders for the third attack, January 23, General Clark, General Keyes, General Wilbur (the assistant division commander), and Col. Walter Hess (division artillery commander) met with General Walker at his division command post. During the meeting the topic of conversation was what had happened.[14] Walker noted, "The conversation was not one in which there was an attempt to blame anyone for the serious check which the Germans had given our operations." At one point in the conversation, Keyes "made a statement generally to the effect that, from the information available before the operation, it seemed to him to be a worthwhile operation." Clark at that point interjected the remark, "It was as much my fault as yours."[15] General Walker "asked Wilbur to verify their statements in writing over his signature." Walker felt Clark and Keyes might attempt to refute the remarks they had made during the conversation.[16]

Years later, General Walker wrote, "I wish he [Clark] had repeated later and publicly what he said then. So far as I know he never did. Neither he nor Keyes ever admitted their error in judgment. They had sent the 36th Division into an attack with too little regard for the difficulties, with too much confidence. Their wishful thinking had obscured their ability to take heed of the facts."[17]

Walker listed his casualties between 1,681 and 2,128 men — either killed, wounded, or missing.[18] The German "15th Panzer Division which opposed the Rapido crossing, reported having counted 430 American dead and having captured 770 prisoners of war. The 15th Panzer Division reported their own casualties for the same period as 64 dead and 179 wounded."[19] Walker later stated, "It was a tragedy that this fine division had to be wrecked . . . in an attempt to do the impossible. It was ordered to cross the Rapido River directly in front of the strongest German positions under conditions that violated sound tactical principles."[20] 2nd Lt. Carl Strom, B Company, 141st Regiment, stated, "Out of 145 men, fourteen men and two officers returned."[21] T/Sgt. Harry R. Moore, 2nd Platoon, F Company, 143rd Regiment, recalled, "only three were left out of my platoon."[22] T/Sgt. William Allen, E Company, 143rd Regiment said, "I was captured . . . at the Rapido. There were 675 captured there."[23] Pvt. George Purcell, I Company, 141st Regiment, stated, "We lost all of our officers at the Rapido."[24] T/Sgt. William Greg Wiley, I Company, 141st, added, "We lost all of our good officers. Two platoon sergeants got back. We had forty men the next day down from 130."[25] Pfc Rudolph M. Trevino, E Company, 141st Regiment, said, "I was so disgusted and disappointed that they [the Germans] busted up the 36th Division."[26] The 3rd Battalion commander, Maj. Robert E. Mehaffey, said, "No question, the purpose of the attack was to take pressure off the Anzio beachhead and keep the pressure off of them and it succeeded in doing that — but we sacrificed my battalion and I don't know how many others."[27]

On January 24 Lt. Gen. Jacob L. Devers, from Alexander's Headquarters, and General Keyes visited with Walker in Walker's command post around 3:00 P.M. Walker recorded in his journal, "They asked a lot of questions. Devers wanted to know if I had given orders to carry unloaded rifles when they crossed the Rapido. I told him, 'No.' He said some of our wounded, now in hospitals, had made such a report to his interrogators."[28]

General Walker's field orders #42 from January 18 laid out the general plans for various units of the 36th Division during the Rapido attack. He did not make mention of weapons being loaded or unloaded as these orders were concerned with the duties of the engineers, the regiments, the battalions, the artillery, and supply units.[29] However, in a special report which covered "Operations of 141st Infantry in the Crossing of the Rapido River on January 20 to 23, 1944" written by General Wilbur on January 26, two days after the Devers visit, Wilbur stated, "Rifle assault companies will not be loaded but fixed with bayonets."[30] It is possible, though not probable, that Walker did not know about these orders at the time of Devers's visit. However, when Devers stopped by Walker's CP in Maddaloni, Italy, on March 13, 1944, he told Walker "that the investigation by General Clarkson, regarding shortage of ammunition and unloaded rifles at the Rapido, showed that there was nothing to the report." Walker knew better and yet he did not speak up.[31]

The initial plans for patrols on both January 18–19 and 19–20 had been for small patrols of men to silently work their way across the river in succession, dig in, and establish strong points until which time they reached platoon strength. The theory was that once at full strength the platoon could advance further inland.[32]

Walker noted, "When Devers left my truck and was walking to his jeep, Wilbur, who apparently had been waiting for the opportunity, stopped him and engaged him in conversation. Wilbur was saying some things that Devers did not like, for Devers' face became flushed. He kept moving toward his jeep as Wilbur followed along, still talking. Devers climbed into the jeep, but Wilbur put his hands on the vehicle, determined to make Devers hear him out.

Devers nudged the driver to move on, but he hesitated, apparently not in the habit of driving off in the midst of a conversation. However, after the third or fourth poke by Devers' riding crop, the driver pulled away." Walker did not hear the whole conversation but he distinctly heard Wilbur say, "The whole trouble is that you people in the rear do not know what goes on up here." Walker continued, "Under the circumstances, something may come of this conversation."[33]

Devers was not a man to be meddled with lightly and without consequences. He did not have a singularly spectacular personality. Eisenhower "characterized Devers as '.22 caliber.' " Bradley "found him to be overly garrulous (saying very little of importance), egotistical, shallow, intolerant, not very smart, and much too inclined to rush off half-cocked."[34] Despite his personality flaws, he was in a position to bring grief to those under him who opposed him. And in this case, Devers was right on the mark. Orders had been given to cross the river with unloaded weapons, though not every company complied.

Wilbur "wasn't scared of anything"[35] but it is odd that Wilbur decided to have this discussion with Devers rather than Keyes. Wilbur and Keyes were close friends and had spent several months together in General Patton's quarters in North Africa in 1943.[36]

January 25 was a day of contrast for the 36th Division. Walker received orders "to conduct a demonstration" along his front as well as "orders to be prepared to cross the Rapido again." In addition, there was a two- to three-hour truce called between the 36th Division and the Germans across the Rapido River. Until that time, the 36th had been unable to retrieve their dead and wounded from across the river. General Walker noted in his journal that around 10:00 A.M. "Capt. Joel Cunninghamm, medical officer of the 141st Infantry, went to the near bank of the Rapido with an ambulance, parlied with a German officer, and requested that he and his medical personnel be permitted to evacuate our dead and surviving wounded west of the river. The German commander agreed to a two-hour period provided both sides withhold all fire in that area." Walker approved the agreement and also notified the 143rd of the truce, during which they, too, could collect their dead and wounded. Later, the time period of the truce was extended an additional hour.[37] Many of the men from the 36th were still in defensive positions along the river bank but others were sent out during the truce to bring back as many dead and wounded as they could.

Prior to the truce, attempts had been made to rescue the wounded and recover the dead. 2nd Lt. William Everett, C Company, 141st Regiment, described one such attempt. Part of C Company had been in defensive positions even before the night of the 22nd. Immediately upon their return to the company area after the first crossing attempt, a number of men from C Company were sent to defensive positions near the river.

Everett's platoon was in this position for two or three days after their first attempt. Everett recalled, "We got shelled constantly there." Everett and his men were to hold a road. He said, "I had this hole dug in and down on the side of a ditch of the road. It went down and it went underneath the bank and it . . . kept [caving] in . . ."

The second day, Everett was in position at the road. Lieutenant Ortman from C Company was sent on a patrol to try and rescue some men that were trapped on the other side of the river. Ortman jumped in Everett's hole and he told Everett, " 'Man, there is no way I can get out there.' He said, 'Damn it, there ain't no way — they're crazy — we can't do that.'" Everett looked at him and saw "two big tears running down out of his eyes." Then Ortman said, "'Oh, but the hell with it — we've got to get it done.'" Ortman jumped out of Everett's foxhole and headed toward the river. Everett recalled, "He got to the river bank . . . and he couldn't get across because though they had thrown some smoke to cover him there was no way they could get across there. They did manage to get some people that were wounded and lying there." Everett continued, "It was the bravest thing I ever saw."[38]

Litter bearers from the 111th Medical Collecting Companies A and C "were not permitted to go beyond the barbed wire barrier to make a search of the area." The German litter bearers carried the American wounded to the barbed wire and the Americans took over from there. The Operations Report from the 111th Medical Battalion recorded, "The German representatives stated that most of our wounded had been evacuated to their own hospitals and offered to take a representative of [our unit] to one of their hospitals where they had eighteen of our wounded, but there was not time enough to accept this. A large percentage of our dead were also removed at this time but no accurate count can be given as they did not clear through our hands."[39] The clearing station had already "processed a record number of casualties" on January 21 and 22 during the two crossing attempts when they admitted 971 soldiers "of which 599 were battle casualties. Due to the difficulty in obtaining medical officer replacements, the clearing station had only five medical officers on duty to handle this heavy flow of casualties."[40]

During the truce the men from the 36th talked to the Germans while the Germans helped the Americans retrieve their casualties. The Germans told the Americans they could not believe there had been such an attack at that point on the river.[41] Several of the men who crossed the river during the truce recalled conversations that they had with German soldiers as they worked together to retrieve the casualties.

1st Sgt. Enoch Harold Terry, 3rd Battalion, 143rd Regiment, crossed the river during the truce. His company commander, Captain Volheim, had been listed as missing in action since the early morning hours of January 22. Terry said, "Captain Volheim had a .45 pistol . . . On [the] handle he had his . . . daughter's picture on one side and his wife's picture on the other . . . When we got there I [ran] into this German captain and I saw he had the gun." Terry asked the captain where he got the gun. The German captain informed Terry that Volheim had been captured. Terry asked the captain to give the gun to him and explained that he wanted to mail it back to Volheim's wife. The German refused to turn over the pistol. Terry said, "I kept on talking to him and . . . He wanted cigarettes — he wanted to know if I had any candy . . . I asked him, 'Were you in Africa?' He said, 'Yes — see these scars on my face? I got them when a tank was shot out from under me.' We picked up all of our dead and we had two or three wounded that we got back across. He told me, 'Sergeant, you be good.' And I said, 'Well, I'm going to try to.' I said, 'I hope this thing can finish up.' And he said, 'Me too — I'm ready to get out of here.'" Terry continued to say that later, while in France, they captured a "bunch of Germans and I heard somebody holler, 'sergeant, sergeant.' And I looked and it was that danged German captain. They'd captured him. So I went over and talked to him and I said, 'Hey, where's my gun?' And he said, 'Some GI got the gun.' " Terry never did find Captain Volheim's pistol. He lamented, "I sure would have liked to have it to send back to Volheim's wife."[42]

Cpl. Zeb Sunday, B Company, 143rd Regiment, stayed on the American side of the river, where he helped evacuate the dead and wounded during the truce. He said, "This German came to our side and I got the medico and I [gave] him a cigarette, a Lucky Strike cigarette. I talked to him just a few minutes. He talked pretty good English. He said he had a brother in Brooklyn named Heinz. He seemed to be just common people like we [were]. He was just doing his job."[43]

During the truce, 1st Lt. Julian Quarles, S-3, 2nd Battalion, 143rd Regiment, "was directed to secure our side of the river so that if the Germans decided to counter attack the 2nd Battalion would be in proper defensive position. Thus during the truce I was busy on the American side directing the installation of machine gun positions and defensive positions along the low ridge which ran anywhere from fifty yards to one hundred yards from the actual banks of the river, making certain that the machine guns had full field of fire and seeing that we were prepared for artillery concentrations and mortar concentrations at strategic points."[44]

Maj. Theodore H. Andrews, executive officer of the 2nd Battalion, 143rd Regiment, had briefly crossed the Rapido during the attack but he remained on the American side during the truce. Andrews had gone down to the river bank to observe the rescue effort. A German officer, also observing the truce, spotted Andrews and came across the river to talk to him. The German officer said, as Andrews remembered, " 'You lads certainly don't conduct river crossings like I was taught at Leavenworth' . . . He had been at our Command and Staff College at Leavenworth. He was all clean and with a perky little cap and clean shined boots . . . flipping his swagger stick." Andrews said, "I just shook my head. It wasn't funny to me. He was right. I would never conduct a river crossing that way. A surprise, yes. If you were going to slip up there and all of a sudden throw this across, but they had already probed it with reconnaissance. They knew what and where we would strike. We were trying to overwhelm them with bodies. That's pretty hard to do with machine guns, mortars and artillery firing at you." He continued, "What we probably should have done was capture him when he got over there, even during the truce, with him being so cocky. That was all of the conversation because I wasn't going to talk with him."[45]

Pfc Tommy V. Davis, D Company, 141st Regiment, remembered, "At the truce, a German told me in English that they would have us out of Italy in thirty days. And I believed him because of the beating we had taken. But it didn't happen. It made you think about it. You know you never thought about losing — I never thought about losing before, but it made you think."[46]

T/Sgt. Sammie D. Petty, F Company, 141st Regiment, could see the river from his company area. He recalled he watched as "our people went down to the river and across and the Germans came out of their positions and went over there and they shook hands. They talked while the rest of the people gathered up the bodies. They didn't give them time [to get all the dead and wounded]. It would have taken longer than [three hours]. You know war's a funny thing anyway. You get these people fighting each other. They're going to kill each other. Then they go down and shake hands — they're the best of buddies. And five minutes later you'll be trying to kill him or he'll be trying to kill you."[47]

During the truce, "each of the two regiments working as rapidly as possible brought back about sixty bodies and a small number of wounded who had survived three days, during which they had lain among the German mine fields and barbed wire, exposed to the cold January weather, with no food or water, except what they were carrying with them when they crossed the river. Prior to the cessation of fire they could not be approached by friend or foe."[48]

While the truce was still in force, General Walker had problems with II Corps trying to enter the area to fire shells toward the Rapido in a "feinting action" in support of the 34th Division further down the river. "One of the target areas was that in which the 143rd Infantry medical parties were collecting the wounded," Walker reported.[49] On three separate occasions during the truce, the tanks had to be turned away, much to the chagrin of II Corps.[50]

Plans for the 36th attack across the Rapido on January 25 never developed.[51] The German commander, General von Senger und Etterlin, viewed the 36th attack at the Rapido as a "side show," and two intercepted messages demonstrated the high morale of the German troops.[52] On the 25th, General Walker recorded in his journal "two messages were received by pigeon from west of the river." Walker thought the first message had probably arrived on the 24th. It read, "Everyone is giving up pig wounded. I may as well do the same unless I die first. Headquarters, 3rd Battalion,

141st Inf."[53] The second message arrived on the morning of the 25th and it read, "To the American 36th Division: herewith a messenger pigeon is returned. We have enough to eat and what's more, we look forward with pleasure to your next attempt."[54]

Years later, in 1955, former Field Marshal Albert Kesselring stated he felt the frontal attack across the Rapido by the 36th Division "should never have been made." He said, "If the U.S. general who ordered that attack [Gen. Mark W. Clark] had been under my command I would not have treated him very politely."[55]

The 141st and 143rd Infantry Regiments had suffered heavy losses in their officers, non-coms, and enlisted men. There was an immediate need to transfer officers and platoon sergeants into the depleted units. The 142nd Infantry Regiment, which had been held in reserve on both January 20 and 21, was notified that one experienced officer from each rifle company and one platoon sergeant from each rifle platoon, as well as two officers with staff capabilities from each battalion headquarters, would be transferred to begin to fill the vacancies in the other two regiments. On January 26 four of these officers were assigned to and joined the 143rd Regiment; the other eleven officers were assigned to and joined the 141st Regiment. Four days later, on January 30, thirty-six rifle platoon sergeants were equally divided with eighteen platoon sergeants sent to "each of the two stricken regiments." The officers lost to the 142nd in this transfer were "partially replaced" on January 28 when they received ten officer replacements.[56]

On January 27 Major Stovall put into action a plan he had devised to explode personnel mines without injury to his men or alerting the Germans across the river. Stovall had between 230 and 300 sheep trucked into the division area. After the sheep arrived, he dressed five of his men, Lt. Bill Dold, Lt. Jim Mueller, T-5 Frank Conversano, S/Sgt. Ed Haynes, and S/Sgt. James White, in clothing suitable to that worn by Italian shepherds. The five disguised engineers and two Italians herded the sheep three miles along the river during the daylight hours of January 27. Stovall hoped the sheep, rather than soldiers, would step on the mines and set them off. The sheep set off a few mines and the Germans seemed to pay no attention to the shepherds until the men turned to retrace their steps. Then the Germans opened fire on the men. Fortunately, all seven men escaped injury. The experiment was not tried again. The sheep were not quite heavy enough to set off a sufficient number of mines to merit another attempt. Later that night, Major Stovall lost six men during conventional mine-clearing operations at the river.[57]

General Clark wrote a letter to General Keyes on January 27 which read in part, "In accordance with a carefully prepared and coordinated plan you have launched and sustained a series of attacks which have accomplished with outstanding success their principal objective, namely, to engage in severe combat the maximum number of enemy forces and thus prevent their interference with our landings and the establishment of the Anzio beachhead. While doing so you have driven the enemy back along the Rapido front and inflicted heavy losses on his already weary troops."[58]

The next day, January 28, the 36th Division received another pigeon with a message that dispelled Clark's comments concerning the success of the II Corps plans and attacks along the Rapido River. The message had been written on January 26 and it read, "To the 36th Division: You poor night watchmen, here is another pigeon No. 2, back so that you won't starve. What do you plan in front of Cassino, with your tin can armor? Your captured syphlitic comrades have shown us the quality of the American soldier. Your captains are too stupid to destroy secret orders before being captured. At the moment, your troops south of Rome are getting a kick in the nuts. You poor nosepickers. The German troops."[59]

On the morning of January 29, General Clark telephoned Walker and told him that he wanted to meet him "near the little village of Mignano." The two men met and walked out of hearing range of their drivers. Clark felt the morale of the division was low and that the time had arrived for some changes to be made. Clark decided that General Wilbur, along with Walker's chief of staff, Col. Clayton Price Kerr, 141st Infantry Commander Col. Richard Werner, and Walker's two sons, G-3, Lt. Col. Fred L. Walker, Jr., and Lt. Charles W. Walker, who served as his father's aide, were all to be replaced. Werner, who was in the hospital, had not been in command of the 141st at the time of the Rapido attack. Two days before this meeting, Clark had removed Col. William H. Martin from his command of the 143rd Infantry. Walker noted in his journal, "Clark had no fault to find with any of these officers and did not point out deficiencies, except to say that Wilbur was a bad influence in the division." The presence of Walker's sons in the division was a particular irritant to Clark, and he took advantage of an opportunity to remove them.[60] Colonel Walker was well qualified for the position of G-3, having graduated from West Point in the class of 1936.[61] Clark's assessment of Wilbur is of particular interest in light of the fact that Wilbur had been on Clark's staff at Salerno.[62]

Walker wanted to keep all of these officers and felt that they were "scapegoats" of the failure at the Rapido.[63] By January 31, Walker had sent both Wilbur and Werner to the hospital. Walker asked Clark to send Fred, Jr., back to the States "because Fred [felt] that he [would] be handicapped in the Italian theater. Clark said he would do so."[64]

CHAPTER EIGHT

Consequences

On March 2, 1944, twenty-five members of the 36th Division who met in an Italian cattle barn to celebrate Texas Independence Day drew up a resolution which dealt with their experiences at the Rapido River a few weeks before. Their resolution called for "an investigation of the Rapido River crossing and General Mark Clark's order that caused so many useless and unnecessary casualties." Due to "censorship and concern that controversy might endanger the war effort" the men decided to postpone any action until the 36th Division Association could hold its first meeting.[1]

The association first met in Brownwood, Texas, on January 19, 1946. There the men formulated a resolution on "the eve of the second anniversary of the crossing of the Rapido River, a military undertaking that will go down in history as one of the colossal blunders of the Second World War."[2] The resolution petitioned Congress to investigate "the Rapido River fiasco and take the necessary steps to correct a military system that will permit an inefficient and inexperienced officer, such as General Mark W. Clark, in a high command to destroy the young manhood of this country and to prevent future soldiers being sacrificed wastefully and uselessly."[3] Not everyone in the association was in favor of this resolution, but there were enough present who were, for the resolution to pass. With the help of a carefully timed "Scripps-Howard newspaper article by

Frank Aston"[4] and several politicians, the 36th Division was able to persuade Congress to investigate the association's allegations.[5]

Four men from the 36th Division testified at the hearing held on March 18, 1946. Col. H. Miller Ainsworth, Col. William H. Martin, Col. Carl L. Phinney, and Maj. Gen. Fred L. Walker testified before the Committee on Military Affairs, House of Representatives, during the 79th Congress.[6]

Although Ainsworth had no firsthand knowledge of the events that took place at the Rapido River in January 1944, he testified first because he was the president of the association that year. Ainsworth had serious aspirations toward the office of governor in Texas and he had pushed hard for this hearing. The fact that Ainsworth was in the States at the time of the Rapido crossing did not help the association's case, and neither did Ainsworth's record while in Italy. Between the 36th's action at Salerno and Naples, the new commanding officer of the 142nd Infantry Regiment, Lt. Col. George E. Lynch, recommended to General Walker that Ainsworth be relieved of his duties as the executive officer of the 142nd for "unsatisfactory performance."[7] General Walker approved Lynch's request and sent Ainsworth back to the States. Nevertheless, Ainsworth testified before the committee that he felt Mark Clark violated two basic rules of tactics for a diversionary attack because such an attack "must have some chance to succeed and that it should be conducted in a manner that you will have a minimum amount of losses."[8]

General Walker's testimony was critical of Clark and Keyes. He stated, "Every soldier realized . . . a frontal attack should not be made against a well-fortified position if it is . . . possible to attack from the flank. To attack a well-organized defensive position with an unfordable river in front . . . would be considered poor judgement from a tactical point of view."[9] He also testified that the men of the 36th failed through no fault of their own. "Their courage and determination [at the Rapido] was far greater than" any other battle they were in while under his command.[10] Walker addressed the lack of time and equipment and the loss of many key leaders. He stated he felt the failure of the 36th Division at the Rapido was the result of "poor tactical judgement on the part of high commanders to carry out the instructions they received from General Alexander." He felt the result of these poor tactics was the "unnecessary loss of life and did not assist . . . the landing at Anzio."[11] Walker also testified that Clark and Keyes indicated to him that the French and British failure to effectively complete their assignments just prior to the Rapido crossing made it "all the more important that the Thirty-sixth Division succeed."[12]

Colonel Phinney testified, "The only way the . . . crossing could have been successful . . . where it was ordered would have been for the Germans to have withdrawn and the crossing to have been made without opposition." He stated, "Our reports indicated the Germans had no such intentions." Phinney told the committee about an American officer the Germans captured. While this officer was a prisoner of war, the Germans ridiculed him and "asked why the Americans insisted on making a crossing where the Germans were holding it so strongly." Phinney went on to say, "Even to our enemies the attack seemed stupid."[13]

Maj. Robert Mehaffey was subpoenaed to appear before the committee, but Mehaffey's chest surgeon said, "They don't need you there. They have all of the information they need, especially if they have your journal." Mehaffey sadly noted, "But we haven't located my journal. Nobody has it. The report that we got — whether it was right or wrong — was that the man who had it dropped it in the river or fell in the river or something. Sergeant Marion was my battalion sergeant major and he didn't tell me this, but I think he has a question in his mind about what might have happened to that journal. Because this conversation with General Keyes was entered in there, the conversation with Colonel Price, our regimental executive officer, would have been recorded there. And all the other events that pertained to the Third Battalion 141 that bore any weight would have been included in this journal."[14]

There were other notable absences from the hearings and some chose only to respond by letter. General Clark did not return from Vienna to appear at the hearing. Eisenhower, as Clark's chief of staff, did not feel it was necessary for Clark to go to the hearing.[15] Long before the hearing, in fact sixteen days before the Aston article came out, Clark got wind of it and he knew he had a problem. Clark repeatedly wrote to Eisenhower, Maj. Gen. Alfred M. Gruenther, who was Eisenhower's deputy chief of staff, and others he thought would help refute the charges that the 36th Division Association had made in its resolution. Clark wrote to Gruenther that the failure of the British Tenth Corps to successfully cross the Garigliano the night before the Rapido attack "was a major contributing factor to the failure of the Rapido crossing." Clark went on, "While this is now of historical record I should consider it advisable to utilize this angle unless pressed for details." Clark wrote again three days later: "Will you represent me in asking the War Department to put the squeeze on Walker as you suggested. If you get no results, please represent me in presenting the matter to the Chief of Staff." [16]

On January 14, 1946, Clark wired Gruenther again, "I have no reply from you to my radios . . . of January 7th and 10th. I assume you are complying with my request as time does not permit of much further delay. If War Department will not refute this story . . . and if time does not permit you to carry the ball for me, please advise immediately for I will carry it from here. Tone of Aston article indicates deliberately biased story designed to misrepresent military actualities. I feel the War Department must go on record and if they will not, I will." [17] As time went on, Clark became more and more desperate to try to avoid a congressional hearing.

On January 11 Gruenther wrote a letter to Col. R. J. Woods, who was on the general staff of the War Department. Clark received a copy of the letter which stated in part, "It is my belief that the War Department, possibly through the Bureau of Public Relations, should put the squeeze on General Walker in a big way. A statement should be prepared for General Walker to the effect that now he has had a chance to study the operation from the big picture, he realizes that the orders issued by the Commanding General of the Fifth Army were correct and fully justified." The letter went on to say that the statement prepared for Walker should also state that Walker recanted "any quotation or informal comments" that he had made either at the time of the battle or at any later date. The letter continued on, "if such a statement were sent to the Scripps-Howard paper that there would be a reasonable good chance of having the story killed. If the main actor in the plot withdraws his interest in an active way, it seems to me that the story will fall flat." [18]

On January 22 Congressman Henry M. Jackson, a Democrat from Washington, made a speech on the House floor during which he defended Clark. The next day Gruenther informed Clark that the "chairman of the House Military Affairs Committee, Congressman Andrew J. May, as well as other members, were favorably disposed toward him." Gruenther also stated that Congressman John

E. Lyle, a Democrat from Texas, did not think that Congress would authorize an investigation into the matter.[19]

Since none of these efforts averted the hearing, Robert P. Patterson, secretary of war, wrote a letter to the chairman of the Committee on Military Affairs, A. J. May, in which he stated, "The division reported its casualties for a period in which the attacks were made as 155 killed, 1,052 wounded, and 921 missing — a total of 2,128."[20] May wrote that he had examined the reports of the case and "it is my conclusion that the action to which the Thirty-sixth Division was committed was a necessary one and that General Clark exercised sound judgment in planning and ordering it."[21]

Major Mehaffey summed up the situation years later when he said, "Well, I think about it [the investigation] just like any other 36th individual — it was a cut and dried thing before there ever was an investigation. General Clark was a brilliant man — there's no question about that. And he was of the regular establishment and had to be backed under all cost."[22]

As most observers outside the 36th expected, the Board of Inquiry completely exonerated Clark, but the Rapido affair would always haunt his career. Fred Sheehan wrote, "Many years later, Texas legislators in Washington succeeded in blocking the appointment of General Clark as Army chief of staff purely because of the disaster suffered in Italy in January 1944, by the Texas National Guard Division."[23] And Adleman and Walton made this evaluation: "It is almost indisputable that Mark Clark failed to become chief of staff of the American Army because so many Texans were slaughtered on the banks of that obscure Italian river."[24]

The probability of the inquiry leading to the censure of Clark was remote due to his rank and close friendship with Eisenhower. If Congress had found him guilty of incompetence, it would have opened the door for innumerable hearings involving past and future wars. For Congress to have found a four-star general of a victorious army guilty of incompetence was inconceivable.

CHAPTER NINE:

Conclusion

Had the Committee on Military Affairs been privy to information declassified in 1974 concerning Clark's sporadic use or disuse of Ultra, the British cryptanalitic section that broke the German Enigma code, Clark's case before Congress might not have fared so well. Clark's failure to use Ultra intercepts apparently was a reprehensible result of his inherent dislike for the British and his arrogant nature.

Soon after America entered the war, the British attempted to brief Clark on Ultra's capabilities. F. W. Winterbotham, creator of the Scientific Intelligence Unit of the Secret Intelligence Service (SIS), described Clark's first encounter with Ultra: "Eisenhower came in with Lieutenant-General Mark Wayne Clark and his principal Intelligence officers." Eisenhower stayed long enough to introduce the members of his intelligence staff and "then he excused himself since, he said, he and his chief of staff, Major Walter Bedell Smith, had already been told about it by the Prime Minister; Clark was restless from the start."[1] Winterbotham explained to Clark how Ultra came about and gave him "some pertinent examples of what it would do." Had Clark spent more time at the briefing he would have heard "how the information would reach him, and the security regulations which accompanied its use. But Mark Clark didn't appear to believe the first part and after a quarter of an hour he excused himself and his officers on the grounds that he had something else to do."[2]

Ultra intercepted messages that let Clark know he had been successful in pinning down the Germans and in attracting additional German forces "when the British crossed the Garigliano on January 17."[3] Ultra advised General Clark that Kesselring sent a message that expressed confidence he could hold the Cassino Line, at least for some time.[4] Winterbotham reported, "At the end of the third week in January, in fact, right up to the moment of landing, General Clark was assured of complete strategic surprise and the probability that no new opposition could be brought to bear for forty-eight hours."[5]

General Clark failed on numerous occasions to heed the advice of Ultra and General Walker, and in doing so, he unnecessarily delayed the Allied capture of Rome. It was understandable that Clark might doubt the authenticity of the Ultra reports at the time of the Garigliano crossing, given Ultra's newness and his basic dislike of the British.[6] However, when the second British crossing failed to break through the German defenses not far from the Rapido River site, he should have questioned the wisdom of the Rapido crossing. With the information he had about Anzio, he could have delayed the scheduled Rapido crossing and allowed time for General Walker to break the Gustav Line north of the Rapido on the German flank. Walker suggested this plan to Clark and Keyes on several occasions prior to January 20.[7] This approach would have been no more risky than the attack. Again, Clark's insecurity may have influenced his decision. Although Clark was then the one in charge, there had been a time, in the 1930s, when Walker was the one to lead and Clark the one to follow when Walker was Clark's instructor at the War College. Perhaps the former teacher-student relationship between the two men created a barrier that could not be surmounted.[8] Friction between the two men was fueled further by the presence of Walker's two sons in the division. Certainly, when Clark's troops landed on the beaches of Anzio and found no resistance, he should have made use of the Ultra information and ordered General Lucas to advance to Rome immediately.

Rome could have been Clark's four months earlier, and the courageous men of the 36th would not have found themselves with too little time and too few supplies to prepare to meet the Germans at the Gustav Line if Clark had utilized the Ultra messages.

Jane Scrivener, an American living in Rome during the war, recorded in her diary on January 22 that the Germans seemed nervous and many of them had left Rome. "There were few armored cars and no tanks, all the officers appeared to be clearing out."[9] While Clark failed to use Ultra to create a brilliant offensive triumph, the Germans were in position to take advantage of the inexperience of Clark and his corps commander at the Rapido.

Clark and Keyes apparently failed to consider the adverse effect of the muddy conditions on armor and the German defensive control over both the Rapido River and the Liri Valley when they repeatedly ordered the construction of the Bailey bridge during the 36th attack. The Bailey bridge that Clark kept urging Keyes to put up would not have helped. Each section of Bailey bridge was ten feet long and weighed over 5,000 pounds. The men of the 36th would have had to carry each section to the river. The engineers could not put the bridge up until the 36th took the river, which they were unable to do. If the engineers had erected the bridge, tanks and trucks would not have been able to get to it because of the depth of the mud near the river. All of the turmoil about the Bailey bridge was merely the result of inexperience on the part of Clark and Keyes. They did not have enough experience in command of a battle situation to know they could not effectively get tanks into the Liri Valley. Without artillery and tank support on the newly taken bridgehead, the mission would have been doomed. If the tanks had been able to get into the Liri Valley, they would not have gotten far before the Germans destroyed them from their vantage points in the valley.[10]

Likewise, there was no reasonable excuse for Keyes's order to attack by noon on the 22nd. In fact, there seems to be no excuse for the second attack order at all. It should have been apparent to any commander, whether new to battle or not, that the German defenses at the Rapido were too strong to break at that time. Wilbur recorded in his personal notes, "I believe that this action was Jeff's [Geoffrey Keyes's] first experience in command of a battle — in fact the first real battle experience of his life. Naturally he wanted it to succeed. When the crossing failed, I believe he began to look for some one to blame and struck out in his great and very tragic disappointment."[11]

If Clark had seen any chance of success at the Rapido he would not have canceled Keyes's third order for the attack, because

General Clark desperately wanted to be the first to conquer Rome from the south in 2,000 years. He wanted the Rapido crossing to succeed. His pride and love for publicity fanned the flames of his ambition and obscured his judgment. His lack of command experience in combat tempted him to try to go through the Liri Valley on his way to Rome, just as Bellisarius had done in A.D. 536.[12] It was General Walker, not Clark, who came up with and executed the plan that led to the breakthrough at Velletri and the Allied capture of Rome.[13]

Although General Walker and the men of the 36th Division handed Clark the keys to Rome, for Walker the celebration was short-lived. Soon after Rome was liberated, General Walker received a letter from Clark which informed him that General McNair had requested Walker for assignment as commandant of the Infantry School. Walker had expected such an action from Clark. As he noted, "It [Clark's letter] is cleverly worded to save Clark's and my faces, and to give the impression of a choice, but there is no choice. It is a reassignment."[14] On July 7, 1944, almost ten months to the day after the 36th stormed ashore, General Walker received his farewell review from the troops at Paestum, where it had all begun.[15]

Unfortunately, Clark had outranked his capabilities. He had reached the apex of his abilities when he so efficiently organized the new recruits in the States. When plans were drawn for Clark to lead the invasion into Italy, General Bradley had reservations about Clark's abilities. Bradley recalled, "I was not certain that Mark Clark was the best choice for this rather bold leap into Italy. I had come to know Clark well by now. He had commanded a battalion in combat in World War I and had been wounded in action. But he had not yet commanded large-scale forces in combat in World War II. Moreover, I had serious reservations about him personally. He seemed false somehow, too eager to impress, too hungry for the limelight, promotions and personal publicity. Patton didn't trust him either. He thought Clark was 'too damned slick' and more preoccupied with bettering his own future than winning the war."[16] General Truscott said of Clark, "[H]is concern for personal publicity was his greatest weakness. I have sometimes thought it may have prevented him from acquiring that 'feel of battle' that marks all top-flight battle leaders."[17] This shortcoming would seldom be more evident than at the Rapido.

Against a deadly merger of the inexperience of Clark and Keyes with tactical error, superior enemy defensive position, and constraints of nature, time, and materiel, the men who wore the T-Patch fought with quiet courage and unhesitating devotion to duty at the Rapido. However, they could not accept such great losses in an ill-conceived operation. They finished the business of the war as they fought through Italy, France, Germany, and Austria, and then they took on the U.S. Army, in the person of Gen. Mark Clark, for allowing such a fiasco. They lost that battle too, but not without damage to the career of the one man they held most responsible. Perhaps the greatest tribute to the men of the "Texas Army" was that they served with courage and loyalty to each other that no enemy could defeat.

Appendix A

CASUALTY REPORTS

The 36th Division Battle Casualty Section was composed of four men who worked "under the direction of three officers of the 36th's Adjutant General, Lt. Col. John J. Deane." His assistants were Maj. Harry Kelton, 2nd Lt. William T. Steger, and WO D. C. McClenahan. These men were assisted by T/Sgt. Luther Johnson, T/4 Jerry Frangella, and T/5 Vadaus Carmack.[1]

Casualty lists were compiled from several sources. Each morning the first sergeant of each company would include a list of the prior day's casualties in his morning report. Men were listed as missing in action until they were found to be either wounded in a hospital, dead, AWOL, or POW. Hospitals were contacted every day to gain information about new admissions and to upgrade or downgrade the condition of the men. When a man was confirmed to be a POW, his records were updated from MIA to POW.

As late as October 19, 1944, "the battle casualty section [was] still receiving reports of bodies found in and near the Rapido River, where the division suffered heavy losses [the previous] January."[2]

The roster of casualties compiled in February 1944 was as accurate as could be expected so soon after the Rapido battle.

Code for Casualty Rosters

KIA — Killed in Action	LIA — Lightly Injured in Action
DOW — Died of Wounds	MIA — Missing in Action
SWA — Seriously Wounded in Action	SIA — Seriously Injured in Action
LWA — Lightly Wounded in Action	

Roster of Casualties
141st Infantry Regiment[3]
January 1–31, 1944*

*Not included are 605 names that were listed as missing in action (18 officers and 587 enlisted men)

Name	Rank	Type	Date of Casualty	Residence
Regimental Headquarters				
Alspaugh, Robert R. L.	Capt.	KIA	16 Jan. 44	Tulsa, OK
Anti-Tank Company				
Cox, Lexie L.	Pfc	SWA	18 Jan. 44	Jumping Branch, WV
England, Alfred NMI	Pfc	SWA	18 Jan. 44	Lesterville, MO
Jackson, James W.	Pfc	SWA	18 Jan. 44	Prysorburg, MO
Purcell, Fred H.	Pvt.	LWA	26 Jan. 44	Kingsport, TN
Seaver, Joe F.	Pfc	SWA	18 Jan. 44	Leesville, Texas
Cannon Company				
Stevenson, Floyd C.	Cpl.	LWA	28 Jan. 44	Weslaco, Texas
Walsh, Peter R.	Pfc	KIA	28 Jan. 44	Royal Oak, MN
Medical Detachment				
Aebrah, James J.	Pvt.	LWA	21 Jan. 44	Dunle, PA
Briscoe, Robert J.	Pfc	SWA	21 Jan. 44	Trenton, NJ
Caiarneau, Jospeh A.	Pvt.	SWA	22 Jan. 44	Eastwalters, ME
De Angelo, Howard NMI	Pvt.	LWA	21 Jan. 44	Yonkers, NY
Hayes, John M.	Pvt.	LWA	21 Jan. 44	Bronx, NY
Hicks, Frank E.	Pvt.	LWA	22 Jan. 44	Morlina, NC
Izzo, Lawrence M.	Pvt.	LWA	21 Jan. 44	Brooklyn, NY
Johnson, Herbert F.	Pvt.	LWA	19 Jan. 44	Onsett, MA
Le Grand, James H., Jr.	Pvt.	SWA	21 Jan. 44	Medford, MA
Smith, David J.	Pvt.	LWA	18 Jan. 44	Newington, CT
Sweatman, Louis G.	Pvt.	LWA	21 Jan. 44	Atlanta, GA
A Company				
Artymovich, Clarence M.	1st Lt.	KIA	21 Jan. 44	Detroit, MI
Beasley, Warren G.	1st Lt.	LWA	21 Jan. 44	North Vernon, IN
Bumbalough, Elbert E.	Pfc	KIA	21 Jan. 44	Columbus, IN
Checkston, Albert L.	Pvt.	KIA	21 Jan. 44	Washington, DC
Goode, Joel D., Jr.	T/Sgt.	LWA	21 Jan. 44	San Antonio, Texas
Guy, Edward F.	Pfc	LWA	21 Jan. 44	New York, NY
Henderson, Leon L., Jr.	Pvt.	LWA	21 Jan. 44	Trenton, NC
Hewitt, Frank V.	Pvt.	KIA	21 Jan. 44	North Adams, MA
Hill, Herbert R.	Pvt.	KIA	21 Jan. 44	South Shaftsburg, VT
Hosey, Carl O.	Pfc	LWA	21 Jan. 44	Richwood, WV
Karpinski, Robert B.	Pvt.	LWA	21 Jan. 44	Montreal, WI
Keats, Gordon E.	Pvt.	LWA	21 Jan. 44	Milwaukee, WI
Rose, Julian NMI	Pvt.	LWA	21 Jan. 44	Bronx, NY
Seidaker, Harry R.	Pfc	LWA	21 Jan. 44	Brenom, IN
Seidesimer, Ben F.	Pfc	DOW	23 Jan. 44	Hamilton, Texas

Seilhekimer, Phillip G.	Pfc	LWA	21 Jan. 44	Hamilton, Texas
Sicurelia, Nicholas J.	Pvt.	LWA	21 Jan. 44	East Rockford, NJ
Son Grant, William E.	Sgt.	LWA	21 Jan. 44	Adrian, MI
Stratton, Jospeh P.	S/Sgt.	LWA	21 Jan. 44	San Antonio, Texas
Taylor, Gordon NMI	S/Sgt.	DOW	22 Jan. 44	Newburg, NY
Traugott, Stefan R.	Pvt.	LWA	21 Jan. 44	New York, NY
Turner, Covey E.	Pfc	LWA	21 Jan. 44	Munitions, WV
Williamson, Frinnie NMI	Pfc	LWA	21 Jan. 44	Litcreek, KY

B Company

Harmonson, Selsar R.	Capt.	KIA	21 Jan. 44	Wharton, Texas
Tully, Martin J.	1st Lt.	LWA	21 Jan. 44	Chicago, IL
Bouresseau, Dale S.	2d Lt.	LWA	20 Jan. 44	Chagrin Falls, ID
Abonitz, Richard S.	Pvt.	KIA	21 Jan. 44	Providence, RI
Bavusg, Matteo NMI	Pvt.	LIA	24 Jan. 44	Brooklyn, NY
Bialceak, Stanley P.	Pfc	LWA	21 Jan. 44	Brooklyn, NY
Bonerman, Willard B.	Sgt.	LWA	21 Jan. 44	Houston, Texas
Borbell, George R.	Pfc	LWA	21 Jan. 44	Philadelphia, PA
Brazeel, Carl NMI	Pfc	LWA	21 Jan. 44	Banger, AL
Briggs, George F.	Pvt.	LWA	21 Jan. 44	Durham, NC
Bruce, Robert W.	Pfc	LWA	21 Jan. 44	Bronx, NY
Claplie, William NMI	Pfc	LWA	21 Jan. 44	Villanova, PA
Colby, Charles D.	Pvt.	KIA	21 Jan. 44	Alma, GA
Compton, Joe N.	Pfc	LWA	21 Jan. 44	Bluffton, IN
Conrad, Erwin L.	Pfc	KIA	21 Jan. 44	Tulsa, OK
Cook, Bob P.	Pvt.	LWA	21 Jan. 44	Dalton, WV
Coppinger, Edmund H.	Pvt.	KIA	21 Jan. 44	Hoboken, NJ
Crabtree, Allen J.	Pfc	LWA	21 Jan. 44	Inglewood, CO
Craig, Dayron C.	Pvt.	KIA	21 Jan. 44	Kennett, MO
Crawford, Archie P., Jr.	Pvt.	LWA	23 Jan. 44	Eden, WI
Dangier, Charles R.	Sgt.	LWA	21 Jan. 44	Byron, OH
Davis, Alfred W.	Pvt.	LWA	21 Jan. 44	Lynchburg, VA
Dressman, Allen A.	Pfc	LWA	21 Jan. 44	Covington, KY
Emsley, John H.	Pvt.	LWA	23 Jan. 44	Pinecastle, FL
Estep, Paul R.	Pfc	LWA	21 Jan. 44	Greenbryer, WV
Fangher, Howard H.	S/Sgt.	LWA	21 Jan. 44	Johnson City, NY
Fritz, Ralph J.	Pvt.	KIA	21 Jan. 44	South Bend, IN
Gaiko, Rudolph A.	Pvt.	LWA	21 Jan. 44	Milwaukee, WI
Gamble, Raleigh NMI	Pfc	LWA	21 Jan. 44	Flatcreek, KY
Gassert, Kenneth H.	Pvt.	KIA	21 Jan. 44	Dearpark, OH
Glover, Lester F.	Pfc	KIA	21 Jan. 44	Chelsia, MA
Goldstein, Sam NMI	Pfc	LWA	21 Jan. 44	Bronx, NY
Graham, Frank M.	Pvt.	LWA	26 Jan. 44	Tocoa, GA
Hakes, Ross N.	Pfc	LWA	21 Jan. 44	Mansfield, OH
Hantman, Alex NMI	Pfc	LWA	21 Jan. 44	Brooklyn, NY
Haun, William M.	Pvt.	LWA	21 Jan. 44	Prospect, KY
Heintz, Frederick NMI	Pvt.	LWA	21 Jan. 44	Brooklyn, NY
Herring, Bossman NMI	Pvt.	LWA	21 Jan. 44	Loris, SC
Howard, Lewis NMI	Pvt.	KIA	21 Jan. 44	Anneston, AL
Hudson, Jess C.	Pvt.	KIA	21 Jan. 44	Denison, Texas
Huie, Ken NMI	Pfc	LWA	21 Jan. 44	New York, NY
Jones, Richard W.	Pfc	LWA	21 Jan. 44	Rochester, NY
Lanoreauox, Donald NMI	Pfc	KIA	21 Jan. 44	Sparta, MI
Laurant, Edward E.	Pvt.	LWA	21 Jan. 44	Detroit, MI
Leek, Jernwood NMI	Pvt.	KIA	21 Jan. 44	Middlebourne, WV
Long, Caidle O.	Pfc	LWA	21 Jan. 44	Julian, WV

Meimhardt, Fred NMI	Pvt.	LWA	21 Jan. 44	Brooklyn, NY
Mergenovich, George NMI	Pfc	LWA	21 Jan. 44	Hollisdayscove, WV
McClafferty, Paul G.	Pfc	LWA	21 Jan. 44	Etna, PA
McCune, Robert C.	1st Sgt.	LWA	21 Jan. 44	San Antonio, Texas
McCutcheron, Cecil D.	Pfc	LWA	21 Jan. 44	Pavetvill, VA
Newsome, William NMI	Pfc	KIA	21 Jan. 44	Louise, KY
Prentice, Jim A.	Sgt.	LWA	21 Jan. 44	Whitney, Texas
Robertson, Earl L.	Pvt.	DOW	22 Jan. 44	Santa Monica, CA
Rodemheiser, Earl A.	Pvt.	LWA	21 Jan. 44	New Port, DE
Serna, Francisco NMI	Pvt.	LWA	20 Jan. 44	Harlingen, Texas
Sousa, Albert E.	Pfc	LWA	21 Jan. 44	Pawtucket, RI
Sparks, Willie C.	Pvt.	LWA	21 Jan. 44	South Irving, KY
Vasher, Joseph R.	Pvt.	LWA	23 Jan. 44	Wyandott, MI

C Company

Boucher, Robert A.	Pvt.	DOW	20 Jan. 44	Lewston, MI
Cruze, William G.	Sgt.	LWA	22 Jan. 44	Driftwood, Texas
Czarnescki, John F.	Pfc	LWA	23 Jan. 44	Newark, NJ
Daniel, Milford E.	Pvt.	SWA	23 Jan. 44	Helenwood, TN
Deckeduane, William G.	Pvt.	SWA	24 Jan. 44	New Orleans, LA
Dick, Volber L.	Pfc	SWA	21 Jan. 44	Nancy, KY
Domarnite, Roscoe R.	Pfc	SWA	21 Jan. 44	Stewart, VA
Duffey, Paul H.	Pvt.	SWA	21 Jan. 44	Lancaster, PA
Edwards, John L.	Pvt.	LWA	20 Jan. 44	Toledo, OH
Ferguson, Herman R.	Pfc	LWA	21 Jan. 44	Ashland, KY
Frankenburg, Paul W.	Pfc	SWA	21 Jan. 44	Dayton, OH
Hays, Stanley NMI	S/Sgt.	SWA	21 Jan. 44	Loustcreek, KY
Hile, Paul F.	Pvt.	LWA	23 Jan. 44	Clearfield, PA
Holliday, Paul F.	Pvt.	SWA	23 Jan. 44	Roseburg, WV
Hope, William D.	Pvt.	SWA	21 Jan. 44	Ridgewood, NJ
Horstman, Oran E.	S/Sgt.	SWA	21 Jan. 44	Winchester, KY
O'Conner, Daniel O.	S/Sgt.	SWA	21 Jan. 44	Portsmouth, OH
Parsons, Harvey NMI	Pfc	LWA	19 Jan. 44	Gallup, KY
Quick, Monty W.	S/Sgt.	SWA	21 Jan. 44	Richlands, WV
Roberts, Rufford NMI	Pfc	SWA	21 Jan. 44	Cowcreek, KY
Santina, Harry NMI	Pvt.	KIA	21 Jan. 44	Cucumber, WV
Serna, Alejandro R.	Sgt.	KIA	23 Jan. 44	Harlingen, Texas
Vasquez, Frank C.	Pfc	SWA	21 Jan. 44	Los Angeles, CA
Wright, Berry A.	Pvt.	SWA	23 Jan. 44	Fresque, ME
Zastrow, Harry W.	Pvt.	SWA	21 Jan. 44	Manwantosa, WI

D Company

Conway, Franklin NMI	Sgt.	LWA	21 Jan. 44	Baytown, Texas
Rodenhauser, William B.	Pfc	LIA	21 Jan. 44	Freemont, OH
Schilling, William T.	Pvt.	LIA	24 Jan. 44	Philadelphia, PA
Steinle, Albert W.	Cpl.	LWA	23 Jan. 44	Mountain Lake, MN

2nd Battalion Headquarters

Landry, Milton J.	Maj.	SWA	22 Jan. 44	San Antonio, Texas
Lehman, Henry E.	Capt.	LWA	22 Jan. 44	San Antonio, Texas
Baldwin, Reynolds D.	2d Lt.	LWA	22 Jan. 44	Philadelphia, PA
Haraison, Chesney Q.	2d Lt.	SWA	22 Jan. 44	Baltimore, MD
Becktold, Melvin P.	Pvt.	DOW	23 Jan. 44	Wampa, ID
Bishop, Eddie M.	Pvt.	LWA	22 Jan. 44	Lodge, SC
Carolia, Ralph NMI	Pvt.	LWA	20 Jan. 44	Oliver, PA
Clark, Rollie D.	Pvt.	LWA	22 Jan. 44	Marshall, Texas

Copeland, Harold E.	Pvt.	LWA	17 Jan. 44	Nashville, TN
De Leon, Pascual NMI	Pfc	LWA	22 Jan. 44	Laredo, Texas
Hartman, Arthur G.	1st Sgt.	SWA	22 Jan. 44	San Antonio, Texas
Svosoda, Frank A.	Pfc	KIA	15 Jan. 44	Wolford, IA

E Company

Chapin, John L.	Capt.	KIA	22 Jan. 44	El Paso, Texas
Barker, William R.	1st Lt.	SWA	23 Jan. 44	Lexington, MA
Navarrete, Gabriel L.	2d Lt.	LWA	19 Jan. 44	El Paso, Texas
Batten, Alfred N.	Pfc	LWA	19 Jan. 44	Saint Simons Island, GA
Blansett, John R.	Pvt.	LWA	22 Jan. 44	Houston, MS
Cohn, Joseph NMI	Pvt.	LWA	19 Jan. 44	Trenton, NJ
Demers, Raymond A.	Sgt.	LWA	19 Jan. 44	Washington, RI
Dominguez, Benito G.	S/Sgt.	LWA	19 Jan. 44	San Antonio, Texas
Dunn, John E.	Pvt.	LWA	19 Jan. 44	Detroit, MI
Engrette, Albert F. T.	Pvt.	LWA	22 Jan. 44	San Jose, CA
Gangi, Paul P.	Pfc	LWA	20 Jan. 44	Winchester, MA
Gonzales, Julio R.	Cpl.	LWA	22 Jan. 44	El Paso, Texas
Goodheart, Bruce E.	Pvt.	LWA	22 Jan. 44	Ilion, NY
Hermandee, Manuel C.	Pfc	LWA	22 Jan. 44	San Antonio, Texas
Hernandez, Jose NMI	Sgt.	LWA	19 Jan. 44	Carrizo Springs, Texas
Hubble, John A.	Pfc	LWA	22 Jan. 44	Shavenna, IL
Pavlonic, John M.	Pvt.	LWA	19 Jan. 44	Russelton, PA
Richards, Cecil D.	Pfc	LWA	22 Jan. 44	Fairland, OK
Rivera, Manuel R.	S/Sgt.	LWA	19 Jan. 44	El Paso, Texas
Rosales, Jose A.	Pfc	LWA	22 Jan. 44	Raymondville, Texas
Segura, Roque O.	S/Sgt.	KIA	22 Jan. 44	El Paso, Texas
Silvas, Jose NMI	Pfc	LWA	22 Jan. 44	Taft, Texas
Smith, Vance NMI, Jr.	Pfc	LWA	19 Jan. 44	Statesville, NC
Spangler, William G., Jr.	Pfc	LWA	22 Jan. 44	Holden, WV
Sulik, Edward NMI	Pvt.	LWA	22 Jan. 44	Youngstown, OH
Walsh, Robert N.	Pvt.	LWA	19 Jan. 44	Carmichael, PA
Wescott, Russell E.	Pvt.	LWA	19 Jan. 44	Tampico, IL
Wildham, William E.	Pvt.	LWA	19 Jan. 44	Yazoo City, MA
Wilson, Carl E.	Pvt.	LWA	19 Jan. 44	Calhoun, GA
Yavorsky, John J.	Pfc	LWA	18 Jan. 44	Toledo, OH
Young, William E., Jr.	Pvt.	LWA	22 Jan. 44	Jamaica, L.I., NY
Zelazko, Frank E.	Pfc	LWA	18 Jan. 44	Inkster, MI

F Company

Potts, John R.	1st Lt.	LWA	22 Jan. 44	Levelland, Texas
Seibert, William F.	2d Lt.	LWA	22 Jan. 44	Washington, DC
Barber, Howard L.	Pfc	LWA	21 Jan. 44	Bolscott, NY
Bullock, James M.	Pvt.	LIA	22 Jan. 44	Piedmont, AL
Cartwright, Alvin D.	Pfc	LIA	22 Jan. 44	Nettie, WV
Culpepper, Dean W.	S/Sgt.	LWA	19 Jan. 44	Lockhart, Texas
Curry, Ralph W.	Pvt.	LIA	22 Jan. 44	Granite City, IL
DePalna, Anthony J.	Pfc	KIA	15 Jan. 44	Brooklyn, NY
Edmonson, Luther M.	Pfc	LWA	22 Jan. 44	Athens, TN
Edwards, Oren C.	Pvt.	LWA	16 Jan. 44	Woodlawn, VA
Ferguson, Ezra M.	Cpl.	LIA	22 Jan. 44	McCarr, KY
Ferry, Joseph F.	Pvt.	LIA	22 Jan. 44	Philadelphia, PA
Fulginiti, Salvatore J.	Sgt.	KIA	15 Jan. 44	Brooklyn, NY
Gibbs, Woodsie C.	Pvt.	LWA	16 Jan. 44	Lilly, WI
Howard, Percy D.	Pvt.	LWA	19 Jan. 44	Salisbury, NC
Mishler, Louis G.	Pfc	LWA	19 Jan. 44	Mantua, OH

Montefusco, Robert NMI	Pvt.	LWA	21 Jan. 44	Brooklyn, NY
McGhee, James H.	Pvt.	LIA	16 Jan. 44	Norfolk, VA
McKnight, Randall	S/Sgt.	LWA	22 Jan. 44	Wills Point, Texas
Norris, Vern D.	Pvt.	LIA	22 Jan. 44	Coffee, IL
Pandetti, Domenico NMI	Pvt.	KIA	16 Jan. 44	Providence, RI
Schnolninski, Bruno NMI	T/Sgt.	LWA	22 Jan. 44	Lockhart, Texas
Scholnineli, Bennie NMI	Sgt.	LIA	22 Jan. 44	Lockhart, Texas
Shively, Wilfred W.	T/5	LWA	16 Jan. 44	Lewistown, PA
Starr, Charles H.	Pfc	LWA	16 Jan. 44	Lincolnton, NC
Stull, Henry A.	Pvt.	LWA	16 Jan. 44	Owingsville, KY
Sunderman, Herman H.	Sgt.	LWA	21 Jan. 44	Columbia, IL
Sylvestee, Angelo J.	Pvt.	KIA	16 Jan. 44	Cornwall, NY
Tucker, James G.	Pvt.	KIA	16 Jan. 44	Eastport, MD
Vogt, Milton S.	S/Sgt.	KIA	16 Jan. 44	St. Louis, MO
Walker, Edward B.	Pvt.	LWA	16 Jan. 44	Matteon, IL
Walker, John M.	Pvt.	LWA	20 Jan. 44	Ripley, MS
Weatherwax, Albert R.	Pvt.	LWA	15 Jan. 44	Cadillac, MI
Young, Linus A.	S/Sgt.	LIA	22 Jan. 44	Elvins, MO

G Company

McCord, Rex T.	1st Lt.	LWA	22 Jan. 44	Leavenworth, KS
Phillips, John R.	2d Lt.	LWA	22 Jan. 44	Willinsburg, PA
Anderson, Hal N.	2d Lt.	SWA	17 Jan. 44	Conroe, Texas
Adams, Clifford NMI	Sgt.	LWA	25 Jan. 44	Broadhead, KY
Baker, Warren G.	Pvt.	LWA	18 Jan. 44	Cradborchard, KY
Baril, Edgar L.	Pvt.	KIA	22 Jan. 44	Woonschot, RI
Beargie, Raymond J.	Pvt.	LWA	22 Jan. 44	Cleveland, OH
Blumbaugh, Raymond L.	Pfc	LWA	18 Jan. 44	Plymouth, IN
Brooks, Robie W.	Pfc	KIA	20 Jan. 44	Kovenbranch, ME
Bussant, Byesing B.	Pfc	KIA	22 Jan. 44	New York, NY
Ceccarini, Ronzo T.	Pvt.	LWA	18 Jan. 44	North Agawam, MA
Chapman, Leonard E.	Pfc	LWA	22 Jan. 44	Oakdale, TN
Dias, John F.	Pvt.	SWA	17 Jan. 44	Portsmouth, RI
Dingledine, Robert V.	Pvt.	LIA	22 Jan. 44	Battlecreek, MI
Funnell, Richard T.	Pvt.	LIA	22 Jan. 44	Eaggerloville, NY
Gardner, Warren H.	Pfc	LWA	22 Jan. 44	Exeter, RI
Heimbold, William G.	Pvt.	LWA	22 Jan. 44	Troy, NY
Hiatt, Elam C.	Pvt.	SWA	17 Jan. 44	Marion, IN
Hinton, Willie B.	Pfc	SWA	17 Jan. 44	Hobbsville, NC
Holt, Edward J.	Pvt.	SWA	17 Jan. 44	Holdenwald, TN
House, Edward R.	Pfc	LWA	22 Jan. 44	Buffalo, NY
Kulach, Chester J.	Sgt.	LWA	18 Jan. 44	Chicago, IL
Letters, Daniel P.	Pfc	LWA	22 Jan. 44	Detroit, MI
Long, Ralph D.	Pvt.	LWA	22 Jan. 44	Bloomsburg, PA
Louch, Charles F.	Pvt.	LIA	22 Jan. 44	Woodside, NY
Martin, Cyril L.	Pfc	LWA	22 Jan. 44	New Ballemara, PA
Reese, William NMI	Pfc	LWA	22 Jan. 44	New Port, TN
Rosenburg, David NMI	Pvt.	SWA	18 Jan. 44	Brooklyn, NY
Sczozech, Joseph B.	S/Sgt.	LWA	22 Jan. 44	Chicago, IL
Smith, Elmer R.	Pvt.	LWA	22 Jan. 44	Covington, VA
Sutton, Raymond NMI	Pfc	LWA	18 Jan. 44	Cosby, TN
Swodish, Charles H.	S/Sgt.	LWA	18 Jan. 44	Jamacia, NY
Synkal, Stanley J.	Pfc	LWA	22 Jan. 44	Brooklyn, NY
Tate, Frankie NMI	Pfc	LWA	22 Jan. 44	Olenmorgan, VA
Tepatti, William F.	Pfc	LWA	22 Jan. 44	Pekahomas, IL
Tinko, Andrew NMI	S/Sgt.	LWA	22 Jan. 44	Bronx, NY

Vigne, Willett E.	Pfc	LWA	22 Jan. 44	Key Port, NJ
Vincent, James W.	Pvt.	LWA	18 Jan. 44	Streator, IL
Webster, Claudie L.	S/Sgt.	LWA	22 Jan. 44	Corpus Christi, Texas
Wynn, William R.	T/Sgt.	SWA	17 Jan. 44	Robstown, Texas

H Company

Glenn, James R., Jr.	Capt.	KIA	22 Jan. 44	San Benito, Texas
Alvarez, Daniel NMI	Sgt.	SWA	23 Jan. 44	Marfa, Texas
Bradford, Edwin E.	Pfc	LWA	16 Jan. 44	Liberal, KS
Everett, Rillace H.	Pfc	LIA	22 Jan. 44	Peterville, TN
Flynt, Aubrey NMI	Pvt.	LWA	22 Jan. 44	Griffin, GA
Fryman, Kenneth L.	Pvt.	KIA	22 Jan. 44	Ashland, OH
Gruber, George NMI	Pvt.	LWA	16 Jan. 44	Brooklyn, NY
Harms, Howard H.	Pvt.	LWA	24 Jan. 44	Brooklyn, NY
Henlsy, Morton C.	Pvt.	LWA	24 Jan. 44	Chicago, IL
Jones, Everett NMI	Sgt.	LWA	24 Jan. 44	Cowsprings, MD
Stockman, Marshall H.	Pvt.	SWA	23 Jan. 44	Frederick, MD
Tozzi, Mario A.	Pvt.	LWA	22 Jan. 44	Pittsburg, PA
Vacanti, Charles A.	Pvt.	LIA	22 Jan. 44	Buffalo, NY
Wickware, Harry E.	Pvt.	LWA	16 Jan. 44	Franksville, WI

3rd Battalion Headquarters

Richardson, Edwin W.	Lt. Col.	LWA	21 Jan. 44	Westbrook, ME
Goss, Henry A.	Lt. Col.	KIA	22 Jan. 44	Grand Rapids, MI
Mehaffey, Robert E., Jr.	Maj.	SWA	22 Jan. 44	Breckenridge, Texas
Ford, Edgar NMI	Capt.	LWA	21 Jan. 44	Rusk, Texas
Aldridge, Shona K.	1st Lt.	KIA	22 Jan. 44	Banner Elk, NC
Adamovich, Paul A.	Pfc	KIA	25 Jan. 44	Monongah, WV
Albright, Eugene W.	Pvt.	LWA	21 Jan. 44	Logansport, IN
Celsner, Fred NMI	Pvt.	LWA	21 Jan. 44	Jackson Heights, NY
Feidman, Robert N.	Pvt.	KIA	21 Jan. 44	Chicago, IL
Garner, Claudie E.	S/Sgt.	LWA	21 Jan. 44	Gonzales, Texas
Kelley, James B.	Pfc	LWA	21 Jan. 44	Lake Butler, FL
Krieger, Joseph D.	Pvt.	LWA	21 Jan. 44	Claymont, DE
Meeker, Mark F.	Sgt.	LWA	21 Jan. 44	Danville, IL
Oatley, Eugene J.	Pvt.	LIA	23 Jan. 44	Toledo, OH
Sanchez, Concepcion NMI	S/Sgt.	LWA	21 Jan. 44	San Antonio, Texas
Sanchez, Joaquin G.	Pfc	LWA	21 Jan. 44	Mission, Texas
Wightman, James S.	Pfc	LWA	21 Jan. 44	Saluda, SC

I Company

Rogers, William E.	2d Lt.	DOW	22 Jan. 44	Elberton, GA
Durban, Frank G.	2d Lt.	LWA	21 Jan. 44	Chicago, IL
Zulberti, John J.	2d Lt.	KIA	21 Jan. 44	Syracuse, NY
Alexander, Glenn W.	Sgt.	KIA	16 Jan. 44	Lancaster, PA
Appling, A. J. (i.o.)	S/Sgt.	LWA	16 Jan. 44	Kingsbury, Texas
Di Filippo, Chester L.	Pfc	LWA	22 Jan. 44	Detroit, MI
Edgar, James H.	Pvt.	KIA	16 Jan. 44	Utica, NY
Ervin, Miles G.	Sgt.	LWA	22 Jan. 44	Desdemenia, Texas
Foreman, Paskell L.	Pfc	LWA	21 Jan. 44	Newcastle, Texas
Gilliland, William C.	Pvt.	LWA	21 Jan. 44	Brookneal, VA
Godfrey, Howard L.	Pvt.	LWA	21 Jan. 44	Hanapolis, NC
Gonzales, Rafael NMI	Pfc	LWA	21 Jan. 44	Hebbronville, Texas
Hall, David A.	Pvt.	LWA	21 Jan. 44	South Bend, IN
Hardy, Warren G.	Pfc	LWA	23 Jan. 44	Barr, TN
Jackson, Carl E.	Pvt.	LWA	16 Jan. 44	Flint, MI

Johnson, Charles J.	Pvt.	LWA	15 Jan. 44	Freeport, NY
Knight, Louis J.	Pfc	KIA	24 Jan. 44	Brooklyn, NY
La Feance, Normand L.	Pfc	LWA	21 Jan. 44	Detroit, MI
Latham, Monroe W.	Pvt.	SWA	18 Jan. 44	Lewisburg, KY
Marlow, Chris NMI, Jr.	Pfc	LWA	23 Jan. 44	Bristol, VA
Medina, Faustino B.	Pfc	LWA	21 Jan. 44	Zapata, Texas
Moore, Marlin V.	S/Sgt.	LWA	18 Jan. 44	Luling, Texas
McMullen, Russell W.	Pvt.	LWA	21 Jan. 44	Columbus, OH
Quintanillo, Gerardo T.	Sgt.	LWA	21 Jan. 44	Kleberg, Texas
Richter, Samuel W.	Pvt.	LWA	22 Jan. 44	Philadelphia, PA
Rohr, Ralph R.	Pvt.	LWA	21 Jan. 44	Baltimore, MD
Rosen, Seymour C.	Pvt.	KIA	22 Jan. 44	Brooklyn, NY
Santoro, Hector NMI	Pvt.	LWA	16 Jan. 44	Phillipsburg, NJ
Schafer, Henry NMI	Pvt.	LWA	22 Jan. 44	Vancover, WA
Smith, Isaac S.	Pvt.	LWA	21 Jan. 44	Danville, VA
Vicino, James J.	Pfc	LWA	21 Jan. 44	Brooklyn, NY

K Company

Davey, Robert L.	1st Lt.	LWA	22 Jan. 44	West Frankfort, IL
Albright, Floyd A.	Pvt.	LIA	22 Jan. 44	Milwaukee, WI
Anderson, Dewey M.	Pvt.	LWA	15 Jan. 44	Opp, AL
Anderson, Gaylord R.	Pvt.	KIA	23 Jan. 44	Maywook, NV
Bennett, Earnest C.	Pfc	LWA	20 Jan. 44	Madesville, WV
Blauchfield, Charles F.	Pfc	KIA	23 Jan. 44	Chester, PA
Brand, Roy	Pfc	KIA	15 Jan. 44	Brooklyn, NY
Brown, James R., Jr.	Pvt.	LWA	23 Jan. 44	Pokeepskie, NY
Cauley, Herbert W.	Sgt.	LWA	22 Jan. 44	Alice, Texas
Chaney, Robert M.	Pvt.	LWA	20 Jan. 44	Spray, NC
Conem, Henry NMI	Pfc	LWA	22 Jan. 44	Brooklyn, NY
Culliton, John P.	Pfc	LWA	22 Jan. 44	Brooklyn, NY
Czardwicki, Ferdinand F.	Pvt.	DOW	22 Jan. 44	Jersey City, NJ
Gomes, Joseph NMI	Pfc	KIA	26 Jan. 44	Brooklyn, NY
Gray, Owen M.	Pfc	LWA	20 Jan. 44	Detroit, MI
Griffin, Quercus M., Jr.	1st Sgt.	SWA	25 Jan. 44	Gonzales, Texas
Hebber, William R.	Pvt.	LWA	21 Jan. 44	Caspian, MI
Henricks, Lawrence A.	Pfc	LWA	22 Jan. 44	Houston, Texas
Jones, Clinton E.	Pvt.	LWA	21 Jan. 44	Tarboro, NC
Klavin, Rodrigo A.	Pvt.	LWA	22 Jan. 44	Boston, MA
Kulscar, Joseph NMI	Pfc	LIA	22 Jan. 44	Reegisville, PA
Lipscomb, Henry P.	Pvt.	KIA	23 Jan. 44	Chase City, FL
Malott, John R.	Pvt.	LWA	23 Jan. 44	Marion, IN
Mayo, Roy R.	Pfc	LWA	15 Jan. 44	Electra, Texas
Miller, John F.	Pvt.	LWA	22 Jan. 44	Deplains, VA
Moore, Paul A.	Pvt.	LWA	15 Jan. 44	Baldwin, MS
McCarthy, Robert NMI	Pfc	LWA	15 Jan. 44	Shernorn, MA
McDonald, Jack W.	Pvt.	LWA	22 Jan. 44	Nemoka, OK
Nicoulin, Peter F.	Pfc	LWA	21 Jan. 44	Union City, NJ
Pellegrime, Louis NMI	Pfc	LWA	22 Jan. 44	Chicago, IL
Poskosky, John NMI, Jr.	Pfc	LWA	23 Jan. 44	Atlasburg, PA
Scales, Robert J., Jr.	Sgt.	LWA	15 Jan. 44	Dayland, NY
Schafer, George F., Jr.	Pfc	KIA	23 Jan. 44	Camden, NJ
Shelley, James E.	Pvt.	KIA	20 Jan. 44	Gotherburg, MD
Smith, Ira F.	Sgt.	LWA	21 Jan. 44	Gonzales, Texas
Spradlin, Earnest E.	Pfc	LIA	22 Jan. 44	Vinton, VA
Sun, Leo J.	Pfc	LWA	22 Jan. 44	Long Island, NY

Terkin, Marvin D.	Pfc	LWA	21 Jan. 44	Gonzales, Texas
Vassel, Michael NMI	Pfc	LWA	21 Jan. 44	Mexico, ME
Velkovar, Stanley NMI	Pvt.	LWA	22 Jan. 44	Cleveland, OH

L Company

Epperson, James E.	Capt.	LWA	22 Jan. 44	Rocksprings, Texas
Williams, Joseph N.	2d Lt.	LWA	22 Jan. 44	Shelbourne, MA
Bryan, Juneious W.	Pvt.	LWA	22 Jan. 44	Lumberton, NC
Calabria, John H.	Pvt.	LWA	22 Jan. 44	Stubenville, OH
Colloton, Richard I.	Pvt.	LWA	22 Jan. 44	Milwaukee, WI
Daugbery, Chester T.	Pfc	KIA	23 Jan. 44	Raleigh, NC
Domanick, Michael S.	S/Sgt.	LWA	25 Jan. 44	Beachurst, NY
Doss, John D.	Pvt.	LWA	25 Jan. 44	Hoolbra, MS
Garcia, Adam R.	Pfc	KIA	21 Jan. 44	Kingsville, Texas
Garcia, Natividad S.	Pfc	KIA	23 Jan. 44	Abraham, Texas
Hall, William L.	S/Sgt.	LWA	22 Jan. 44	Iowa Park, Texas
Halliburton, Floyd F.	Pvt.	SWA	16 Jan. 44	Melder, Texas
Kettleson, Herman V.	Pvt.	LWA	16 Jan. 44	Jamesville, WI
Lessord, Leroy E.	Pvt.	SWA	22 Jan. 44	Rochester, NY
Migacz, Henry J.	Pvt.	LWA	22 Jan. 44	Chicago, IL
Morray, Alvis NMI	Pfc	LWA	22 Jan. 44	Comfort, TN
Phillips, Roy W.	Pfc	LWA	22 Jan. 44	Nashville, TN
Richter, Edmund J.	Pfc	LWA	22 Jan. 44	Flatonia, Texas
Riggs, Arnold R.	Pvt.	LWA	16 Jan. 44	Dawson Springs, KY
Ropelia, Maynard C.	Pfc	LWA	25 Jan. 44	Mineola, IL
Sadler, Robert A.	Pvt.	LWA	22 Jan. 44	Lynn, MA
Sanchez, Roman NMI	Pfc	LWA	22 Jan. 44	San Saba, Texas
Sesulski, Joseph NMI	Pvt.	LWA	25 Jan. 44	Wilkesbar, PA
Smith, Mark E.	Pvt.	LWA	25 Jan. 44	Peterstown, WV
Sunbon, Robert G.	Pvt.	LWA	25 Jan. 44	Freeport, IL
Surrett, Lucious G.	Pfc	LWA	22 Jan. 44	Canton, NC
Taylor, Charles E.	Pfc	LWA	22 Jan. 44	Evansville, IN
Taylor, Coy M.	Pvt.	LWA	16 Jan. 44	High Point, NC
Volante, Arthur G.	Sgt.	LWA	16 Jan. 44	Bronx, NY
Wiggins, Benson A., Jr.	Pvt.	LWA	22 Jan. 44	St. Ignace, MI

M Company

Mazzeo, John NMI	1st Lt.	LWA	22 Jan. 44	Easton, PA
Adeloni, Emileo NMI	Pfc	LWA	18 Jan. 44	Brooklyn, NY
Bryant, Lester D.	Pvt.	DOW	21 Jan. 44	Centralia, IL
Conley, James F.	Pfc	LWA	22 Jan. 44	Centralia, IL
Crepice, Anthony F.	Pvt.	LWA	22 Jan. 44	New York, NY
Gilman, Mark E.	Pvt.	LWA	21 Jan. 44	Albany, NY
Hood, John V., Jr.	Pfc	LWA	22 Jan. 44	Knoxville, TN
Jordan, Paul J.	Pfc	LWA	21 Jan. 44	Queens Village, NY
Lemaire, Augustine A.	Pfc	LWA	21 Jan. 44	Albino, NY
Menna, Angelo J.	Sgt.	LWA	21 Jan. 44	Brooklyn, NY
Menra, Angelo J.	Sgt.	LWA	26 Jan. 44	Jamacia, L.I., NY
Nietzel, Walter A.	Pvt.	LWA	22 Jan. 44	Lowell, MA
Ramsey, Aubrey E.	Pfc	LWA	26 Jan. 44	Vernon, Texas
Riley, Dean A.	Pfc	KIA	21 Jan. 44	Avora, IA
Rivera, Alfredo NMI	Pfc	LWA	22 Jan. 44	Taft, Texas
Rockrich, Daniel D.	Pfc	LWA	21 Jan. 44	Akron, OH
Sherrill, Paul B.	Pfc	SWA	21 Jan. 44	Evansville, IN
Siwicki, John S.	Pfc	KIA	21 Jan. 44	West Rutland, VT
Smith, William F.	Pvt.	LWA	21 Jan. 44	Bangor, MI

Roster of Casualties
143rd Infantry Regiment[4]
January 1–31, 1944

Name	Rank	Type	Date of Casualty	Residence

Headquarters and Headquarters Company

Name	Rank	Type	Date of Casualty	Residence
Cushing, William P.	Pfc	LWA	18 Jan. 44	Ft. Worth, Texas
Nelson, William T., Jr.	S/Sgt.	LWA	24 Jan. 44	Longview, Texas

Service Company

Name	Rank	Type	Date of Casualty	Residence
Sorensen, Helvig M.	1st Lt.	LWA	22 Jan. 44	Chicago, IL

Anti-Tank Company

Name	Rank	Type	Date of Casualty	Residence
Bessarab, Peter NMI	Sgt.	MIA	21 Jan. 44	Chicago, IL
Bruce, Darwin D.	Pfc	SWA	20 Jan. 44	Salina, OK
Holland, J. D. (i.o.)	Pfc	SWA	21 Jan. 44	Mineola, Texas
Holt, Johnnie R.	Sgt.	LWA	22 Jan. 44	McGregor, Texas
Pratt, Charles K.	Pfc	KIA	19 Jan. 44	Baltimore, MD
Sullivan, James J.	Pfc	LWA	22 Jan. 44	Roxbury, MA
Taylor, Alcott E.	Pfc	LWA	22 Jan. 44	Monmouth Center, ME
Traywick, Edward A.	Pfc	LWA	22 Jan. 44	Waco, Texas
Verducci, Joseph D.	Pfc	LWA	23 Jan. 44	Brighton, MA

Cannon Company

Name	Rank	Type	Date of Casualty	Residence
McDonald, Thomas T.	T/5	SWA	30 Jan. 44	Maysville, KY

Medical Detachment

Name	Rank	Type	Date of Casualty	Residence
Alvey, James W.	Pvt.	MIA	23 Jan. 44	Charleston, MO
Baker, Leon C.	Pvt.	KIA	29 Jan. 44	Wickes, AR
Ballard, Chesterfield NMI	Pvt.	MIA	21 Jan. 44	Jayess, MS
Beaudin, Elmer J.	Pvt.	LWA	21 Jan. 44	Detroit, MI
Birdsong, Otha C.	Pfc	MIA	23 Jan. 44	Sand Springs, OK
Boring, Joseph W.	Pfc	KIA	20 Jan. 44	Thornville, OH
Bridge, Jack E.	Pfc	LWA	21 Jan. 44	Addison, MI
Buynak, Elmer J.	Pfc	KIA	24 Jan. 44	Cleveland, OH
Caldwell, Ezell J.	Pvt.	MIA	24 Jan. 44	Lincolntown, NC
Cox, Oscar W.	Pfc	LWA	30 Jan. 44	Breckenridge, Texas
Dulabone, Guy L.	Pvt.	MIA	22 Jan. 44	Schaefferstown, PA
Durlester, Gene NMI	Pvt.	LWA	22 Jan. 44	Bronx, NY
Gavin, Frank J.	Pfc	LWA	22 Jan. 44	Chicago, IL
Hamilton, Delbert L.	Pfc	LWA	19 Jan. 44	Alton, IL
Holland, Aubrey NMI	Pvt.	LWA	24 Jan. 44	W. Conshohocken, PA
Kelley, Woodrow W.	T/5	MIA	24 Jan. 44	Milford, Texas
LeClair, Romeo A.	Pfc	MIA	21 Jan. 44	Charlotte, VT
Mancheras, James G.	T/5	LWA	20 Jan. 44	Lynchburg, VA
Porter, James J.	Pvt.	SWA	22 Jan. 44	Winter Beach, FL
Snapka, Method R.	T/4	LIA	22 Jan. 44	Abbott, Texas
Tome, Raymond D.	Pvt.	SWA	22 Jan. 44	Woodbine, PA
Valenzuela, Felizardo M.	Pvt.	MIA	22 Jan. 44	Bisbee, AZ
Weiner, Jacob NMI	Pfc	KIA	25 Jan. 44	Brooklyn, NY

Headquarters and Headquarters Company First Battalion

Frazior, David M.	Maj.	LWA	22 Jan. 44	Houston, Texas
Steffen, Milton H.	Capt.	MIA	21 Jan. 44	Huntsville, Texas
Bean, William C.	Pvt.	LWA	17 Jan. 44	Lowell, MA
Cayton, Huxley L.	Pfc	LIA	21 Jan. 44	Mexia, Texas
Dubb, Michael NMI, Jr.	Pvt.	LIA	21 Jan. 44	Giardville, PA
Ek, Max NMI	Pvt.	LWA	21 Jan. 44	Kokomo, IN
Ellison, Samuel F.	Cpl.	LIA	21 Jan. 44	Groesbeck, Texas
Humphries, Hurshel D.	Pfc	LWA	21 Jan. 44	Clifton, Texas
Kinsman, Raymond NMI	Pvt.	LWA	16 Jan. 44	Brooklyn, NY
Kuskowski, Edward NMI	Pfc	KIA	21 Jan. 44	Roslyn, NY
Lorenzini, Battista NMI	Sgt.	LIA	21 Jan. 44	Roanoke, IL
Palma, Salvatore P.	Pvt.	LWA	21 Jan. 44	Brooklyn, NY
Rozycki, Edmund J.	Pvt.	SWA	21 Jan. 44	New York, NY
Snokhous, George O.	T/5	LWA	21 Jan. 44	West, Texas
Stein, Samuel J.	T/4	SWA	22 Jan. 44	Brooklyn, NY

A Company

Baird, Burnes T.	2d Lt.	SWA	22 Jan. 44	Clairton, PA
Gorman, Francis J.	1st Lt.	SWA	22 Jan. 44	Lynn, MA
Pliska, Richard J.	2d Lt.	LWA	22 Jan. 44	Two Rivers, WI
Upchurch, Richard J.	2d Lt.	SWA	22 Jan. 44	Chicago, IL
Walker, David M.	2d Lt.	LWA	22 Jan. 44	Andover, NJ
Ables, James W.	Pvt.	LWA	21 Jan. 44	Athens, TN
Ahl, Floyd A.	Pvt.	LWA	21 Jan. 44	Schenectady, NY
Albanese, John J.	Pvt.	MIA	22 Jan. 44	Brooklyn, NY
Albano, Gaetano T.	Pvt.	SWA	27 Jan. 44	Brooklyn, NY
Alexander, Raymond NMI	Pvt.	SWA	22 Jan. 44	Quincy, IL
Allonardo, Frank NMI	Pvt.	LWA	21 Jan. 44	Philadelphia, PA
Anderson, Anders G.	Pvt.	SWA	22 Jan. 44	Lynn, MA
Andriola, Vincent J.	Pvt.	LWA	23 Jan. 44	Newark, NJ
Armstrong, Lewis H.	Pfc	MIA	22 Jan. 44	Pilot Mountain, NC
Aylor, Robert L.	Pvt.	MIA	22 Jan. 44	Lawrenceburg, IN
Barnes, Homer E.	Pfc	LWA	21 Jan. 44	Ossing, NY
Bartko, Emil J.	Pvt.	LWA	22 Jan. 44	Cleveland, OH
Bastian, Ralph A.	Pvt.	SWA	20 Jan. 44	Cleveland, OH
Baugher, Harold O.	Pvt.	LWA	22 Jan. 44	Warsaw, IN
Beaver, Charles L.	Pvt.	SWA	22 Jan. 44	Lewner, GA
Beaver, Rufus L.	Pvt.	DOW	24 Jan. 44	Lincolnton, NC
Bender, Wesley E.	T/Sgt.	MIA	22 Jan. 44	Easton, PA
Betke, Albert H.	Pvt.	SWA	22 Jan. 44	Beaver Falls, PA
Blankenship, Clifton NMI	Pvt.	LWA	27 Jan. 44	Ashland, KY
Blanton, Gary F.	Pfc	MIA	22 Jan. 44	Tabor City, NC
Blaschak, Frank A., Jr.	Pvt.	MIA	22 Jan. 44	Russellton, PA
Blewett, David G.	Pfc	SWA	22 Jan. 44	Dalton, PA
Bloch, Joseph NMI	Pvt.	LWA	21 Jan. 44	Chicago, IL
Boeglin, Eugene R.	Pvt.	LWA	22 Jan. 44	N. Andover, MA
Bouchard, Lawrence A.	Pfc	LWA	22 Jan. 44	Sherman Station, ME
Boucher, Samuel R.	Pvt.	MIA	22 Jan. 44	Bloomington, IN
Bowen, James C.	Pvt.	LWA	22 Jan. 44	Lugoff, SC
Boyles, Grady J.	Pvt.	SWA	27 Jan. 44	Russelville, AL
Brann, Newton R.	Pfc	LWA	22 Jan. 44	Anderson, IN
Breeden, Lawrence NMI	Pvt.	SWA	23 Jan. 44	Seiverville, TN
Brennan, George R.	Pvt.	SWA	22 Jan. 44	Clearspring, MD
Brewer, William S.	Pfc	SWA	22 Jan. 44	Chicago, IL
Budd, Alfred G.	Pvt.	LWA	22 Jan. 44	Delaplane, VA

Buzard, Frederick A.	Pvt.	LWA	22 Jan. 44	Cochranton, PA
Camello, Anthony J.	Pvt.	SWA	22 Jan. 44	Brooklyn, NY
Chapman, Campbell N.	Pfc	MIA	25 Jan. 44	Honea Path, SC
Coggins, James C., Jr.	Pvt.	LWA	25 Jan. 44	Elizabethton, TN
Coleman, Lee A.	Pfc	MIA	22 Jan. 44	Missouri Valley, IA
Collins, Clarence E.	S/Sgt.	LWA	22 Jan. 44	Pueblo, CO
Conn, Norman D.	Pvt.	MIA	22 Jan. 44	Kankakee, IL
Cook, Bill G.	Pvt.	SWA	27 Jan. 44	Kansas City, KS
Counts, Clyde D.	Pvt.	LWA	22 Jan. 44	Flintville, TN
Dansicker, Herbert NMI	Pfc	SWA	21 Jan. 44	Baltimore, MD
Davis, Jerry W.	T/Sgt.	LWA	22 Jan. 44	Paris, Texas
Defazio, Albert NMI	Pfc	SWA	22 Jan. 44	Vernon, PA
DeSanto, Joseph M.	Pvt.	KIA	22 Jan. 44	Plainfield, NJ
DeSimone, Salvatore P.	Pvt.	LWA	21 Jan. 44	Bronx, NY
Dittman, Meredith E.	Pfc	SWA	21 Jan. 44	Buffalo, NY
Dixon, Arthur M.	Pvt.	MIA	22 Jan. 44	Dorchester, MA
Edwards, Albert E.	Pvt.	LWA	22 Jan. 44	Miami, OK
Fallon, Gerard M.	Pvt.	KIA	26 Jan. 44	Brooklyn, NY
Fields, Delbert M.	Pvt.	SWA	21 Jan. 44	Springfield, IN
Frederick, William O.	S/Sgt.	SWA	22 Jan. 44	Tyler, Texas
Galloway, Harold L.	S/Sgt.	SWA	22 Jan. 44	Alto, Texas
Gannon, Edward C.	Pvt.	LWA	21 Jan. 44	Canton, OH
Graniere, Frank NMI	S/Sgt.	LWA	22 Jan. 44	San Antonio, Texas
Gray, Orval NMI	Pvt.	LWA	22 Jan. 44	Henshaw, KY
Jellick, Charles T.	S/Sgt.	LWA	25 Jan. 44	Philadelphia, PA
Kaiser, Howard H.	Sgt.	MIA	22 Jan. 44	Brooklyn, NY
Kemp, John W.	Pfc	SWA	22 Jan. 44	Ft. Wayne, IN
Kieczkajlo, Martin S.	Sgt.	SWA	22 Jan. 44	New York, NY
Laiche, Anicet A.	S/Sgt.	MIA	22 Jan. 44	Paulina, LA
Lake, Scott NMI	Pfc	LWA	21 Jan. 44	Jamestown, IN
Lebeis, Bertram H.	1st Sgt.	LWA	22 Jan. 44	New York, NY
Long, Jerry T.	Pvt.	MIA	22 Jan. 44	Corning, IA
McClintock, Archie S.	Pvt.	LWA	21 Jan. 44	Carlilse, PA
Markiewica, Walter J.	S/Sgt.	SWA	22 Jan. 44	Hamtramck, MI
Michalak, John J., Jr.	Pvt.	LWA	24 Jan. 44	Chicago, IL
Mitchell, James L.	Pvt.	LWA	21 Jan. 44	Hamilton, AL
Moffitt, Harvey L.	Pvt.	SWA	22 Jan. 44	Ripley, MS
Monaco, Anthony R.	Sgt.	LWA	21 Jan. 44	Chicago, IL
Nahodil, Robert S.	Sgt.	SWA	22 Jan. 44	Berea, OH
Naill, Kenneth B.	Pvt.	LWA	22 Jan. 44	Rockford, IL
Nuhfer, Eugene E.	Pvt.	SWA	27 Jan. 44	Toledo, OH
Parrott, William F.	T/Sgt.	LWA	24 Jan. 44	Garrison, Texas
Phillips, Frederick W.	Pfc	LWA	21 Jan. 44	Long Branch, NJ
Pierco, Claude H.	Pvt.	MIA	22 Jan. 44	Coustok, MI
Roycroft, Alton R.	Cpl.	SWA	22 Jan. 44	Rusk, Texas
Sipes, James B.	Pvt.	MIA	22 Jan. 44	Hornsby, TN
Smith, Clarence W.	Pvt.	SWA	25 Jan. 44	Parkers Landing, PA
Sniezek, Edward A.	Pfc	SWA	22 Jan. 44	Detroit, MI
Southard, Rodney N.	Pvt.	MIA	22 Jan. 44	Rochester, NH
Spencer, Kenneth R.	Pvt.	LWA	21 Jan. 44	Bemis, TN
Stackhouse, Walter C.	Pfc	LWA	22 Jan. 44	Coatsville, PA
Stalnaker, Thomas NMI	Pvt.	LWA	22 Jan. 44	E. Tallassee, AL
Sternberg, William R.	Pvt.	MIA	22 Jan. 44	Newark, NJ
Stubblefield, James E.	Pfc	LWA	21 Jan. 44	Troup, Texas
Stults, Barney N.	Pfc	LWA	25 Jan. 44	Weatherford, Texas
Sweatt, Paul L.	Pvt.	SWA	22 Jan. 44	Herald White, IL

Taylor, Joseph H.	Sgt.	SWA	22 Jan. 44	Brooklyn, NY
Tellez, Joe R.	Pvt.	LWA	22 Jan. 44	Los Angeles, CA
Terra, Antone E.	Pvt.	SWA	25 Jan. 44	Taunton, MA
Thomas, Hilary S.	Pvt.	KIA	26 Jan. 44	Reed, KY
Treadway, Walker NMI	Pvt.	LWA	22 Jan. 44	Oak Hill, WV
Turner, John R.	Pvt.	LWA	22 Jan. 44	Heflin, AL
Van Matre, Norman R.	Pvt.	SWA	22 Jan. 44	Kaylong, WV
Vaughan, Jack H.	Pvt.	LWA	20 Jan. 44	Gadsden, AL
Vigil, Joe NMI	Pvt.	LWA	24 Jan. 44	Pueblo, CO
Vincent, Charles L.	Pvt.	SWA	21 Jan. 44	Louisville, KY
Walton, Alvin F.	Pvt.	MIA	22 Jan. 44	Buchannon, WV
Weissemeier, Raymond J.	Pfc	LWA	25 Jan. 44	Richmond Hill, NY
West, Warren J.	Pfc	MIA	22 Jan. 44	Knoxville, TN

B Company

Crute, John M., Jr.	1st Lt.	KIA	21 Jan. 44	Farmville, VA
Sheffler, Abbott M.	2d Lt.	SWA	23 Jan. 44	Baltimore, MD
Andrasi, George NMI	S/Sgt.	LWA	26 Jan. 44	Hazelton, PA
Barfield, Isaac NMI	Pvt.	LWA	27 Jan. 44	Vernon, FL
Bourbeau, Leonard M.	Pvt.	LWA	21 Jan. 44	Ludlow, MA
Bowman, John J.	Pfc	DOW	21 Jan. 44	Apollo, PA
Boyd, Arthur L.	Pvt.	LWA	22 Jan. 44	Darke, WV
Brocato, August G.	Pfc	SWA	21 Jan. 44	Baltimore, MD
Burkemper, Lawrence W., Jr.	Pfc	KIA	21 Jan. 44	Old Monroe, MO
Cardone, Girolomo C.	Pvt.	LWA	22 Jan. 44	New York, NY
Carlone, William D.	Pvt.	SWA	22 Jan. 44	Barrington, RI
Chambers, Walter E., Jr.	Pfc	LWA	21 Jan. 44	Lansdale, PA
Cherban, Mike NMI	Pfc	SWA	21 Jan. 44	Isabella, PA
Crockett, Charles A., Jr.	Pvt.	KIA	21 Jan. 44	Tangier, VA
Demarest, Phillip W.	Pfc	MIA	27 Jan. 44	Owenboro, KY
Di Ruscio, Serafino NMI	Pvt.	LWA	22 Jan. 44	Philadelphia, PA
Dorzan, Alfonse A.	Sgt.	SWA	22 Jan. 44	Newark, NJ
Ferrara, John P.	Pvt.	SWA	21 Jan. 44	Garfield, NJ
Fondakowski, Edward M.	Sgt.	LWA	21 Jan. 44	Chicago, IL
Freeman, Andrew J.	Pvt.	LWA	24 Jan. 44	Converse, SC
Freeman, Will C.	Pvt.	SWA	24 Jan. 44	Berry, AL
Goodlett, John C., Jr.	Pvt.	LWA	21 Jan. 44	Sinai, KY
Goodman, Milton NMI	Pvt.	LWA	21 Jan. 44	Brooklyn, NY
Graves, Clarence W.	Pvt.	MIA	21 Jan. 44	Sommerville, NJ
Green, William L.	Pfc	SWA	21 Jan. 44	Waynesville, MO
Greenhalgh, John C.	Pvt.	LWA	22 Jan. 44	McKeesport, PA
Haliw, Michael NMI	Pfc	LWA	21 Jan. 44	Denver, CO
		MIA	26 Jan. 44	
Herrmann, John D.	Pvt.	SWA	21 Jan. 44	Roselle, NJ
Hoover, Woodrow C.	Pfc	SWA	22 Jan. 44	Toledo, OH
Johnston, James W.	Pfc	LWA	21 Jan. 44	Chicago, IL
Kaczorek, Andrew J.	Pfc	LWA	22 Jan. 44	Milwaukee, WI
Kalabisko, Peter NMI	Pfc	LWA	21 Jan. 44	Bethel, PA
Kielian, Joseph W.	Sgt.	DOW	22 Jan. 44	Sayreville, NJ
King, John A.	Pfc	SWA	22 Jan. 44	McGrann, PA
Koch, Robert J.	Pfc	MIA	21 Jan. 44	Newark, NJ
Kranz, Henry C.	S/Sgt.	SWA	22 Jan. 44	Lancaster, PA
Lagarosse, Ernest R.	Pvt.	LWA	21 Jan. 44	Flushing, NY
Landis, Gale W.	Pvt.	MIA	27 Jan. 44	Dayton, OH
Lee, Pierre I., Jr.	Pvt.	LWA	22 Jan. 44	Marrero, LA
Lytle, Julius F.	Pfc	DOW	22 Jan. 44	Stanley, KY

Moore, Edward B.	Pfc	LWA	23 Jan. 44	Eastman, GA
O'Neal, Jack F.	S/Sgt.	LWA	22 Jan. 44	Mexia, Texas
Perguson, Dee C., Jr.	Sgt.	SWA	21 Jan. 44	Horse Branch, KY
Petrowski, Felix P. B.	Pvt.	LWA	21 Jan. 44	Norwich, CT
Pokrzywa, John NMI	S/Sgt.	MIA	21 Jan. 44	Edwardsville, PA
Rager, Arthur T.	S/Sgt.	SWA	21 Jan. 44	Johnstown, PA
Reich, Carl E.	Sgt.	DOW	26 Jan. 44	Maywood, IL
Riggins, Edward C.	Pvt.	MIA	26 Jan. 44	Woodbury, GA
Rogers, Harvey NMI	Pfc	MIA	21 Jan. 44	Harbeson, DE
Rosen, Samuel NMI	Pfc	MIA	22 Jan. 44	Brooklyn, NY
Sepanek, Casimer J.	Sgt.	SWA	21 Jan. 44	Bayonne, NJ
St Clair, Joseph K., Sr.	Pvt	LWA	24 Jan. 44	Bluefield, WV
Taylor, Phillip R.	Pvt.	SWA	21 Jan. 44	Charleston, WV
Tiberi, Ralph NMI	Pvt.	MIA	21 Jan. 44	Columbus, OH
Tompkins, Holden NMI	Pvt	LWA	22 Jan. 44	Fairview, NJ
Tompkins, Thomas A.	S/Sgt.	LWA	22 Jan. 44	Mexia, Texas
Tortora, Pasquale NMI	Pvt.	SWA	22 Jan. 44	Brooklyn, NY
Triplett, Jack F.	Pfc	LWA	21 Jan. 44	Huntington, WV
Trusty, Paul E.	Pfc	SWA	21 Jan. 44	E. St. Louis, IL
Ujazdowski, Stanley A.	S/Sgt.	KIA	21 Jan. 44	Philadelphia, PA
Walsh, Kenneth F.	Pfc	LWA	21 Jan. 44	W. New York, NY
Williams, Herbert R., Jr.	Pfc	LWA	22 Jan. 44	Clio, IA
Williams, Ralph P.	Pfc	LWA	22 Jan. 44	Pauline, SC
Wyzykowski, Stanley P.	S/Sgt.	LWA	22 Jan. 44	Trenton, NJ

C Company

Fink, Irving NMI	2d Lt.	LWA	22 Jan. 44	Brooklyn, NY
Nobles, General J.	2d Lt.	SWA	22 Jan. 44	Danville, GA
Barr, Irwin G.	Pfc	LWA	22 Jan. 44	Pine Grove, GA
Biddy, Homer L., Jr.	Pvt.	SWA	22 Jan. 44	Cartersville, GA
Daniel, Calvin G.	Pfc	LWA	22 Jan. 44	Woodland, AL
Depew, Lewis NMI	Pvt.	LWA	22 Jan. 44	Manchester, KY
Dow, James E.	Pfc	KIA	23 Jan. 44	Hope Valley, RI
Downs, William H.	Pfc	LWA	22 Jan. 44	Princess Anne, MD
Fancher, Luke H.	Pvt.	MIA	22 Jan. 44	Belmont, MS
Garszczynski, John NMI	Pfc	LWA	21 Jan. 44	Reading, PA
Glorius, Lawrence E.	Pvt.	LWA	22 Jan. 44	Wauchula, FL
Goodwin, Jack D.	Pfc	LWA	22 Jan. 44	Asheville, AL
Jerstad, James H.	Pfc	SWA	22 Jan. 44	Racine, WI
Johnson, Lewis R.	Pfc	SWA	22 Jan. 44	McColl, SC
Kendall, Frank H., Jr.	Pvt.	LWA	22 Jan. 44	Providence, RI
Latal, Raymond F.	Pvt.	LWA	22 Jan. 44	Chicago, IL
Lindsay, Charles L.	Pfc	LWA	19 Jan. 44	Dondolk, MD
Lorenz, Robert F.	Pfc	SWA	25 Jan. 44	Columbus, OH
McCarthy, John T.	Pvt.	LWA	22 Jan. 44	Philadelphia, PA
McClintic, James W.	S/Sgt.	LWA	22 Jan. 44	Groesbeck, Texas
McDermott, James W.	Pfc	LWA	22 Jan. 44	Cleveland, OH
Maliborsky, Paul NMI	Pfc	DOW	22 Jan. 44	Wilkes Barre, PA
Matousek, Rudolph C.	Pfc	LWA	22 Jan. 44	Baltimore, MD
		MIA	31 Jan. 44	
Meehan, John A.	S/Sgt.	MIA	19 Jan. 44	Altoona, PA
Moracco, Angelo A.	Pvt.	SWA	24 Jan. 44	Utica, NY
Moss, Kenneth F.	Pvt.	LWA	19 Jan. 44	Girard, OH
Nemitz, Franklin L.	Pfc	SWA	22 Jan. 44	Elmhurst, IL
Osborne, Earl NMI	Pvt.	SWA	22 Jan. 44	Pine Hill, NJ
Price, Howard Q.	Pfc	LWA	22 Jan. 44	Wheel Wright, KY

Quiroz, Manuel G.	Pfc	LWA	23 Jan. 44	Joliet, IL
Rhodes, Robert R.	Pvt.	LWA	22 Jan. 44	Cumberland, MD
Richins, Lynn E.	Pfc	LWA	21 Jan. 44	Coalville, UT
Romano, Salvatore J.	S/Sgt.	LWA	22 Jan. 44	Brooklyn, NY
Ruiz, Gabriel NMI	S/Sgt.	MIA	22 Jan. 44	San Antonio, Texas
Shincovich, Thomas J.	Pfc	SWA	19 Jan. 44	Hunker, PA
Simpson, Robert A.	Pfc	KIA	19 Jan. 44	Los Angeles, CA
Sloan, William F.	Pvt.	LWA	22 Jan. 44	Agnos, AR
Smith, Billy R.	Pfc	MIA	22 Jan. 44	Royston, GA
Smith, Harold L.	Pfc	SWA	25 Jan. 44	Hartford, AL
Smith, Henry C., Jr.	Pvt.	LWA	22 Jan. 44	Parkersburg, WV
Sowers, Don R.	Pfc	SWA	23 Jan. 44	Greenup, IL
Spale, Erwin J.	Pfc	LWA	21 Jan. 44	Cicero, IL
Stumfoll, Robert F.	Pvt.	SWA	22 Jan. 44	Chicago, IL
Sturdevant, Luther L.	Pvt.	SWA	22 Jan. 44	Eagleville, MO
Swackhammer, Morris E.	Pfc	LWA	22 Jan. 44	Binghamton, NY
Szollosi, John F.	Pfc	LWA	22 Jan. 44	Akron, OH
Wells, Edison E.	Pfc	SWA	20 Jan. 44	Potsdam, NY
West, Casey NMI	Pfc	LWA	22 Jan. 44	Tarplin, WV
Wilton, John NMI	Pvt.	LWA	22 Jan. 44	Franklin, NJ
Yates, George D.	T/Sgt.	MIA	19 Jan. 44	Beaumont, Texas

D Company

Wirtz, John J.	2d Lt.	SWA	22 Jan. 44	Cleveland, OH
Castle, Luther T., Jr.	Pvt.	SWA	21 Jan. 44	Lucasville, OH
Fenstermaker, George NMI	Pvt.	LWA	22 Jan. 44	Lemay, MO
Gravatt, Melvin F.	Pvt.	SWA	25 Jan. 44	Vicksburg, MS
Haro, Augustine H.	Pvt.	SWA	22 Jan. 44	San Francisco, CA
Herbig, William A.	Pvt.	LIA	21 Jan. 44	Cedarville, IL
Holtgreven, Joseph A.	Pvt.	SWA	22 Jan. 44	Maimisburg, OH
Hunt, Thomas E.	Pvt.	LIA	22 Jan. 44	Mohawk, WV
Lanctot, Leonide NMI	Pvt.	LWA	22 Jan. 44	Boston, MA
Leggett, Jim NMI	Pvt.	LWA	25 Jan. 44	Point, Texas
Long, Eldon D.	Pvt.	LWA	24 Jan. 44	Telephone, Texas
Martin, James A.	Pfc	SIA	21 Jan. 44	Sweetwater, Texas
Meagher, Francis E.	Sgt.	LWA	22 Jan. 44	New Brunswick, NJ
Parnell, Franklin H.	Pvt.	LWA	24 Jan. 44	Philadelphia, PA
Perry, Wetzel NMI	Pvt	SWA	22 Jan. 44	East Lynn, WV
Rauvola, Carl H.	Pvt.	SWA	25 Jan. 44	Detroit, MI
Sayers, Francis H.	Pvt.	SWA	22 Jan. 44	New Haven, CT
Singleton, Joseph J.	Pvt.	LWA	21 Jan. 44	South Bend, IN
Warwick, William W.	Pvt.	LWA	22 Jan. 44	Newton Grove, NC
Wicks, Alvin M.	Pfc	LWA	22 Jan. 44	Watertown, MA
Wilson, Bill D.	S/Sgt.	LWA	21 Jan. 44	Wolfe City, Texas
Wiltrout, Robert W.	Pvt.	LIA	21 Jan. 44	Mansfield, OH
Yuhas, Joseph B.	Pvt.	LWA	24 Jan. 44	Trenton, NJ

Headquarters and Headquarters Company Second Battalion

Amos, Clyde C.	Pvt.	LWA	22 Jan. 44	Hyrum, UT
Badi, Raymond J.	Pfc	SWA	21 Jan. 44	Euclid, OH
Benik, Ivan E.	Pvt.	LWA	22 Jan. 44	Miles City, MT
Bivins, Donald G.	Pvt.	LWA	22 Jan. 44	Plainview, NE
Blackwood, John B.	Pvt.	LWA	27 Jan. 44	Cullman, AL
Chulack, Peter J.	Sgt.	SWA	27 Jan. 44	Pittsburg, PA
Clyden, Kenneth L.	Pvt.	SWA	27 Jan. 44	Hoopsten, IL
Conlogue, Andrew J.	Sgt.	SWA	22 Jan. 44	Mamaronack, NY

Earl, Finis R.	Pvt.	LWA	22 Jan. 44	Whitney, Texas
Elliott, Floyd J.	Pvt.	SWA	21 Jan. 44	Baltimore, MD
Evanich, Steve NMI	Pfc	SWA	28 Jan. 44	Canton, OH
Fletcher, Luther E.	Pvt.	LWA	23 Jan. 44	Chicago, IL
Fodor, John S.	Pvt.	SWA	23 Jan. 44	Stockbridge, MI
Fox, Keith E.	Pvt.	LWA	27 Jan. 44	Syracuse, NY
Furberg, Lester NMI	Pvt.	KIA	21 Jan. 44	Brooklyn, NY
Gennara, George F.	Pvt.	SWA	21 Jan. 44	Amasa, MI
Gerland, George C.	Pfc	SWA	22 Jan. 44	Caldwell, Texas
Kowalczyk, Alexander S.	Pfc	SWA	27 Jan. 44	Baltimore, MD
Lyda, Homer P.	Pvt.	SWA	27 Jan. 44	Hendersonville, NC
Martin, Raymond A.	Pvt.	SWA	22 Jan. 44	Eutaw, AL
Peters, John E.	Pvt.	MIA	22 Jan. 44	S. Allehany, NY
Short, Robert E.	Cpl.	SWA	27 Jan. 44	Houston, Texas
Six, Joseph S.	Pfc	SWA	22 Jan. 44	Princeton, WV
Spescha, William P.	Pvt.	SWA	23 Jan. 44	Philadelphia, PA
Trudelle, Florian NMI	Pvt.	LWA	22 Jan. 44	Fall River, MA
Valcourt, Isidore NMI	Pvt.	SWA	27 Jan. 44	N. Chelmsford, MA
Wallstein, Ralph M.	S/Sgt.	SWA	31 Jan. 44	Brooklyn, NY

E Company

Bergman, Eben C.	Capt.	MIA	22 Jan. 44	Clifton, Texas
Kelsey, Oren L.	1st Lt.	SWA	22 Jan. 44	Elk Falls, KS
Bredael, Frederick B.	2d Lt.	MIA	22 Jan. 44	Green Bay, WI
Lisenbe, James C.	2d Lt.	MIA	22 Jan. 44	Temple, Texas
Kader, John NMI	2d Lt.	MIA	22 Jan. 44	Congo, OH
Wilkerson, William R.	2d Lt.	LWA	22 Jan. 44	Charlottville, VA
Aguilera, Tony NMI	Pfc	MIA	22 Jan. 44	Los Nitos, CA
Aktarian, John P.	Pfc	KIA	24 Jan. 44	Long Island City, NY
Albers, Robert G.	Pfc	KIA	22 Jan. 44	Canton, OH
Alexander, Herman D.	Pvt.	MIA	22 Jan. 44	Utica, NY
Allen, William S.	Sgt.	MIA	22 Jan. 44	Dresden, TN
Ammons, Bunnie J.	Pvt.	MIA	22 Jan. 44	Andalusa, AL
Anderson, Gerald R.	Pvt.	MIA	22 Jan. 44	Oak Park, IL
Angell, Harold F.	Pfc	MIA	22 Jan. 44	W. Tulsa, OK
Anger, William H.	Pvt.	MIA	22 Jan. 44	Milwaukee, WI
Annis, Carl E.	Pvt.	KIA	25 Jan. 44	Abilene, KS
Arnold, James E.	Pvt.	MIA	22 Jan. 44	Centralia, IL
Arpin, Leo NMI	Pvt.	MIA	22 Jan. 44	Chicopee, MA
Atkins, Carlies R.	Cpl.	MIA	22 Jan. 44	Martinsville, VA
Baker, Marvin A.	Pvt.	MIA	22 Jan. 44	Bonnie, IL
Balardini, Arthur A.	Pfc	KIA	25 Jan. 44	Adams, MA
Barkley, Hollis D.	Pvt.	MIA	22 Jan. 44	Massena, NY
Belanger, John D.	Pfc	SWA	20 Jan. 44	Caribou, ME
Berg, Adolph F.	Pvt.	MIA	22 Jan. 44	Oak Park, IL
Binder, George NMI	Pvt.	MIA	22 Jan. 44	Bronx, NY
Binnion, Prentice L.	Pvt.	MIA	22 Jan. 44	Red Boiling Spr, TN
Blevens, Frank E.	Pfc	KIA	21 Jan. 44	Lamar, CO
Bobbitt, James M.	Pfc	MIA	22 Jan. 44	Southside, TN
Bolt, Dillard L.	Pvt.	MIA	22 Jan. 44	Liberty, KY
Borejko, Henry T.	Pvt.	MIA	22 Jan. 44	Providence, RI
Bouffard, Alfred A.	Pvt.	MIA	22 Jan. 44	Chicopee Falls, MA
Bozsa, Louis NMI	Pvt.	SWA	22 Jan. 44	E. St. Louis, IL
Brand, Joseph G.	Pvt.	MIA	22 Jan. 44	Westmont, NJ
Brown, Don J.	Pvt.	MIA	22 Jan. 44	Detroit, MI
Brown, John J.	Pvt.	KIA	27 Jan. 44	Chester, PA

Brumfield, Harold L.	Pvt.	MIA	22 Jan. 44	Proctorville, OH
Brush, Joseph W.	Pvt.	MIA	22 Jan. 44	Newark, NJ
Bucello, Louis P.	Pfc	MIA	22 Jan. 44	New York, NY
Budnick, Edward J.	Pvt.	KIA	24 Jan. 44	New Britain, CT
Burski, Raymond F.	Pfc	MIA	22 Jan. 44	Natrona, PA
Butcher, William T.	Pvt.	MIA	22 Jan. 44	Plymouth, PA
Butts, Emory T.	Pvt.	SWA	22 Jan. 44	Hedgesville, WV
Canniff, Richard D.	Pfc	KIA	24 Jan. 44	Orange, NJ
Capie, Robert M.	Pfc	SWA	22 Jan. 44	Buffalo, NY
Carr, Leo J.	Pvt.	MIA	22 Jan. 44	Massena, NY
Caruso, Frank NMI	Cpl.	SWA	22 Jan. 44	Ambler, PA
Cary, Robert W.	Pvt.	MIA	22 Jan. 44	Carrollton, MO
Cooper, George F.	Pvt.	MIA	22 Jan. 44	Concord, TN
Cormano, Anthony M.	Pvt.	MIA	22 Jan. 44	Jamaica, NY
Crawford, Walter G.	S/Sgt.	MIA	22 Jan. 44	E. St. Louis, IL
Cummings, Rayford F.	Pvt.	MIA	22 Jan. 44	Moultrie, GA
Chacke, Joseph S.	Pvt.	MIA	22 Jan. 44	Plymouth, PA
Czapla, Theodore P.	Pvt.	MIA	22 Jan. 44	Chicago, IL
Davis, James E.	Pvt.	MIA	22 Jan. 44	Spartanburg, SC
Dechene, Richard C.	Pvt.	KIA	21 Jan. 44	Minneapolis, MN
Dunham, Walter L.	Pvt.	SWA	22 Jan. 44	Fords, NJ
Earnest, Hugh NMI	Pfc	SWA	22 Jan. 44	Lawrenceville, IL
Elmore, Mike W.	Pfc	MIA	22 Jan. 44	Rising Fawn, GA
French, Wilbur G.	Pvt.	MIA	22 Jan. 44	Torrington, CT
Gosse, John E.	Pvt.	MIA	22 Jan. 44	Chicago, IL
Grubbs, Delbert L.	Pvt.	LWA	28 Jan. 44	Christopher, IL
Hallahan, John F.	Sgt.	SWA	22 Jan. 44	Little Ferry, NJ
Harwood, Gerald S.	Pvt.	MIA	22 Jan. 44	Brattleboro, VT
Hearn, James J.	Pvt.	MIA	22 Jan. 44	Auburn, MA
Henderson, Horace E.	S/Sgt.	SWA	22 Jan. 44	Texarkana, Texas
Holoduek, Frank NMI	Pvt.	MIA	22 Jan. 44	Troy, NY
Huffman, Charles J.	Pvt.	MIA	22 Jan. 44	Louisville, KY
Hutzell, Leroy A.	Pvt.	MIA	22 Jan. 44	Boonesboro, MD
Kattleman, Joseph E.	Pvt.	LWA	22 Jan. 44	Pittsfield, IL
Klimek, Joseph H.	Pvt.	LWA	19 Jan. 44	Chicago, IL
Kocher, Joseph H.	Pvt.	MIA	22 Jan. 44	Wilkes Barre, PA
Kolczak, Charles J.	Sgt.	MIA	22 Jan. 44	Hobart, IN
Konzen, Lawrence F.	Pvt.	SWA	22 Jan. 44	Earlville, IA
Loudermilk, James A.	Pvt.	MIA	22 Jan. 44	Akron, OH
McDonald, Robert L.	Pfc	KIA	24 Jan. 44	Brillant, AL
Malek, Edward A.	Pvt.	MIA	22 Jan. 44	Detroit, MI
Marconi, Victor E.	Pvt.	MIA	22 Jan. 44	St. Marys, PA
Maxon, Lee R.	Pvt.	KIA	21 Jan. 44	Madison, IL
May, Darrel E.	Pvt.	MIA	22 Jan. 44	Purdy, MO
Iacovelli, Ernest R.	Pvt.	MIA	22 Jan. 44	Milford, MA
Kasmark, Frank M., Jr.	Pvt.	MIA	22 Jan. 44	Chicago, IL
Lagasse, Raymond NMI	Pvt.	MIA	22 Jan. 44	Fall River, MA
Lesatz, Francis M.	Pvt.	MIA	22 Jan. 44	Engadine, MI
Pedota, Edward NMI	Pfc	MIA	22 Jan. 44	Newark, NJ
Pinkston, James F.	Pvt.	MIA	22 Jan. 44	Shelbyville, TN
Roberts, Chester A.	Pvt.	MIA	22 Jan. 44	Lawrenceburg, TN
Roush, Ray NMI	Pfc	SWA	22 Jan. 44	Mason, WV
Sager, Paul R.	Pvt.	KIA	27 Jan. 44	Newark, OH
Sequine, William P.	Pvt.	SWA	22 Jan. 44	Phillipsburg, NJ
Stallone, Joseph NMI	Pvt.	LWA	22 Jan. 44	Brooklyn, NY
Van Gaasbeck, Charles M.	Pvt.	SWA	22 Jan. 44	Kingston, NY

Volz, Frank J.	Sgt.	MIA	22 Jan. 44	Robstown, Texas
Wagner, Lewis E.	Pvt.	MIA	22 Jan. 44	Galesburg, IL
Waller, Curtis C.	Pvt.	MIA	22 Jan. 44	Leenoir City, TN
Webb, Harold W.	Pvt.	MIA	22 Jan. 44	Topton, PA
Weidman, Donald L.	Pvt.	KIA	21 Jan. 44	Martinsburg, WV
Weis, Frank NMI	Pvt.	KIA	21 Jan. 44	Brooklyn, NY
Welton, Kenneth W.	Pvt.	MIA	22 Jan. 44	Brennerton, WA
Wenrich, Roy E.	Pvt.	KIA	21 Jan. 44	Harrisburg, PA
Whitlock, Robert G.	Pvt.	MIA	22 Jan. 44	Rocky Hill, NJ
Wrenn, Daniel M.	Pfc	MIA	22 Jan. 44	Louisville, KY
Zavor, Charles J.	Pvt.	LWA	22 Jan. 44	Mishawaka, IN
Zeppi, Frank M.	Pvt.	MIA	22 Jan. 44	Orange, NJ

F Company

Bayne, Carl R.	Capt.	KIA	21 Jan. 44	Yoakum, Texas
Hughes, Nathan A.	2d Lt.	LWA	22 Jan. 44	Cincinnati, OH
Lindstrom, John K.	2d Lt.	SWA	22 Jan. 44	N. Walpoe, NH
Spencer, Robert F.	2d Lt.	SWA	22 Jan. 44	Charlestown, IN
Zebrowski, Bernard J.	2d Lt.	LWA	23 Jan. 44	Bronx, NY
Barker, Bert NMI	Pfc	MIA	22 Jan. 44	Halcom, KY
Bell, Arnold T.	T/Sgt.	MIA	22 Jan. 44	Huntsville, Texas
Blevins, Harry R.	S/Sgt.	MIA	22 Jan. 44	Newport News, VA
Brown, Grady NMI	S/Sgt.	MIA	22 Jan. 44	Conroe, Texas
Carey, Augustine J.	Pvt.	MIA	22 Jan. 44	E. Providence, RI
Carey, Henry W.	Pvt.	MIA	22 Jan. 44	Ivyland, PA
Carlo, Pasquale T.	Sgt.	MIA	22 Jan. 44	Taterson, NJ
Carter, Foy NMI	PFC	KIA	21 Jan. 44	Red Boiling Spr., TN
Casady, Edgar L., Jr.	Pvt.	MIA	22 Jan. 44	Lafayette, TN
Casey, James I.	Pvt.	SWA	22 Jan. 44	Newport, RI
Cassidy, Clyde G., Jr.	Pfc	MIA	22 Jan. 44	Barton, VT
Cassidy, Richard A.	Pfc	MIA	22 Jan. 44	Bethlehem, PA
Chaconas, Angelo NMI	Pfc	MIA	22 Jan. 44	Bronx, NY
Chastang, Henry J.	Pvt.	MIA	22 Jan. 44	Mobile, AL
Chiusano, Ralph R.	Pfc	MIA	22 Jan. 44	Brooklyn, NY
Choate, Marshall D.	Sgt.	MIA	22 Jan. 44	Huntsville, Texas
Choma, Peter L.	Pvt.	MIA	22 Jan. 44	Stanford, CT
Christeno, Rosario M.	Pvt.	KIA	21 Jan. 44	Pawtcatuck, CT
Cieslak, Chester J.	Pvt.	MIA	22 Jan. 44	Detroit, MI
Clapp, Hazell NMI	Pvt.	MIA	22 Jan. 44	Detroit, MI
Clark, Raymond T.	Sgt.	MIA	22 Jan. 44	Cookville, Texas
Clay, Joseph B.	Pfc	MIA	22 Jan. 44	Savannah, TN
Closo, Charles W.	Pfc	MIA	22 Jan. 44	Ft. Wayne, IN
Coats, Max E.	Pvt.	MIA	22 Jan. 44	Arkansas City, KS
Collins, Shelby NMI	Pfc	MIA	22 Jan. 44	Witesburg, KY
Combs, Leon J.	Pvt.	MIA	22 Jan. 44	Erin, NY
Comes, Herbert E.	Pvt.	MIA	22 Jan. 44	Ilion, NY
Conte, Alfred NMI	Pfc	MIA	22 Jan. 44	Amesbury, MA
Coon, Raymond NMI	Pvt.	MIA	22 Jan. 44	Noank, CT
Cornwall, Edward G.	Pfc	MIA	22 Jan. 44	Barrington, NJ
Cottrell, John C.	Pvt.	MIA	22 Jan. 44	Clarksburg, NJ
Couture, Donald P.	Pvt.	MIA	22 Jan. 44	Winooski, VT
Cromer, Basil H.	Pfc	MIA	22 Jan. 44	Fairmont, WV
Cummings, James L.	Pvt.	MIA	22 Jan. 44	Portage, PA
Cychner, Max J.	Pfc	MIA	22 Jan. 44	Chicago, IL
Dean, Robert K.	S/Sgt.	MIA	22 Jan. 44	Huntsville, Texas
DeAngelis, Albert NMI	Pvt.	LWA	23 Jan. 44	Weirton, WV

Denov, Joseph NMI	Pfc	MIA	22 Jan. 44	Chicago, IL
Desko, John NMI, Jr.	Pvt.	LWA	17 Jan. 44	Youngstown, OH
Dick, Melvin J.	Pfc	MIA	22 Jan. 44	Mauston, WI
Dileo, Alfred NMI	Pvt.	SWA	22 Jan. 44	New Brunswick, NJ
Dinanzio, Hugo J.	Pvt.	MIA	22 Jan. 44	Yonkers, NY
Doub, Landon A.	Pvt.	LWA	22 Jan. 44	LaBelle, FL
Eglin, Ernest E.	Pvt.	MIA	22 Jan. 44	New York, NY
Engstrom, Robert D.	Pfc	MIA	22 Jan. 44	Grove City, PA
Ervin, James H.	Pvt.	KIA	24 Jan. 44	Mattoon, IL
Estes, John D.	Pfc	SWA	22 Jan. 44	Fisk, MO
Faber, Paul NMI	Pfc	MIA	22 Jan. 44	Daytona Beach, FL
Farne, Robert G.	Pfc	MIA	22 Jan. 44	Berwind, WV
Felosi, John R.	Pfc	MIA	22 Jan. 44	Liggett, KY
Fine, Albert J.	Pvt.	MIA	22 Jan. 44	Mononganela, PA
Freeman, Hubert L.	Pfc	MIA	22 Jan. 44	Chicago, IL
Frena, John M.	Pvt.	SWA	22 Jan. 44	Munhall, PA
Frye, Thomas D.	Pfc	MIA	22 Jan. 44	Frisco City, AL
Gaken, Stephen J.	Pvt.	MIA	22 Jan. 44	Saratoga Spr., NY
Gallagher, Jack D.	Pvt.	MIA	22 Jan. 44	Reidsville, NC
Gallagher, William E.	Pfc	SWA	22 Jan. 44	Easton, KS
Garber, Melvin J.	Pfc	MIA	22 Jan. 44	Clairton, PA
Gardner, Charles H.	Pvt.	MIA	22 Jan. 44	York Springs, PA
Gates, Guiford B.	Pfc	MIA	22 Jan. 44	Medford, MA
Gauntt, Milton L.	Sgt.	SWA	22 Jan. 44	Huntsville, Texas
Graham, James E.	Pfc	MIA	22 Jan. 44	Austinville, VA
Grondski, Thomas J.	Pfc	MIA	22 Jan. 44	Trenton, NJ
Heredia, Catarino M.	S/Sgt.	MIA	22 Jan. 44	Pecos, Texas
Hinkley, Chester E.	Sgt.	MIA	22 Jan. 44	Independence, MO
Hoover, John L.	T/Sgt.	MIA	22 Jan. 44	Monongahela, PA
Jones, Marvin E.	F/Sgt.	MIA	22 Jan. 44	Huntsville, Texas
Keef, Charles D.	Pfc	MIA	22 Jan. 44	Lincoln, NE
Lambeth, Robert D.	Pfc	MIA	22 Jan. 44	Los Angeles, CA
Lange, Raymond E.	Pfc	MIA	22 Jan. 44	Ludington, MI
LeBanc, Joseph V.	Pvt.	MIA	22 Jan. 44	Oldtown, ME
Lebo, Marvin W.	Pfc	MIA	22 Jan. 44	Reading, PA
Lennon, Kenneth J.	Pvt.	MIA	22 Jan. 44	Chicago, IL
Lichtenbaum, Joseph B.	Pvt.	MIA	22 Jan. 44	Hartford, CT
Linegar, Bryan NMI	Pvt.	MIA	22 Jan. 44	Evansville, IN
MacFarland, Willis V.	Pvt.	LWA	22 Jan. 44	St. Louis, MO
McArthur, Clifford E.	Pvt.	SWA	22 Jan. 44	S. S. Marie, MI
McCall, Thomas E.	S/Sgt.	MIA	22 Jan. 44	Veedersburg, IN
McConehy, Cleo L.	Pvt.	MIA	22 Jan. 44	Clinton, IA
McGirr, James N.	Pvt.	MIA	22 Jan. 44	Saratoga Spr., NY
McLaughlin, John D.	Pfc	MIA	22 Jan. 44	New York, NY
McLaughlin, John M.	Pvt.	MIA	22 Jan. 44	Dubuque, IA
McMaster, Buster C.	Sgt.	MIA	22 Jan. 44	Winifrede, WV
McNamara, Bernard J.	S/Sgt.	MIA	22 Jan. 44	Bronx, NY
McNamara, Joseph T., Jr.	Pvt.	MIA	22 Jan. 44	New York, NY
Maly, Johnnie E.	Sgt.	MIA	22 Jan. 44	Bryan, Texas
Malone, Joseph T.	Pvt.	MIA	22 Jan. 44	Trenton, NJ
Martin, Allen A.	Pvt.	LWA	22 Jan. 44	Milwaukee, WI
Maslowski, Ted F.	Pfc	MIA	22 Jan. 44	Chicago, IL
Mazza, Michael A.	Pvt.	MIA	22 Jan. 44	Haverville, MA
Meiczkowski, Thaddeus S.	Pvt.	SWA	22 Jan. 44	Steubenville, OH
Metsa, Arthur H.	Pvt.	MIA	22 Jan. 44	Baltic, MI
Miller, Gordon B.	Pvt.	MIA	22 Jan. 44	Duluth, MN

Molongoski, Edmund P.	Pvt.	MIA	22 Jan. 44	Montague City, MA
Mongeau, Elmer M.	Pvt.	MIA	22 Jan. 44	Ontonagon, MI
Moore, Harry R.	S/Sgt.	LWA	22 Jan. 44	Ft. Worth, Texas
Moran, Frank C.	Pvt.	MIA	22 Jan. 44	Cleveland, OH
Morgan, Thomas W.	Pfc	MIA	22 Jan. 44	Macon, GA
Muise, Francis W.	Pfc	SWA	22 Jan. 44	Wakefield, MA
Nicola, Ernest NMI	Pfc	MIA	22 Jan. 44	Providence, RI
Payne, Russell H.	Pfc	MIA	22 Jan. 44	Secretary, MO
Potts, George E.	Pfc	MIA	22 Jan. 44	Philadelphia, PA
Ratliff, Burla L.	Pfc	MIA	22 Jan. 44	Belcher, KY
Redding, Richard M.	S/Sgt.	MIA	22 Jan. 44	Rahway, NJ
Ress, Peter G.	Pvt.	MIA	22 Jan. 44	Racino, WI
Romberger, Ralph C.	Pvt.	MIA	22 Jan. 44	Harrisburg, PA
Sage, Robert C.	S/Sgt.	MIA	22 Jan. 44	Tampa, FL
Santalucia, Joseph NMI	Pvt.	MIA	22 Jan. 44	Garfield, NJ
Santasiero, Roscoe A.	Pfc	MIA	22 Jan. 44	Port Chester, NY
Schafer, Raymond H.	Pfc	MIA	22 Jan. 44	Pittsburg, PA
Schalch, William K., Sr.	Pfc	MIA	22 Jan. 44	Paris, KY
Schumer, Joseph P., Jr.	Pfc	MIA	22 Jan. 44	Evanston, IL
Sensabaugh, William L.	Pvt.	MIA	22 Jan. 44	Church Hill, TN
Shull, Prober R.	Pfc	MIA	22 Jan. 44	Clarksdale, MS
Singer, Frederick R.	Pvt.	MIA	22 Jan. 44	Detroit, MI
Smith, Claude NMI	S/Sgt.	MIA	22 Jan. 44	Gunlock, KY
Sullenberger, John W.	Pfc	MIA	22 Jan. 44	Parr, PA
Sullivan, Jack E.	Pfc	MIA	22 Jan. 44	Starke, FL
Szela, Hermin A.	Pvt.	MIA	22 Jan. 44	Elizabeth, NJ
Tretter, Alexander NMI	Pfc	MIA	22 Jan. 44	Monessen, PA
Tropeano, James A.	Sgt.	MIA	22 Jan. 44	Wakefield, MA
Tuszynski, Raymond J.	Pvt.	MIA	22 Jan. 44	Erie, PA
Valentine, John J.	Pfc	MIA	22 Jan. 44	Jackson Heights, NY
Valjato, John D.	Pfc	MIA	22 Jan. 44	Cleveland, OH
Velo, Anthony C., Jr.	Pfc	MIA	22 Jan. 44	Hollis, NY
Verrett, Gilbert A.	Pfc	MIA	22 Jan. 44	Morgan City, LA
Wallace, Bowers H.	Pfc	MIA	22 Jan. 44	Sturgis, KY
Wargin, Edward F.	Pfc	MIA	22 Jan. 44	Milwaukee, WI
Waugh, Melvin C.	Pfc	MIA	22 Jan. 44	Hiddenite, NC
Whipple, Ralph R.	Pfc	MIA	22 Jan. 44	Wexford, PA
Wissman, Carl G.	Pfc	MIA	22 Jan. 44	New Bremen, OH
Wolfe, William L.	Pvt.	MIA	22 Jan. 44	Butler, TN
Yates, Charles M.	Pvt.	MIA	22 Jan. 44	Cobb, TN
Zanotti, Leo J.	Sgt.	MIA	22 Jan. 44	Wilmington, MA

G Company

Bierley, David H.	2d Lt.	LWA	26 Jan. 44	Corington, KY
Adamezyk, Leonard S.	Pvt.	SWA	22 Jan. 44	Glouster, NJ
Adams, Donald L.	Pfc	LWA	21 Jan. 44	Cleveland, OH
Burger, Matthew K.	Pvt.	KIA	21 Jan. 44	New York, NY
Coles, Kirk K.	Pvt.	LWA	29 Jan. 44	Charlestown, WV
Coolong, Hadley J.	Pfc	SWA	22 Jan. 44	Patten, ME
Czapozynski, Walter E.	Pvt.	LWA	22 Jan. 44	Toledo, OH
Davis, Leroy NMI	Pvt.	SWA	23 Jan. 44	Durand, IL
Deal, Rexford W.	Pfc	LWA	21 Jan. 44	Muskegon, MI
Gibson, Glenn G.	Pfc	LWA	21 Jan. 44	Statesville, NC
Grill, Danis NMI	Pvt.	SWA	20 Jan. 44	New York, NY
Hadzick, Ralph E.	Pvt.	SWA	22 Jan. 44	Long Island, NY
Hammel, Ralph E.	Pvt.	DOW	22 Jan. 44	S. Ozone Pk., NY

Hansbury, Francis J.	Pfc	LWA	21 Jan. 44	Cohoes, NY
Hashman, Russell NMI	Pfc	LWA	21 Jan. 44	Indianapolis, IN
Helton, Ray B.	Pvt.	SWA	22 Jan. 44	Sevierville, TN
Heyer, Frank E.	Pfc	LWA	21 Jan. 44	Mobile, AL
Hill, Howard NMI	Pfc	LWA	22 Jan. 44	Cambridge, MD
Hughes, Harvey H.	Pvt.	LWA	22 Jan. 44	Compton, CA
Minehart, Andrew A.	Pvt.	SWA	22 Jan. 44	Butler, PA
Mullins, Arvid E.	Pvt.	LWA	21 Jan. 44	Coal Run, KY
Nored, William A.	Pvt.	LWA	21 Jan. 44	Quilin, MO
Prahl, George L.	Pvt.	LWA	22 Jan. 44	Monogan, WV
Staats, David L.	Pvt.	SWA	29 Jan. 44	Ottumwa, IA
Steere, Warren A.	Pvt.	LWA	24 Jan. 44	Oakland Beach, RI
Stevenson, Vernon R.	Pvt.	LWA	21 Jan. 44	Quimby, IA
Story, Odis T.	Sgt.	SWA	22 Jan. 44	Sulphur Spr., Texas
Toll, Carl R.	Pfc	LWA	21 Jan. 44	Rockford, IL
Villano, John S.	S/Sgt.	SWA	22 Jan. 44	Somerville, NJ

H Company

Kilmer, Christopher NMI	2d Lt.	SWA	23 Jan. 44	Tuscon, AZ
Shaneberger, Robley D. W.	2d. Lt.	LWA	22 Jan. 44	Easton, PA
Vierheller, Thomas E.	2d Lt.	MIA	23 Jan. 44	Parkersburg, WV
Acevedo, Angel G.	Sgt.	KIA	17 Jan. 44	El Paso, Texas
Alley, Paul NMI	Pvt.	MIA	23 Jan. 44	Wytheville, VA
Anderson, Harold S.	Pvt.	MIA	23 Jan. 44	E. Weymouth, MA
Auler, Russel J.	Pfc	LWA	22 Jan. 44	Alexandria, IN
Badman, James F.	Sgt.	KIA	22 Jan. 44	Baltimore, MD
Barnes, Charles W.	Pfc	MIA	23 Jan. 44	Brownfield, PA
Bell, Ben NMI	Pfc	MIA	23 Jan. 44	Ridgeway, VA
Bell, David A.	Sgt.	MIA	23 Jan. 44	Sheridan, WY
Benham, John E.	Pfc	SWA	22 Jan. 44	Dorchester, MA
Berger, Paul E.	Pvt.	MIA	23 Jan. 44	New Alexander, PA
Casebier, Earl S.	Pfc	MIA	23 Jan. 44	Greenville, KY
Cornett, Marhall E.	Pvt.	MIA	23 Jan. 44	High Splint, KY
Cotropia, Joseph A.	Sgt.	MIA	23 Jan. 44	Rochester, NY
Cox, Clifford E.	Pvt.	MIA	23 Jan. 44	Portage, PA
Crossman, Ervin NMI	Sgt.	LWA	25 Jan. 44	Detroit, MI
Cucinotta, Joseph J.	Pfc	MIA	23 Jan. 44	Gibbstown, NJ
Daley, Lorne H.	Sgt.	MIA	23 Jan. 44	Stratford, NY
Derrick, William H.	Pfc	MIA	23 Jan. 44	Portage, PA
Eldridge, Joseph A.	Pfc	MIA	23 Jan. 44	Elizabeth, NJ
Esliger, William J.	Pfc	MIA	23 Jan. 44	Groveton, NH
Fisher, Robert J.	Pfc	LWA	22 Jan. 44	Philadelphia, PA
Franklin, Donald M.	Pvt.	SWA	22 Jan. 44	Ellenton, SC
Gamache, Charles H.	Pfc	MIA	23 Jan. 44	Westfield, MA
Hanscom, Lincoln H.	Pfc	MIA	23 Jan. 44	Portsmouth, MA
Hatcher, Howard W.	Pfc	LWA	22 Jan. 44	Roswell, GA
Hendricks, Jack V.	Pvt.	MIA	23 Jan. 44	Raleigh, NC
Hoffman, Charles C.	Pfc	MIA	23 Jan. 44	W. Columbia, WV
Horner, Mahlon M.	Pvt.	MIA	23 Jan. 44	Florence, NJ
Huber, Phillip A.	Pfc	LWA	23 Jan. 44	Valencia, PA
Joseph, Vernard L.	Pfc	MIA	23 Jan. 44	Gloversville, NY
King, Raymond M.	Pfc	MIA	23 Jan. 44	Mitchell, IN
Kintopp, Henry J.	Pfc	LWA	22 Jan. 44	Iron Ridge, WI
Kirby, Albert C.	Pvt.	MIA	23 Jan. 44	Belmont, NC
Kociara, John NMI	Pfc	LWA	23 Jan. 44	Chicago, IL
Krager, Ross D.	Pfc	MIA	23 Jan. 44	Siloam Springs, AR

Levenson, Herschel L.	Pfc	MIA	23 Jan. 44	Bronx, NY
Linkes, Sylvester R.	Pfc	MIA	23 Jan. 44	N. Vandergrift, PA
Love, George W.	Pvt.	SWA	22 Jan. 44	Clay, WV
Lupo, Salvatore J.	Pfc	KIA	24 Jan. 44	Richmond, NY
Melancon, Howard R.	Pfc	LWA	22 Jan. 44	Lutcher, LA
Monteith, Fremont D.	Pvt.	MIA	23 Jan. 44	Everett, WA
Thomas, Robert S.	Pfc	MIA	23 Jan. 44	E. Liverpool, OH
Valdez, Leonides NMI	Pfc	LWA	22 Jan. 44	Concepcion, Texas
Wuestman, John H., Jr.	Sgt.	LWA	29 Jan. 44	Brooklyn, NY

Headquarters and Headquarters Company Third Battalion

Volheim, Herman M.	Capt.	MIA	22 Jan. 44	Venice, CA
Reed, Myron W.	2d Lt.	SWA	22 Jan. 44	Mono, IN
Bledsoe, Vernon NMI	Pfc	LWA	19 Jan. 44	Loogootee, IN
Bocchino, William NMI	Pvt.	LWA	22 Jan. 44	Raritan, NJ
Cassidy, Floyd R.	Pvt.	LWA	17 Jan. 44	Gladstone, MI
Connell, John C.	T/5	DOW	18 Jan. 44	W. Orange, NJ
Cox, George D.	Pvt.	LIA	21 Jan. 44	Moshein, TN
Furlo, John V.	Pvt.	MIA	22 Jan. 44	Saginaw, MI
Granowicz, Joseph J.	Pfc	SWA	22 Jan. 44	Detroit, MI
Hartford, Homer J.	Pvt.	LWA	22 Jan. 44	Carrier Mills, IL
Kromel, Peter P.	Pvt.	SWA	27 Jan. 44	Chicago, IL
La Corte, Frank NMI	Pvt.	LWA	17 Jan. 44	Elizabeth, NJ
Lofrano, Carlo NMI	Pfc	SWA	22 Jan. 44	Brooklyn, NY
McDonald, John S.	Pvt.	MIA	22 Jan. 44	Peach Creek, WV
Morris, Allen L.	Pfc	SWA	27 Jan. 44	Waco, Texas
Newall, William G.	Pvt.	SWA	22 Jan. 44	Chicago, IL
Phillips, Doyle C.	Pfc	SWA	27 Jan. 44	Hillsboro, Texas
Phillips, Wilson H.	Pvt.	SWA	27 Jan. 44	Waynesville, NC
Prunty, Doy J.	Pvt.	SWA	22 Jan. 44	Lorain, OH
Stark, Arthur E.	Pvt.	DOW	26 Jan. 44	Hendersonville, TN
Szarawarski, Thaddeus NMI	Pvt.	LWA	22 Jan. 44	Garfield, NJ
Viether, Orville O.	Pvt.	LWA	17 Jan. 44	Atlantic, IA

I Company

Gleason, Laurence P.	2d Lt.	KIA	21 Jan. 44	Jersey City, NJ
Skalovsky, Michael NMI	2d Lt.	SWA	22 Jan. 44	San Antonio, Texas
Sternstein, Jack NMI	2d Lt.	SWA	17 Jan. 44	Chicago, IL
Tschantz, Carl C.	2d Lt.	MIA	22 Jan. 44	Akron, OH
Badovick, George NMI	Pvt.	LWA	28 Jan. 44	Cleveland, OH
Black, Joe H.	Pvt.	LWA	19 Jan. 44	Gary, IN
Broad, John A.	Pvt.	LIA	21 Jan. 44	Newburgh, NY
Bufmack, William NMI	Pvt.	LWA	22 Jan. 44	Colorado Springs, CO
Cain, James M.	S/Sgt.	LWA	18 Jan. 44	Atlanta, GA
Camacho, Joseph A.	Pvt.	LWA	21 Jan. 44	Lowell, MA
Camisa, Silvio A.	Pvt.	LWA	21 Jan. 44	Bronx, NY
Cenedella, Kenneth V.	Pvt.	LWA	21 Jan. 44	Berkeley, CA
Corvi, James V.	Pfc	SIA	21 Jan. 44	Newark, NJ
Cronkhite, William H., Jr.	Pvt.	LWA	22 Jan. 44	Lewiston, ME
Czubernat, Michael S.	Pvt.	KIA	19 Jan. 44	Chicago, IL
Dennis, Charles F.	T/Sgt.	LWA	20 Jan. 44	Waco, Texas
Derenzo, Vincent J.	Pvt.	LWA	22 Jan. 44	Brooklyn, NY
Dinko, Nicholas F.	Pvt.	LWA	22 Jan. 44	Brooklyn, NY
Di Raimo, Anthony G.	Pvt.	LWA	22 Jan. 44	Granston, RI
Disperto, Emanuel D.	Pfc	LWA	22 Jan. 44	Elizabeth, NJ
Donihue, Rolland R.	Pfc	LWA	18 Jan. 44	Parma, MI

Drake, Marvin O.	Sgt.	LWA	20 Jan. 44	Belton, Texas
Erickson, Edward S.	Pvt.	DOW	18 Jan. 44	Jersey City, NJ
Farnsworth, William T.	Pvt.	SWA	24 Jan. 44	Sulphur Spr., Texas
Fastenau, Herman H., Jr.	Pvt.	SWA	20 Jan. 44	Union City, NJ
Felty, Lloyd W.	Pvt.	LWA	20 Jan. 44	Port Deposit, MD
Fenter, George H.	Pfc	LWA	17 Jan. 44	Point, Texas
Fields, Victor W.	Pfc	SIA	21 Jan. 44	Limona, FL
Franklin, Earl J.	Pfc	LWA	26 Jan. 44	Globe, AZ
Gabriel, Robert E.	Pfc	LWA	20 Jan. 44	Maspeth, NY
Garcia, Raymond NMI	Pvt.	SWA	24 Jan. 44	Canton, OH
Gelder, Theron A.	Pfc	LWA	22 Jan. 44	Hillsdale, MI
Godlewski, Stanley NMI	Pvt.	LWA	21 Jan. 44	Philadelphia, PA
Gonzales, Richard V.	Pfc	LWA	22 Jan. 44	Los Angeles, CA
Guerie, Lucien E.	Pvt.	LWA	22 Jan. 44	Lewiston, ME
Guidice, Michael P.	Pfc	LWA	20 Jan. 44	Latrobe, PA
Hernandez, Abelardo NMI	Pfc	LWA	21 Jan. 44	New Braunfels, Texas
Hochberg, Sol NMI	Pvt.	LWA	22 Jan. 44	New York, NY
Jaskiewicz, Teddy F.	Pvt.	SWA	21 Jan. 44	E. St. Louis, IL
Jefferess, Charlie R.	Pvt.	SWA	20 Jan. 44	Gary, IN
Johnson, Jerome B.	Pvt.	LWA	21 Jan. 44	Champaign, IL
Kelly, Roland H.	Pvt.	LWA	20 Jan. 44	Alton, IL
King, Cecil O., Jr.	Pvt.	LWA	22 Jan. 44	Geneva, PA
King, Ray L.	Pvt.	SWA	20 Jan. 44	Sevierville, TN
Knauer, Russel P.	Pvt.	LWA	24 Jan. 44	Morristown, PA
Knighten, Marshall F.	Pvt.	LWA	20 Jan. 44	Saxapahaw, NC
Konarek, Albert W.	S/Sgt.	LWA	21 Jan. 44	Thrall, Texas
Lloyd, Donald D.	Pfc	LWA	22 Jan. 44	Eugene, OR
Mack, Warren J.	S/Sgt.	LWA	17 Jan. 44	Bronx, NY
Magazzu, Salvatore D.	Pvt.	LWA	21 Jan. 44	Philadelphia, PA
Maliszewski, Joseph J.	Pfc	LWA	17 Jan. 44	Wilmington, DE
Marianetti, Tony A.	Pvt.	LWA	23 Jan. 44	Rochester, NY
Marchese, Joseph T.	Pvt.	SIA	21 Jan. 44	New York, NY
Markowitz, Alan NMI	Pvt.	SIA	21 Jan. 44	Brooklyn, NY
Martin, George B.	Pvt.	LWA	22 Jan. 44	Dekalb, Texas
Massing, Frank G.	Pfc	LWA	22 Jan. 44	Buffalo, NY
Mekelik, John J.	S/Sgt.	MIA	26 Jan. 44	Taylor, Texas
Milbrath, Donald O.	Pvt.	LWA	22 Jan. 44	Milwaukee, WI
Miller, Ralph W.	Pvt.	KIA	24 Jan. 44	Wallingford, KY
Mitchell, Marvin P.	Pvt.	LWA	22 Jan. 44	Ewing, KY
Mobyed, George M.	Pvt.	LWA	28 Jan. 44	Brooklyn, NY
Moeckler, Harland NMI	Pfc	KIA	19 Jan. 44	Sheboygan, WI
Monkiewicz, Alexander A.	Pvt.	LIA	21 Jan. 44	Canonsburg, PA
Morris, Edward H.	Sgt.	LWA	22 Jan. 44	Philadelphia, PA
Mueller, Albert NMI	Pvt.	LWA	22 Jan. 44	Marcellus, NY
Myers, Wilbert M.	Pfc	LWA	22 Jan. 44	Greenfield, IN
Nardelli, Mario C.	Pvt.	SWA	23 Jan. 44	Arcadia, KS
Niglio, Valentino NMI	Pvt.	LWA	28 Jan. 44	Philadelphia, PA
Nowling, Richard B.	Pfc	LWA	21 Jan. 44	St. Petersburg, FL
Olenick, Paul NMI	Pfc	LWA	28 Jan. 44	New York, NY
Osborne, Charles J., Jr.	Pvt.	SWA	18 Jan. 44	Bluff City, TN
Oswald, George J.	Pvt.	LWA	22 Jan. 44	Altoona, PA
Parker, Owen W.	Sgt.	LWA	24 Jan. 44	Temple, Texas
Payne, John J.	Pvt.	LWA	22 Jan. 44	Summerfield, NC
Poirier, Omer A.	Pvt.	SWA	19 Jan. 44	Hartford, CT
Purpura, Charles F.	Sgt.	LWA	24 Jan. 44	Indianapolis, IN
Register, Charles NMI, Jr.	Pvt.	DOW	18 Jan. 44	White Springs, FL

Rejtmar, Michael J.	T/Sgt.	MIA	26 Jan. 44	Bernardsville, NJ
Repass, Vernon O.	Pvt.	LWA	18 Jan. 44	N. Tazewell, VA
Roblyer, Scott G.	S/Sgt.	LWA	20 Jan. 44	Gillette, PA
Rohan, Julius F.	Pfc	LWA	22 Jan. 44	Yoakum, Texas
Rosenberg, Peter NMI	Pvt.	SWA	22 Jan. 44	New York, NY
Shoff, Lang D.	Pvt.	LWA	22 Jan. 44	Colebrook, NH
Shuler, Arthur L.	Pfc	SWA	30 Jan. 44	Bordentown, NJ
Smith, David H.	Pfc	MIA	26 Jan. 44	Harrisburg, PA
Smith, Richard W., Jr.	Pfc	SWA	22 Jan. 44	Lynchburg, PA
Steward, Jesse E.	Pfc	LIA	22 Jan. 44	Seminole, OK
Stuckley, Woodrow J.	S/Sgt.	LWA	17 Jan. 44	Hubbard, Texas
Terregino, Anthony NMI	Pvt.	LWA	21 Jan. 44	Meadville, PA
Thompson, Russell E.	Pvt.	LWA	28 Jan. 44	Chicago, IL
Tomer, Clifford NMI	Pvt.	LWA	22 Jan. 44	Canton, OH
Torno, Paul J.	Pvt.	LIA	28 Jan. 44	Dorchester, MA
Tworek, Arthur R.	Pvt.	SWA	22 Jan. 44	Chicago, IL
Vairo, Dominic J.	Pvt.	SWA	19 Jan. 44	Lake Linden, MI
Valine, John M.	Pvt.	LWA	22 Jan. 44	Crystal Falls, MI
Valot, Edward W.	Pvt.	SWA	22 Jan. 44	Cheboygan, MI
Vander Heyden, Don A.	Pvt.	LWA	20 Jan. 44	Norway, MI
Venda, Vincent S.	Pvt.	LWA	22 Jan. 44	Ecorse, MI
Vitt, Walter C.	Pvt.	LWA	22 Jan. 44	Boston, MA
Vlastaras, John NMI	Pvt.	LWA	18 Jan. 44	Newark, NJ
Walker, Ralph A.	Pvt.	DOW	18 Jan. 44	Braddock, PA
Warchel, Leonard S.	Pfc	LWA	22 Jan. 44	E. St. Louis, IL
Warschkow, Raymond G.	Pvt.	LWA	22 Jan. 44	W. Allis, WI
Webster, Edgar R.	Pvt.	LWA	19 Jan. 44	Reading, MA
Willoughby, Alfred L.	Pvt.	LWA	17 Jan. 44	Corsicana, Texas
Wolford, Donald L.	Pvt.	SWA	22 Jan. 44	Cokeville, PA
Yokom, William G.	S/Sgt.	DOW	18 Jan. 44	Buffalo, NY
Zawada, Joe E.	Pvt.	SWA	18 Jan. 44	Chicago, IL
Zornes, Howard E.	Pvt.	LWA	17 Jan. 44	Columbus, OH

K Company

Bragaw, Henry C.	Capt.	KIA	22 Jan. 44	Winnabow, NC
Gutting, Robert H.	1st Lt.	LWA	28 Jan. 44	Cincinnatti, OH
Kramer, Robert L.	2d Lt.	LWA	28 Jan. 44	New York, NY
Sherman, Alex NMI	2d Lt.	SWA	22 Jan. 44	Brooklyn, NY
Shulkin, Leslie M.	2d Lt.	LWA	22 Jan. 44	Beverly Hills, CA
Tremalgia, Cesaro F.	2d Lt.	LWA	22 Jan. 44	Bridgeport, CT
Anderson, Bruce H.	Pfc	MIA	23 Jan. 44	Chicago, IL
Bell, Ray J.	Pvt.	SWA	22 Jan. 44	Norfolk, NY
Bohannon, Floyd W.	Pfc	LWA	28 Jan. 44	Dumas, Texas
Cameron, David J.	Pfc	LWA	23 Jan. 44	Hamilton, OH
Cartwright, Robert T.	Pvt.	LWA	22 Jan. 44	Beavers Dam, OH
Chaszar, John J.	S/Sgt.	KIA	24 Jan. 44	Cleveland, OH
Cramer, Harold W.	Pvt.	KIA	18 Jan. 44	Indian Head, PA
Crawford, Wilbur A.	S/Sgt.	LWA	23 Jan. 44	Waco, Texas
Croteau, Roger V.	Pfc	SWA	17 Jan. 44	Portsmouth, NH
D'Andrea, John A., Jr.	Pvt.	SWA	22 Jan. 44	Springfield, NJ
Dickenson, L. M. (i.o.)	T/Sgt.	LWA	21 Jan. 44	Mart, Texas
Dragan, Joseph W.	Pfc	SWA	22 Jan. 44	Plymouth, PA
Dugan, Henry L.	S/Sgt.	SWA	22 Jan. 44	Groesbeck, Texas
Edwards, Willard L.	Pfc	SWA	22 Jan. 44	Kenova, WV
Eppinger, Robert L.	Pvt.	LWA	22 Jan. 44	Evans City, PA
Faulk, Woodrow NMI	Sgt.	LWA	28 Jan. 44	San Antonio, Texas

Fine, Michael NMI	Pfc	LWA	22 Jan. 44	Brooklyn, NY
Galway, Wilbert H.	Pvt.	MIA	23 Jan. 44	Freeport, IL
Garrison, Leonard W.	Pvt.	LWA	22 Jan. 44	W. Milton, OH
Gassaway, Jack D.	Pvt.	SWA	22 Jan. 44	Lincolnton, GA
Gerow, Leland F.	Pfc	MIA	23 Jan. 44	Big Flats, NY
Griffin, Charles F.	Pfc	LWA	23 Jan. 44	Street, MD
Hanson, Lammoth J.	Pfc	SWA	23 Jan. 44	Jefferson, GA
Harper, Loy M.	Pvt.	LWA	22 Jan. 44	Nauvoo, AL
Hauskin, Clessie L.	Pfc.	LWA	22 Jan. 44	Westmoreland, TN
Henry, Dudley O.	T/Sgt.	KIA	24 Jan. 44	Mosheim, Texas
Hooper, Tom E.	Pfc	LWA	23 Jan. 44	Waco, Texas
Jones, Julian C.	S/Sgt.	LWA	22 Jan. 44	Lamesa, Texas
Jones, Orville E.	1st Sgt.	LWA	22 Jan. 44	Waco, Texas
Kirby, Billy E.	S/Sgt.	LWA	22 Jan. 44	Gatesville, Texas
Laird, Merrill B.	Pfc	LWA	28 Jan. 44	Bellwood, PA
Lavezza, John L., Jr.	Pvt.	LWA	23 Jan. 44	Baltimore, MD
Letney, Carl C.	Pfc	MIA	23 Jan. 44	Waterloo, IA
Lewis, I. D. (i.o.)	Pfc	LWA	21 Jan. 44	Erin, TN
Linback, Henry L.	Pvt.	LWA	23 Jan. 44	Francisville, IN
Maddox, Jim C.	T/Sgt.	LWA	29 Jan. 44	Groesbeck, Texas
Maffitt, Kenneth F.	Pfc	LWA	23 Jan. 44	Gary, IN
Maguire, Reginald J.	Pfc	KIA	21 Jan. 44	Youngstown, OH
Manna, Daniel J.	Pvt.	LWA	23 Jan. 44	Philadelphia, PA
Marchington, Wilber A.	Pfc	SWA	17 Jan. 44	Newark, OH
Mendoza, Jose P.	Pfc	LWA	21 Jan. 44	San Antonio, Texas
Owens, Timmons T.	Pfc	SWA	22 Jan. 44	Louisville, KY
Pacenka, Edward J.	Cpl.	SWA	22 Jan. 44	Maspeth, NY
Paulcheck, Edward C.	Pfc	LWA	23 Jan. 44	McKeesport, PA
Pearson, J. B. (i.o.)	Pfc	DOW	22 Jan. 44	Jasper, AL
Pecora, Dominick J.	Pvt.	LWA	22 Jan. 44	Portchester, NY
Person, Charles D.	Pfc	SWA	22 Jan. 44	Fayetteville, NC
Pianka, Joseph NMI	Pfc	LWA	17 Jan. 44	Baldwinsville, MA
Piechocki, Theodore J.	Pvt.	LWA	21 Jan. 44	South Bend, IN
Porter, Barney G.	Pvt.	DOW	31 Jan. 44	Pickens, SC
Priehs, Charles G.	Pvt.	LWA	22 Jan. 44	Ferndale, MI
Qualls, Kyle W.	Pvt.	MIA	23 Jan. 44	Linden, TN
Rasansky, Paul NMI	Pvt.	LWA	23 Jan. 44	Philadelphia, PA
Rector, Robert E.	Pfc	SWA	22 Jan. 44	Hiawassee Dam, NC
Repicky, Joseph F.	Pfc	LWA	28 Jan. 44	Yonkers, NY
Resch, Henry P.	Pvt.	SWA	22 Jan. 44	Milwaukee, WI
Ricketts, Joseph E.	Pvt.	MIA	23 Jan. 44	St. Andrews, TN
Ridinger, John D.	Pfc	LWA	28 Jan. 44	Chambersburg, PA
Rose, Hyman NMI	Sgt.	SWA	22 Jan. 44	Brooklyn, NY
Roseman, Lindsey L.	Pvt.	DOW	22 Jan. 44	Salisbury, NC
Rubin, Lawrence I.	Pvt.	LWA	21 Jan. 44	Brooklyn, NY
Rummel, Charles R.	T/Sgt.	MIA	23 Jan. 44	Waco, Texas
Russell, Lawrence F.	Pvt.	LWA	28 Jan. 44	Gary, IN
Saarloos, Stanley J.	Pvt.	LWA	23 Jan. 44	Bellenille, NJ
Schatz, Lewis NMI	Pvt.	SWA	22 Jan. 44	Dobbin, Texas
Schmidt, Raymond J.	Pfc	LWA	28 Jan. 44	Philadelphia, PA
Shakespeare, Everett L.	Pfc	MIA	23 Jan. 44	Independence, MO
Silva, Maurice E.	Pvt.	MIA	23 Jan. 44	Everett, MA
Sisson, Joe B.	Pfc	LWA	28 Jan. 44	Apple Springs, Texas
Skelley, Joseph T.	Pvt.	LWA	23 Jan. 44	Fort Lee, NJ
Smiley, Paul N.	Pvt.	LWA	22 Jan. 44	Waterford, PA
Souza, Arthur NMI, Jr.	Pvt.	LWA	22 Jan. 44	S. Darthmouth, MA

Spencer, Oran B.	Pvt.	DOW	24 Jan. 44	Milan, MO
Spooner, John NMI	S/Sgt.	KIA	22 Jan. 44	Brooklyn, NY
Strebin, Loren S.	Pfc	SWA	28 Jan. 44	Kokomo, IN
Stubley, Fred J.	Pfc	LWA	24 Jan. 44	Gloucester, NY
Swain, Delmar M.	Pfc	LWA	21 Jan. 44	Levelland, Texas
Talley, Bernard F.	Pfc	LWA	22 Jan. 44	Ellerson, VA
Taylor, Charles B.	Pfc	LWA	22 Jan. 44	Wadsworth, OH
Thompson, Carl W.	Pfc	LWA	22 Jan. 44	Sayre, PA
Trexler, Wallace R.	Pvt.	LWA	23 Jan. 44	Wadesboro, NC
Veselka, Victor V.	Pvt.	LWA	21 Jan. 44	Waco, Texas
Wadsworth, Leroy L.	Pvt.	LWA	22 Jan. 44	Lock Haven, PA
Wolford, Meade K.	Pvt.	LWA	17 Jan. 44	Hedgesville, WV
Worthington, Stanley V.	Pfc	LWA	17 Jan. 44	Newton, PA
Wright, Earl N.	Pfc	MIA	23 Jan. 44	Rickman, TN
Yancey, Burl NMI	Pvt.	LWA	22 Jan. 44	San Antonio, Texas
Zazzali, Gerald F.	Sgt.	SWA	22 Jan. 44	Newark, NJ

L Company

Cassidy, William E.	2d Lt.	LWA	24 Jan. 44	Brooklyn, NY
		LWA	26 Jan. 44	
Keck, Delmar C.	2d Lt.	LWA	18 Jan. 44	Rolla, MO
		MIA	22 Jan. 44	
Mesner, Peter W.	2d. Lt.	SWA	24 Jan. 44	Buffalo, NY
Michael, Simon NMI	2d Lt.	MIA	22 Jan. 44	Athens, GA
Bounds, James E.	Cpl.	SWA	22 Jan. 44	Jacksonville, Texas
Di Donatis, Arthur A.	Pfc	SWA	17 Jan. 44	Wakefield, MA
Dillon, Lawrence W.	Pfc	SWA	23 Jan. 44	Eccles, WV
Dorman, Eugene A.	Pvt.	MIA	26 Jan. 44	Conway, SC
Farrell, Richard J.	Sgt.	SWA	23 Jan. 44	New Briton, CT
Felstrup, Urban M.	Pfc	LWA	22 Jan. 44	Cloquet, MN
Fitzpatrick, Joseph E.	S/Sgt.	SWA	22 Jan. 44	Portland, MO
Fontanini, August J.	Pfc	LWA	18 Jan. 44	E. Brady, PA
Grimmett, Hall W.	T/Sgt.	LWA	21 Jan. 44	Hillsboro, Texas
Hahn, Harlan NMI	Pfc	MIA	18 Jan. 44	Millway, PA
Hilty, Harold D.	Sgt.	MIA	26 Jan. 44	Gary, IN
Hobbs, Everett S.	Pfc	MIA	26 Jan. 44	Englewood, OH
Holland, Joseph R.	Pfc	MIA	26 Jan. 44	Chester, PA
Homesley, Mose J.	Pfc	LWA	27 Jan. 44	Jacksonville, AL
Hornbuckle, Waid F.	Pvt.	LWA	21 Jan. 44	Sarah, MS
Howarth, Kenneth R.	Pfc	MIA	26 Jan. 44	Peru, IL
Howell, Walter L.	Pfc	LWA	24 Jan. 44	Logansport, IN
Jendras, Anthony J.	S/Sgt.	LWA	21 Jan. 44	Cliff Side Park, NJ
Jones, Manuel L.	F/Sgt.	LWA	21 Jan. 44	Eddy, Texas
Kaplowitz, Louis NMI	Pfc	SWA	23 Jan. 44	Brooklyn, NY
Kelly, Raymond T.	S/Sgt.	LWA	21 Jan. 44	Everett, NJ
Kozlak, George A.	Pfc	MIA	21 Jan. 44	Litchford, CT
Lapenta, Joseph M.	Pvt.	MIA	26 Jan. 44	Belleville, NJ
Lavery, John J., Jr.	S/Sgt.	MIA	18 Jan. 44	Philadelphia, PA
Lewis, Joe H.	S/Sgt.	LWA	22 Jan. 44	Hillsboro, Texas
Lynn, Harold W.	Pfc	MIA	18 Jan. 44	Cullman, AL
McGee, George W.	Pvt.	MIA	26 Jan. 44	Kernersville, NC
McGeever, George A.	Pfc	LWA	19 Jan. 44	Needham, MA
McNabnay, William G.	Pfc	SWA	23 Jan. 44	N. Muskegon, MI
MacDonald, David NMI	Sgt.	LWA	21 Jan. 44	Belleville, NJ
Macier, Edward J.	Pvt.	KIA	17 Jan. 44	Chicago, IL
Maples, Clayton W.	Pfc	LWA	20 Jan. 44	Maynardville, TN

Marchillo, Rocco NMI	Pvt.	SWA	22 Jan. 44	Wilmington, DE
Marlow, Russell W.	Pvt.	SWA	22 Jan. 44	Wyandotte, MI
Mattiazza, Dominic L.	Pvt.	LWA	20 Jan. 44	Oglesby, IL
Melovich, Michael NMI	Pfc	MIA	26 Jan. 44	Youngstown, OH
Melton, Grady NMI	Pvt.	SWA	19 Jan. 44	Eva, TN
Meyer, Chester C.	Pfc	SWA	23 Jan. 44	Milwaukee, WI
Moriarty, Richard J.	Pfc	MIA	26 Jan. 44	New York, NY
Patterson, Harry L.	Pfc	MIA	26 Jan. 44	Collierstown, VA
Poparad, John NMI	Pfc	MIA	26 Jan. 44	Chosterton, IN
Radke, Wylie E.	Pfc	LWA	19 Jan. 44	Malone, Texas
Rodriguez, Juste NMI	Pfc	MIA	26 Jan. 44	Tampa, FL
Rose, Henry D.	Pvt.	SWA	23 Jan. 44	Ecorse, MI
Skepew, Joseph A.	Pfc	MIA	26 Jan. 44	Erie, PA
Smith, Peter NMI	Pfc	LWA	18 Jan. 44	Scranton, PA
Stifle, Lester D.	Pfc	LWA	22 Jan. 44	Gary, IN
Stradling, John S.	Pfc	MIA	21 Jan. 44	Mesa, AZ
Swalina, John S.	Pfc	MIA	22 Jan. 44	Shamokan, OH
Tate, Marvin T.	Pfc	MIA	26 Jan. 44	Kingsley, KS
Thompson, John B.	Pfc	LWA	20 Jan. 44	Port Huron, MI
Todd, Seymour NMI	Pfc	SWA	24 Jan. 44	Anne, Texas
Totten, Norman G.	Pfc	MIA	26 Jan. 44	Springfield, MA
Trombley, Harold N.	Pfc	SWA	22 Jan. 44	Adams, MA
Vaughn, Richard C., Jr.	Pfc	MIA	22 Jan. 44	Richmond, VA
Venezio, Fudio J.	Pvt.	SWA	23 Jan. 44	Inwood, NY
Wallace, Regis F.	Pfc	LWA	22 Jan. 44	Uniontown, PA
Ward, Durham O.	Pfc	SWA	24 Jan. 44	Rives, MO
Weaver, Charles R.	Pfc	LWA	21 Jan. 44	Detroit, MI
Weigle, Arthur D.	Sgt.	KIA	20 Jan. 44	Kutztown, PA
Wolf, Henry W.	Pfc	MIA	18 Jan. 44	Baltimore, MD
Wood, Robert F.	Pfc	LWA	26 Jan. 44	Buffalo, NY
Zimmick, Anthony J.	Pfc	MIA	26 Jan. 44	Pittsburg, PA
Zink, Daniel E.	Sgt.	LWA	22 Jan. 44	Marietta, PA

M Company

Ogburn, Loranzy D.	2d Lt.	LIA	21 Jan. 44	Chester, SC
Aceto, Alfred A.	Pfc	LWA	17 Jan. 44	Maspeth, NY
Boze, Eugene NMI	Pvt.	SWA	20 Jan. 44	Atlanta, GA
Chappell, Clair W.	Pvt.	LWA	22 Jan. 44	Portage, PA
Cooke, William A.	Pfc	LWA	23 Jan. 44	Wellsburg, WV
Craggs, Harold L.	Pfc	SWA	22 Jan. 44	Brownsville, PA
Dunmyer, Myron A.	Pvt.	LWA	23 Jan. 44	Elton, PA
Foit, Joe R.	Pfc	LWA	23 Jan. 44	West, Texas
Frank, Edward NMI	Pvt.	LWA	18 Jan. 44	Brooklyn, NY
Groathouse, Louis C.	Pfc	KIA	27 Jan. 44	Columbus, OH
Han, Chester M.	Pvt.	SWA	20 Jan. 44	Brooklyn, NY
Hortsman, Edward F.	Pfc	SWA	22 Jan. 44	Evansville, IN
Kelley, Max G.	Pvt.	SWA	22 Jan. 44	Philadelphia, PA
Kittle, Ray J.	Pfc	SWA	20 Jan. 44	Weston, WV
Koczorowski, Theodore NMI	Pvt.	SWA	19 Jan. 44	Camden, NJ
Leslie, Nathan NMI	Pvt.	LWA	22 Jan. 44	Brooklyn, NY
McClendon, Carl NMI	Cpl.	LWA	22 Jan. 44	Whitesboro, Texas
Meritt, George T.	Sgt.	LWA	22 Jan. 44	Gatesville, Texas
Nevinsky, John NMI	Sgt.	DOW	25 Jan. 44	Somerville, NJ
Nizelski, Edward V.	Pvt.	LWA	17 Jan. 44	Maspeth, NY
Owens, Stanley E.	Pfc	LWA	21 Jan. 44	Wilmore, PA
Poston, Wilburn NMI	Pfc	SWA	22 Jan. 44	Livingston, TN

Pottoroff, William N., Jr.	Pfc	LWA	23 Jan. 44	Lapel, IN
Pruveadenti, Frank D.	Pvt.	LWA	21 Jan. 44	Eric, PA
Salka, Raymond L.	Pfc	LWA	22 Jan. 44	Whitestone, NY
Schab, Stanley J.	Pvt.	LWA	21 Jan. 44	Westfield, MA
Smothers, Jessie L.	Pfc	LWA	24 Jan. 44	Cordova, AL
Sruba, Aloyisus H.	Cpl.	SWA	20 Jan. 44	Chicago, IL
Stevenson, Robert J.	Pvt.	LWA	23 Jan. 44	Circleville, OH
Stolzer, Willard J.	S/Sgt.	LWA	21 Jan. 44	Festus, MO
Thompson, John C.	Pfc	SWA	22 Jan. 44	Monessen, PA
Turney, Wilks W.	Pfc	SWA	20 Jan. 44	Falkville, AL

Roster of Casualties
111th Engineer Battalion[5]
January 1944

Name	Rank	Type	Residence
Company A			
Calabrese, Frank NMI	Pvt.	LWA	E. Hartford, CT
Edge, Okey L.	Pvt.	LWA	New Martinsville, WV
Lubin, Albert NMI	Pvt.	LWA	Detroit, MI
Nichols, Raymond O.	Sgt.	SWA	Jefferson, Texas
Rogers, John R.	Pvt.	SWA	Campbellsville, KY
Rutzisky, Harry NMI	Pfc	KIA	New York, NY
Tekus, John NMI	Cpl.	LWA	Cleveland, OH
Vires, Raymond A.	Pvt.	LIA	Finger, TN
Company B			
Griffin, Altus D.	S/Sgt.	LWA	Bowie, Texas
Feazell, Raymond M.	Pvt.	LWA	Mountain Home, AR
Owenby, John R.	Pfc	LWA	Cleveland, GA
Plechsmid, Frank S.	Pfc	LWA	St. Jospeh, MI

Appendix B

RESOLUTION OF 36TH DIVISION ASSOCIATION
January 1946

This is the eve of the second anniversary of the crossing of the Rapido River, a military undertaking that will go down in history as one of the colossal blunders of the Second World War.

The One Hundred and Forty-first and One Hundred and Forty-third Infantry regimental combat teams caught the brunt of this holocaust. Every man connected with this undertaking knew it was doomed to failure, because it was an impossible situation. The Rapido River was the main line of resistance. The German elements opposing the division had every foot of ground covered with fire. The high ground was all held by Germans, and observation was perfect for them in directing the artillery fire. Patrols had reported that these enemy positions were strongly held and that the area was heavily mined on both sides of the river, and the German positions were wired and strongly fortified, and that the crossing was not tenable.

Notwithstanding this information (which was in possession of the Fifth Army commander), contrary to the repeated recommendations of the subordinate commanders, General Mark W. Clark ordered the crossing of the Rapido at several points.

The results of this blunder are well known. The crossings were made under the most adverse conditions and required two nights to get elements of the two combat teams across. At daylight the Germans shot the bridges out behind the Thirty-sixth Division troops and began a methodical destruction of our troops. The division suffered heavy casualties, amounting to 2,900 men.

It was such a colossal failure that one of the regimental commanders commented as follows: "The river was strongly defended by a German force superior in numbers to our attacking force. The first attack was made at night and was not successful. On the night before, the British attack of the south failed. The last attack by my regiment was made in daylight and was more decisively unsuccessful than the first. Losses from attacks of this sort are tremendous in manpower and materiel and have a devastating, demoralizing effect upon those few troops who survive them. Officers and men lost in the Rapido River crossing cannot be replaced and the combat efficiency of a regiment is destroyed." Now therefore be it

Resolved, That the men of the Thirty-sixth Division Association, in conven-

135

tion assembled in Brownwood, Texas, petition the Congress of the United States to investigate the Rapido River fiasco and take the necessary steps to correct a military system that will permit an inefficient and inexperienced officer, such as General Mark W. Clark, in a high command to destroy the young manhood of this country and to prevent future soldiers being sacrificed, wastefully and uselessly.

I hereby certify that this is a true and correct copy of the resolution passed at the Thirty-sixth Division Association Convention held at Brownwood, Texas, January 19, 20 and 21, 1946.

> H. Miller Ainsworth
> President, Thirty-sixth Division Association

Appendix C

LETTER OF SUBMITTAL
to Committee on Military Affairs

Hon. A. J. May
Chairman, Committee on Military Affairs
House of Representatives

Dear Mr. May: Herewith is submitted, in response to your letter of January 29, 1946, a report of the circumstances under which the Thirty-sixth Division was engaged at the Rapido River in January 1944.

These activities were an element of a large-scale operation in which the United States Fifth and British Eighth Armies were directed to pin down enemy reserves by aggressive action and thus prevent them from imperilling our Sixth Corps as it made its hazardous landings on the beaches at Anzio. The Thirty-sixth Division attacked on the day that the Anzio expedition was definitely committed to making its landings. Preceding attacks on the southern front having met increasing difficulties, unremitting pressure at the Rapido now became essential.

The division reported its casualties for the period in which the attacks were made as 155 killed, 1,052 wounded, and 921 missing — a total of 2,128.

I have carefully examined the reports in this case and it is my conclusion that the action to which the Thirty-sixth Division was committed was a necessary one and that General Clark exercised sound judgment in planning it and ordering it. While the casualties are to be greatly regretted, the heroic action and sacrifices of the Thirty-sixth Division undoubtedly drew the Germans away from our landing at Anzio during the critical hours of the first foothold, thus contributing in major degree to minimizing the casualties in that undertaking and to the firm establishment of the Anzio beachhead.

Sincerely yours,

Robert P. Patterson,
Secretary of War

Notes

Chapter One: Setting the Stage

1. The 36th Infantry Division acquired its identification as the "Texas" Division or "T-Patchers" because it was a Texas National Guard unit before President Franklin D. Roosevelt federalized it on November 25, 1940. The Army transferred men from all of the states into the federalized 36th Division. The 36th Division shoulder patch is a blue arrowhead with an olive-colored T in the center. This design originally signified the combination of Texas and Oklahoma in the 36th. After World War I, the National Guard removed Oklahoma from the 36th Division and placed it in the 45th Division. Also see Headquarters Army Ground Forces, Office of Technical Information, Special Information Section, "Fact Sheet on the 36th Division," Department of the Army, U.S. Military Institute, Carlisle, PA, Mimeo, AGF, 1945, 1. Also see Shelby L. Stanton, *Order of Battle: U.S. Army, World War II* (Novato, CA: Presidio Press, 1984), 119.

2. Omar N. Bradley and Clay Blair, *A General's Life* (New York: Simon and Schuster, 1983), 87–91.

3. Bradley and Blair, *General's Life,* 108. "A high percentage of the junior officers were over-age and physically unfit." (In June 1941 a study found that 22 percent of all Guard first lieutenants were over forty.) Bradley continued, "The situation was so bad that in June 1941 Marshall himself felt compelled to write a 'frank' (but tactful) letter to all Guard division commanders, pointing out some of the grave weaknesses in the discipline and training."

4. *Ibid.,* 80–81, 92.

5. *Ibid.,* 82, 92.

6. *Ibid.,* 109. Also see 70, 78. Marshall served as the senior instructor of the Illinois National Guard in Chicago. Marshall remained in this position for at least four years.

7. S/Sgt. Richard A. Huff, ed., *The Fighting 36th: A Pictorial History of the 36th "Texas" Infantry Division* (Austin: 36th Division Association, n.d.), n.p. Claude V. Birkhead was born in Oregon in 1878. He commanded the 131st Field Artillery with the AEF in World War I. After the war he served in the 36th Infantry Division of the Texas National Guard first as chief of staff and later as the commanding general. He completed "his schooling in Fort Worth" and "entered prominently into Texas law and politics for nearly" fifty years. Major General Birkhead retired from active duty in June of 1942.

8. Fred L. Walker, *From Texas to Rome: A General's Journal* (Dallas: Taylor, 1969), v–vi, 1.

9. Mark Clark, *Calculated Risk* (New York: Harper, 1950), 175.

10. Walker, *Texas*, 1–15.

11. *Ibid.*, 51.

12. *Ibid.*, 54, 57.

13. *Ibid.*, 66, 71.

14. *Ibid.*, 58, 63–99

15. *Ibid.*, 72. Also see Martin Blumenson, *Mark Clark* (New York: Congdon, 1984), 294–295.

16. Walker, *Texas*, 72.

17. *Ibid.*, 91–92.

18. *Ibid.*, 99–103.

19. *Ibid.*, 103–183.

Chapter Two: Baptism of Fire

1. Walker, *Texas*, 183–266.

2. Bradley and Blair, *General's Life*, 146.

3. Clark, *Risk*, 175.

4. War Department Historical Division, *Salerno: American Operations from the Beaches to the Volturno* (Washington, DC: War Dept., 1944), 1.

5. *Ibid.*, 13. Also see Allen Bullock, *Hitler: A Study in Tyranny*, 1960, Abrig. ed. (New York: Harper & Row, 1971), 411–415. The Italian armistice took Hitler by surprise as much as it did the men of the 36th.

6. D. H. "Blackie" Allen, personal interview, August 15, 1986.

7. War Department, *Salerno: American*, 89.

8. Blumenson, *Clark*, 146.

9. War Department, *Salerno: American*, 89.

10. Clark, *Risk*, 3.

11. Kent Roberts Greenfield, *American Strategy in World War II: A Reconsideration* (Baltimore: Johns Hopkins Press, 1963), 5–6.

12. War Department, *Salerno: American*, 89.

13. Winston S. Churchill, *Closing the Ring*, Vol. 5 of *The Second World War* (Boston: Houghton, 1951), 241.

14. B. H. Liddell Hart, ed., *The Rommel Papers* (New York: Harcourt, 1953), 446.

15. *Ibid.*, 242.

16. Christopher Chant, Richard Humble, William Fowler, Jenny Shaw, and Brigadier Shelford Bidwell, consultant, *Hitler's Generals and their Battles* (N.p.: Leisure Books, 1984), 138.

17. Churchill, *Closing*, 241.

18. Martin Blumenson, *United States Army in World War II the Mediterranean Theater of Operations: Salerno to Cassino* (Washington, DC: Office of the Chief of Military History United States Army, 1969), 208.

19. *Ibid.*, 207.

20. *Ibid.*, 207–208.

21. *Ibid.*, 208.

22. Walker, *Texas*, 277.

23. Fred Majdalany, *Battle of Cassino* (Boston: Houghton, 1957), 31–32.
24. Walker, *Texas,* 277, 293.
25. Al Dietrick, personal interview, May 30, 1987.

Chapter Three:　The Allies Plan While the Germans Prepare

1. Office of Military History, *Command Decisions,* ed. Kent Roberts Greenfield (New York: Harcourt, 1959), 243.
2. The 15th Army Group, under the command of Gen. Sir Harold Alexander, consisted of two armies — the British Eighth Army, under Gen. Bernard L. Montgomery, and the newly formed American Fifth Army, under Lt. Gen. Mark Wayne Clark.
3. Sir David Hunt, Alexander's Staff, *Cassino — A Bitter Victory* Part One: Granada Films. No other information available. Also see "Sad Sack Role," *Time,* December 11, 1944, 29.
4. Churchill, *Closing,* 243–247.
5. Dan Kurzman, *The Race For Rome* (Garden City: Doubleday, 1975), 12.
6. David Eisenhower, *Eisenhower: A War 1943–1945* (New York: Random House, 1986), 52–54.
7. Churchill, *Closing,* 427–437. Also see Blumenson, *Clark,* 161; Eisenhower, *Eisenhower,* 52–54; Herbert Feis, *Churchill Roosevelt Stalin: The War They Waged and the Peace They Sought* (Princeton: Princeton UP, 1957), 302–303.
8. Clark, *Risk,* 250.
9. *Ibid.,* 256. Also see Greenfield, *American Strategy,* 41; Blumenson, *Clark,* 163–164; "Churchill had his way. He disregarded the advice of specialists and technicians who questioned the details, who believed the margin of success to be too slim, who preferred to avoid on counting so heavily on good luck. Churchill vanquished and overcame their doubts by the force of his position, character, and will." Majdalany, *Battle,* 44: "The Allies were now openly treating Rome as the next objective. 'If there were no God,' said Voltaire, 'it would be necessary to invent him.' If there is no clearcut objective, The Allied High Command seemed now to be saying, it is necessary to invent one."
10. David Hapgood and David Richardson, *Monte Cassino* (New York: Congdon, 1984), 25.
11. Martin Blumenson, *Bloody River: The Real Tragedy of the Rapido* (Boston: Houghton, 1970), 15.
12. Blumenson, *Clark,* 18.
13. *Ibid.,* 19–21.
14. *Ibid.,* 21.
15. *Ibid.,* 282.
16. *Ibid.,* 21.
17. Hapgood and Richardson, *Monte Cassino,* 20.
18. Blumenson, *Clark,* 46–47.
19. "An American Abroad," *Time,* June 24, 1946: 27.
20. Milton Bracker, "General Mark Clark Gets the Tough Jobs," *New York Times,* September 19, 1943. Also see Blumenson, *Clark,* 57–58.
21. Bracker, "Tough Jobs," 46.
22. Blumenson, *Clark,* 295.

23. Bracker, "Tough Jobs," 46.
24. Blumenson, *Clark*, 295.
25. Hapgood and Richardson, *Monte Cassino*, 20.
26. John Gunther, *Eisenhower: The Man and the Symbol* (New York: Harper, 1952), 66.
27. Blumenson, *Clark*, 54–55.
28. Hapgood and Richardson, *Monte Cassino*, 20.
29. Kurzman, *Race*, 19.
30. Clark, *Risk*, 357.
31. Kurzman, *Race*, 18.
32. Martin Blumenson, *Anzio: The Gamble That Failed* (Philadelphia: Lippincott, 1963), 54.
33. Clark, *Risk*, 271.
34. Blumenson, *Salerno*, 313–314. Also see Military History Department, *Command Decisions*, 253.
35. Col. Oran C. Stovall, personal interview, August 29, 1986. Also see Charles B. McDonald, *The Mighty Endeavor* (New York: Oxford UP, 1969), 195; Hapgood and Richardson, *Monte Cassino*, 110.
36. Blumenson, *Clark*, 165.
37. Majdalany, *Battle*, 36–37.
38. Walker, *Texas*, 296. Also see Clark, *Risk*, 261; Albert Kesselring, Field Marshal, A.D., *A Soldier's Record* (New York: Morrow, 1954), 225–230; Hapgood and Richardson, *Monte Cassino*, 74–75.
39. Majdalany, *Battle*, 36.
40. *Ibid.*, 37.
41. Blumenson, *Salerno*, 208.
42. Maj. Gen. Fred L. Walker, "My Story of the Rapido Crossing," 1.
43. Hapgood and Richardson, *Monte Cassino*, 74.
44. Frido von Senger und Etterlin, "Monte Cassino," *New English Review* April 1949: 250.
45. Richard Collier, *The Freedom Road: 1944–1945* (New York: Anthenum, 1984), 24.
46. Stewart T. Stanuell, personal interview, October 10, 1986.
47. Owen Arnold, personal interview, September 4, 1987.
48. Personal interviews, August 1986. The men interviewed were with the 36th Division at the time of the Rapido River crossing. They were attending the 36th Division Reunion at the AmFac Hotel in Dallas at the time of the interviews. More men were interviewed at the 36th Reunion in Fort Worth in 1987. Everyone interviewed mentioned the Monte Cassino Abbey; the same was true of all who gave telephone interviews.
49. von Senger, "Monte," 251. Kesselring's attempt to save the Abbey was in vain. The Allies bombed it in mid-March of 1944 and completely destroyed it. This action did not cause the Germans to leave the area. The rubble from the bombed building provided excellent cover for German soldiers. Also see Eric Sevareid, "The Price We Pay in Italy," *Nation* 159 (December 9, 1944): 713; Churchill, *Closing*, 499–500; Churchill, *Triumph and Tragedy*, Vol. 6 of *The Second World War* (Boston: Houghton, 1953), 105–106; Robert Wallace and the editors of Time-Life

Books, *The Italian Campaign World War II,* Vol. 11 (Alexandria, VA: Time-Life, 1978), 141–143, 152–153, 158–159.

50. Gen. Frido von Senger und Etterlin, *Neither Fear Nor Hope* (New York: E. P. Dutton & Co., 1964), 202.

51. von Senger, "Monte," 251.

52. Majdalany, *Battle,* 37.

53. *Ibid.,* 38–40. Also see Robert G. Storey, *The Final Judgement: Pearl Harbor to Nuremberg* (San Antonio: Naylor, 1968), 29.

54. Stovall, interview, August 29, 1986. Also see Walker, *Texas,* 294.

55. Stovall, interview, August 29, 1986.

56. *Ibid.* Also see Walker, *Texas,* 295.

57. Stovall, interview, August 29, 1986. Also see Walker, *Texas,* 299.

58. Stovall, interview, August 29, 1986. Also see Walker, *Texas,* 296.

59. Stovall, interview, August 29, 1986. Colonel Stovall still thinks his statement of 1944 is "the best statement that could ever have been made on it" and he has never changed his opinion. Also see [Oran C. Stovall], "The Odyssey of a Texas Citizen Soldier," Robert L. Wagner, ed., *Southwestern Historical Quarterly* 62, No. 1 (July 1968): 69–70.

60. Stovall, interview, August 29, 1986. Also see Wagner, "Odyssey," 70; Col. Joseph O. Killian, telephone interview, May 12, 1987.

61. Killian, interview, May 12, 1987.

62. Walker, *Texas,* 296.

63. *Ibid.,* 302. Also see Maj. Gen. Fred L. Walker, Ret., "Comments on the Rapido River Crossing January 1944" (N.p.: n.p., 1960), 5–6; E. D. Smith, *The Battle for Cassino* (New York: Scribner's, 1975), 48–49; Walker, *Texas,* 297–301.

64. Walker, *Texas,* 297.

65. *Ibid.,* 297.

66. Smith, *Battle,* 50. Also see Walker, "My Story," 3.

67. Gen. Ernest N. Harmon, *Combat Commander: Autobiography of a Soldier* (Englewood Cliffs, NJ: Prentice-Hall, 1970), 152–153.

68. *Ibid.,* 153.

69. *Ibid.*

Chapter Four: Final Preparations for the River Crossing

1. Walker, *Texas,* 300, 304.

2. Maj. Gen. Albert B. Crowther, Ret., personal interview, March 20, 1987.

3. Stovall, interview, August 29, 1986.

4. *Ibid.*

5. *Ibid.*

6. Clifton "Jack" Bellamy, telephone interview, August 28, 1987.

7. Stovall, interview, August 29, 1986.

8. Ernest L. Petree, telephone interview, March 29, 1987.

9. Stovall, interview, August 29, 1986.

10. *Ibid.*

11. Col. Oran C. Stovall, telephone interview, September 4, 1986. Also see Blumenson, *Bloody River,* 86, 90.

12. Donald Barnett, personal interview, September 4, 1987.

13. Luther H. Wolff, M.D., *Forward Surgeon* (New York: Vantage, 1985), 65.
14. Barnett, interview, September 4, 1987.
15. *Ibid.*
16. Petree, interview, March 29, 1987.
17. O. Wayne Crisman, telephone interview, May 11, 1987.
18. *Ibid.*
19. Dietrick, interview, May 30, 1987.
20. Gabriel L. Navarette, telephone interview, January 30, 1988.
21. Richard M. Manton, cassette tape of military experiences, January 1988.
22. Brig. Gen. Armin F. Puck, Ret., personal interview, April 27, 1987.
23. Bvt. Brig. Gen. Richard M. Burrage, telephone interview, July 27, 1987.
24. Dietrick, interview, May 30, 1987.
25. Blumenson, *Anzio*, 69. Also see Blumenson, *Bloody River*, 65.
26. Blumenson, *Anzio*, 69.
27. Former Field Marshal Albert Kesselring interview, "How Hitler Could Have Won," *U.S. News & World Report* 39 (September 2, 1955): 66.
28. Ernst-Georg von Heyking, film interview, *Cassino — A Bitter Victory*, Granada Productions (no other information available).
29. Walker, *Texas*, 305–306.

Chapter Five: The First Attack

1. Walker, *Texas*, 306.
2. *Ibid.*
3. *Ibid.*, 252.
4. Michael J. Krisman, ed., *Register of Graduates and Former Cadets of the United States Military Academy 1802–1876* (New York: Association of Graduates, USMA, 1976), 321.
5. Huff, *Pictorial History*, n.p.
6. James D. Sumner, Jr., telephone interview, September 9, 1987.
7. Sumner, telephone interview, September 10, 1987.
8. Puck, interview, April 27, 1987.
9. Sumner, interview, September 10, 1987.
10. Walker, *Texas*, 306–307.
11. Robert E. Snyder, WO (jg), 142nd Infantry, Headquarters One Hundred Forty Second Infantry APO #36, U.S. Army, *Historical Record of Operations in Italy January 1944*, February 10, 1944. 36th Division Archives, Texas State Library, Austin, Texas.
12. Walker, "Comments," 2. Also Carl Strom, personal interview, August 29, 1986. Strom measured the river when he went back to Italy in 1985.
13. Lt. Col. Julian H. Philips, Ret., telephone interview, November 23, 1986.
14. Majdalany, *Battle*, 63–64.
15. Stovall, interview, August 29, 1986, and September 6, 1986.
16. Smith, *Battles*, 52. Also Stovall interview, August 29, 1986.
17. Walker, *Texas*, 286.
18. *Ibid.*, 107.
19. Col. Milton J. Landry, personal interview, March 20, 1987.
20. Brig. Gen. William H. Wilbur, "APO #36, U.S.A. Special Report, Op-

erations of 141st Infantry in the crossing of the Rapido River on January 20 to 23, 1944." N.p.: Office of the Assistant Division Commander, January 26, 1944. From the files of Lt. Col. Julian H. Philips, Ret.

21. *Ibid.*

22. Lt. Col. John C. L. Adams, "Headquarters Second Battalion 141st Infantry APO #36 Memorandum: To General Walker." January 30, 1944. From the files of Lt. Col. Julian H. Philips, Ret.

23. 2nd Lt. Charles G. Schwartz, Reg. Hq., 141st Infantry Regiment, "APO 36, U.S. Army, Operations in Italy in January 1944, Annex #6, February 12, 1944. 36th Division Archives, Texas State Library, Austin, Texas.

24. C. P. "Buddy" Autrey, telephone interview, April 27, 1987.

25. Operations Report, 141st Infantry Regiment.

26. *Ibid.*

27. Autrey, interview, April 27, 1987.

28. Strom, interview, August 29, 1986.

29. Operations Report, 141st Infantry Regiment.

30. Strom, interview, August 29, 1986. Strom referred to a diary he kept during the war. Also see Robert L. Wagner, *The Texas Army: A History of the 36th Division in the Italian Campaign* (Austin: n.p., 1972), 105–106: "Ralph W. Arnold was made CO of 'B' Company and after being reorganized it continued toward the river."

31. Autrey, interview, April 27, 1987.

32. Strom, interview, August 29, 1986.

33. Autrey, interview, April 27, 1987.

34. *Ibid.*

35. *Ibid.*

36. Chief Warrant Officer E. J. Kahn, Jr. and T/Sgt. Henry McLemore, *Fighting Divisions* (Washington, DC: Infantry Journal Press, 1946), 53. This was a slight exaggeration because "every weapon in warfare" would include bombs, etc.

37. Strom, interview, August 29, 1986. Also Edward Dressel, conversation, August 28, 1986. Dressel was with the 141st Infantry Headquarters. He crossed the river during the truce to help bring back the dead and wounded. He said they "found a whole battalion that had died from concussion."

38. Strom, interview, August 29, 1986. Also William Allen, personal interview, August 28, 1986.

39. Autrey, interview, April 27, 1987.

40. Strom, interview, August 29, 1986.

41. Operations Report, 141st Infantry Regiment.

42. Walker, *Texas*, 307.

43. William E. Everett, telephone interview, July 28, 1987.

44. Mac Acosta, personal interview, March 19, 1987.

45. Everett, interview, July 28, 1987.

46. Acosta, interview, March 19, 1987.

47. Everett, interview, July 28, 1987.

48. *Ibid.*

49. Maj. George Purcell, Ret., personal interview, August 28, 1986.

50. Operations Report, 141st Infantry Regiment.

51. Maj. Robert E. Mehaffey, Ret., personal interview, August 30, 1986. Also

Mehaffey, telephone interview, March 24, 1988; Edgar Ford, questionnaire, September 1987.

52. Purcell, interview, August 28, 1986.

53. Mehaffey, interview, March 24, 1988.

54. Purcell, interview, August 28, 1986.

55. *Ibid.*

56. Col. David M. Frazior, Ret., personal interview, August 23, 1987.

57. *Ibid.*

58. Capt. Douglas N. Boyd, adjutant, 143rd Infantry, "Operations in Italy, January 1944, 143rd Infantry Regiment, Annex No. 8." N.p.: February 12, 1944. 36th Division Archives, Texas State Library, Austin, Texas.

59. Frazior, interview, August 23, 1987. Also Frazior, telephone conversation, May 1988; Operations Report, 143rd Infantry Regiment which states that C Company crossed the river first and was later followed by A and B companies. Colonel Frazior disagrees with the Operations Report concerning this.

60. Frazior, conversation, May 1988. Also see Operations Report, 143rd Infantry Regiment, which states Nunez was in C Company.

61. Operations Report, 143rd Infantry Regiment.

62. Zeb Sunday, personal interview, September 5, 1987.

63. Riley M. Tidwell, personal interview, June 13, 1987. While at San Pietro, Private Tidwell was the soldier who brought Capt. Henry Waskow's body down from the mountain. Ernie Pyle wrote a famous article about the reaction of Waskow's men to their captain's death.

64. Ervald "Wimpy" Wethington, personal interview, September 5, 1987.

65. Frazior, interview, August 23, 1987. Also Maj. Bert Carlton, personal interview, June 19, 1987.

66. Operations Report, 143rd Infantry Regiment.

67. *Ibid.*

68. Frazior, interview, August 23, 1987. Also see Operations Report, 143rd Infantry Regiment.

69. Frazior, interview, August 23, 1987. Also see Operations Report, 143rd Infantry Regiment.

70. Operations Report, 143rd Infantry Regiment.

71. Frazior, interview, August 23, 1987.

72. Robert L. Mallory, personal interview, September 4, 1987.

73. Billy E. Kirby, personal interview, September 4, 1987.

74. Manuel L. "Mexican" Jones, personal interview, June 13, 1987.

75. Jack Bridge, telephone interview, May 22, 1987.

76. Guy Rogers, personal interview, June 13, 1987.

77. Carlton, interview, June 19, 1987. Also see Operations Report 143rd Infantry Regiment. Colonel Martin noted in the Operations Report, "At 2255 I personally went to the river to find out the situation and was accompanied by Brigadier General KENDALL of the 88th Division, and by Captain MILTON H. STEFFAN, . . . Battalion Executive Officer . . ."

78. Carlton, interview, June 19, 1987.

79. Operations Report, 143rd Infantry Regiment.

80. Robert "Buck" Glover, personal interview, August 28, 1986.

Chapter Six: The Second Attack

1. Walker, *Texas*, 309.
2. *Ibid.* Also Stovall, interview, August 29, 1986.
3. Walker, *Texas*, 310–312. Also see Walker, "Comments," 11–12; Walker, "My Story," 5.
4. Operations Report, 141st Infantry Regiment.
5. *Ibid.*
6. *Ibid.*
7. *Ibid.*
8. *Ibid.*
9. Landry, interview, March 20, 1987.
10. Killian, interview, September 4, 1987.
11. Kirby, interview, September 4, 1987.
12. Landry, interview, March 20, 1987.
13. *Ibid.*
14. Operations Report, 141st Infantry Regiment.
15. Landry, interview, March 20, 1987.
16. Sidney E. Lurie, telephone interview, November 22, 1987.
17. Rudolph M. Trevino, telephone interview, November 20, 1986.
18. Rudolph M. Trevino, letter, April 18, 1987.
19. Rudolph M. Trevino, personal interview, March 19, 1987. Also Trevino, interview, November 20, 1986.
20. Bradley and Blair, *A General's Life*, 172.
21. Trevino, interview, March 19, 1987. Also Trevino, interview, November 20, 1986.
22. Trevino, interview, March 19, 1987.
23. Manton, interview, March 29, 1987.
24. Puck, interview, April 27, 1987.
25. Armin F. Puck, telephone interview, March 19, 1987.
26. Puck, interview, April 27, 1987.
27. Puck, interview, March 19, 1987.
28. Puck, interview, April 27, 1987.
29. Sammie D. Petty, personal interview, May 30, 1987.
30. Bill McFadden, telephone interview, September 19, 1987.
31. Petty, interview, May 30, 1987.
32. *Ibid.*
33. Kenneth Saul, personal interview, September 5, 1987.
34. *Ibid.*
35. Landry, interview, March 20, 1987.
36. Operations Report, 141st Infantry Regiment.
37. *Ibid.*
38. *Ibid.*
39. Landry, interview, March 20, 1987.
40. Operations Report, 141st Infantry Regiment.
41. Landry, interview, March 20, 1987.
42. *Ibid.* Landry was wounded seven times while he was in Italy.
43. Landry, letter, December 9, 1987.

44. Lurie, interview, November 22, 1987.

45. Mehaffey, interview, August 30, 1986.

46. Purcell, interview, August 28, 1986.

47. Mehaffey, conversation, March 24, 1988. Also Mehaffey, interview, August 30, 1986.

48. Mehaffey, interview, August 28, 1986.

49. Wagner, *The Texas Army*, 114.

50. *Ibid.*

51. Mehaffey, interview, August 28, 1986.

52. Wagner, *The Texas Army*, 114.

53. Operations Report, 141st Infantry Regiment.

54. *Ibid.*

55. *Ibid.* Also see Savino Manella, statement in 36th Division Collection, Archives Division, Texas State Library, Austin, Texas.

56. Operations Report, 141st Infantry Regiment.

57. *Ibid.*

58. *Ibid.*

59. The Operations Report states that the 143rd took off at 4:00 P.M. and then later states 2:30 P.M. The men in K Company say they crossed the river at 3:00 P.M. on January 21.

60. Operations Report, 143rd Infantry Regiment.

61. Frazior, interview, August 23, 1987.

62. Operations Report, 143rd Infantry Regiment.

63. *Ibid.*

64. Headquarters, 36th Infantry Division, APO #36, U.S. Army, General Orders No. 88, Section I — Award of Silver Star, March 30, 1944. From the files of Col. Julian M. Quarles, Ret.

65. Award of Silver Star.

66. Tidwell, interview, June 13, 1987.

67. Sunday, interview, September 5, 1987.

68. Wethington, interview, September 5, 1987.

69. *Ibid.*

70. Award of Silver Star.

71. Frazior, interview, August 23, 1987.

72. *Ibid.*

73. Operations Report, 143rd Infantry Regiment.

74. *Ibid.*

75. *Ibid.* Also Frazior, interview, August 23, 1987.

76. Lt. Col. Joel W. Westbrook, Ret., telephone interview, September 6, 1987. Also see Operations Report, 143rd Infantry Regiment. Companies A, B, and C had lost their commanders.

77. Operations Report, 143rd Infantry Regiment.

78. Westbrook, interview, September 6, 1987.

79. Operations Report, 143rd Infantry Regiment.

80. Westbrook, interview, September 6, 1987.

81. See Operations Report, 141st Infantry Regiment, for the time.

82. Operations Report, 143rd Infantry Regiment.

83. Wagner, *The Texas Army*, 116. Wagner noted that Carter did not remain in

command of the 3rd Battalion for a very long time. Ressijac, who had commanded the battalion during the first attack, was returned to command of the 3rd Battalion after the second crossing attempt was made. Carter did not work out well.

84. Operations Report, 143rd Infantry Regiment.

85. *Ibid.*

86. Gerald L. "Mac" McAfee, personal interview, June 13, 1987.

87. Wilbur Crawford, personal interview, June 13, 1987.

88. Lewis "Dude" Evans, telephone interview, October 5, 1987.

89. Kirby, interview, September 4, 1987.

90. Alvin Amelunke, telephone interview, September 14, 1987.

91. Kirby, interview, September 4, 1987.

92. Carlton, interview, June 19, 1987.

93. Evans, interview, October 5, 1987.

94. Charles Rummel, Sr., telephone interview, November 20, 1986.

95. Operations Report, 143rd Infantry Regiment.

96. Robert Wallace and the editors of Time-Life, *The Italian Campaign: World World War II,* Vol. 11 (Alexandria, VA: Time-Life, 1970), 117.

97. Paul Blackmer, telephone interview, July 12, 1987.

98. Jim C. "Bug Eyes" Maddox, personal interview, September 4, 1987. Also Jim C. Maddox, telephone conversation, June 14, 1988.

99. Mallory, interview, September 4, 1987. Also Lloyd D. Riley, conversation, September 3, 1987. Riley was a forward observer, Battery C, 155th Field Artillery, 36th Division. He said the life expectancy of a forward observer was thirty minutes.

100. Maddox, interview, September 4, 1987. Also Maddox, conversation, June 14, 1988; Mallory, interview, September 4, 1987.

101. Maddox, interview, September 4, 1987. Also see Walker, *Texas,* 86. Walker noted in his journal on May 23, 1942: "We have begun instruction and tests in swimming. About 10% of our men cannot swim, and we must teach them so they meet minimum swimming standards."

102. Maddox, interview, September 4, 1987.

103. Mallory, interview, September 4, 1987.

104. Blackmer, interview, July 12, 1987.

105. Lt. Col. Guy L. Rogers, Ret., questionnaire, June 1987.

106. Lt. Col. Guy L. Rogers, Ret., personal interview, June 13, 1987.

107. Carl McClendon, personal interview, June 13, 1987.

108. Amelunke, interview, September 14, 1987.

109. *Ibid.* Zerk Robertson "was in L Company and he was a platoon sergeant . . . he was one of the first three to receive a battlefield commission out of the entire 36th Division."

110. Amelunke, interview, September 14, 1987.

111. Award of Silver Star.

112. *Ibid.*

113. Maj. Gen. Charles J. Denholm, Ret., telephone interview, November 11, 1987.

114. Historical Record 2nd Battalion, 143rd Infantry from 212334 Jan. 44 to 221200 Jan. 44. From the files of Lt. Col. Julian H. Philips, Ret.

115. Operations Report, 143rd Infantry Regiment.

116. Historical Record, 2nd Battalion.
117. Operations Report, 143rd Infantry Regiment.
118. Historical Record, 2nd Battalion.
119. *Ibid.*
120. *Ibid.*
121. Col. Julian M. Quarles, Ret., written interview, June 1987.
122. William Allen, personal interview, August 28, 1986.
123. Award of Silver Star.
124. Historical Record, 2nd Battalion.
125. Harry R. Moore, questionnaire, September 1986.
126. *Army Times,* April 28, 1945, 16. From the files of Col. Julian M. Quarles, Ret. Also see "Army Hero Loses Life in River," AP, Conowengo, MD, September 23, 1965. From the files of Col. Julian M. Quarles, Ret. M/Sgt. Thomas McCall drowned in the Susquehanna River in Maryland in September 1965. At the time of his death he was the senior army advisor to the District of Columbia National Guard.
127. Joseph Cotropia, personal interview, September 3, 1987.
128. Award of Silver Star.
129. Historical Record, 2nd Battalion.
130. Quarles, letter, June 13, 1987.
131. Don Wharton, "Escape From a Prison Train," *The Fighting 36th Quarterly,* Texas 36th Division Association, Spring 1982, Vol. 2, No. 1:13–18.
132. Operations Report, 143rd Infantry Regiment.
133. *Ibid.*
134. Walker, "My Story," 6.
135. Walker, *Texas,* 312.
136. Strom, interview, August 29, 1986.

Chapter Seven: Again and Yet Again

1. Walker, *Texas,* 314. Also see Walker, "My Story," 6; Walker, "Comments," 14–15.
2. Walker, *Texas,* 313.
3. *Ibid.*
4. *Ibid.* Also see Walker, "My Story," 5.
5. Clark, *Risk,* 283.
6. *Ibid.,* 288.
7. Blumenson, *Clark,* 172.
8. Office of Chief of Military History, *Command,* 262.
9. McDonald, *Mighty,* 194.
10. Blumenson, *Anzio,* 197.
11. Eric Sevareid, *Not So Wild a Dream* (New York: Knopf, 1946), 393–394.
12. Churchill, *Triumph,* 800.
13. Sevareid, "The Price," 713–714.
14. Walker, *Texas,* 316.
15. *Ibid.* Also see Walker, "My Story," 6.
16. Walker, *Texas,* 316.
17. *Ibid.,* 311–312. Initial reports from the 141st — 1,050 killed, wounded,

missing; 143rd — 969 killed, wounded, missing. Total — 2,019. Also see Feder, "They'll Never Forget," 20, which records 2,900 men killed, missing, wounded. He seems to have over-estimated. He had the same amount as the 36th Division Association resolution had. Kesselring, "How," 66 (1,681); "Murder at the Rapido?" *Time* 47, January 28, 1946: 24 (2,000 killed, wounded, missing); United States Congressional Committee on Military Affairs, House of Representatives, on the Rapido River Crossing, *Hearing*, 79 Cong., 2nd Sess., H Vol 1147–8 (Washington: GPO, 1946) — 2,128 killed, missing, wounded.

18. Walker, "My Story" (more than 2,100); Fred L. Walker [Jr.], "Mission Impossible at Cassino," N.p.: n.p., n.d. (1,681 k.m.w.)

19. Walker, "Comments," 26.

20. Fred L. Walker, "The 36th Was a Great Fighting Unit," *Southwestern Historical Quarterly* 72, no. 1 (July 1968): 42.

21. Strom, interview, August 29, 1986.

22. Moore, questionnaire, September 1986.

23. William Allen, interview, August 28, 1986.

24. Purcell, interview, August 28, 1986.

25. William Greg Wiley, personal interview, August 29, 1986.

26. Trevino, interview, March 19, 1987.

27. Mehaffey, interview, August 30, 1986.

28. Walker, *Texas*, 317.

29. Appendix "A" FO 42, Hq. 36th Div., January 18, 1944.

30. Wilbur, Special Report, January 26, 1944.

31. Walker, *Texas*, 340.

32. Operations Report, 141st Infantry Regiment.

33. Walker, *Texas*, 317.

34. Bradley and Blair, *A General's Life*, 210.

35. Puck, interview, April 27, 1987.

36. Sumner, interview, September 10, 1987.

37. Walker, *Texas*, 318–320. Also see Walker, "Comments," 16–17; Strom, interview, August 29, 1986. Strom and Pfc Henry von Holland, C Company, 141st Infantry Regiment, crossed the river for C Company and negotiated a six-hour truce.

38. Everett, interview, July 28, 1987.

39. Operations in Italy, January 1944, Headquarters 111th Medical Battalion, APO #36. From the 36th Division Collection, Archives Division, Texas State Library, Austin, Texas.

40. Operations in Italy, 111th Medical Battalion.

41. Herman Vlock, 4th Parachute Division, German Army, taped interview, *Cassino — A Bitter Victory*, Part One, Granada Productions (no other information available). "An attack in such difficult terrain, though it can't be seen so well, was surprising. We on the German side were astonished at such a strong attack here."

42. Enoch Harold Terry, telephone interview, September 29, 1987.

43. Sunday, interview, September 5, 1987.

44. Quarles, letter, June 13, 1987.

45. Dr. Terry Andrews, interview, Brig. Gen. Theodore H. Andrews [1986?], 28–34. From the files of Col. Julian M. Quarles, Ret. Andrews said during the next truce, which the Germans requested because so many German troops had

been killed or wounded, that he talked quite a bit. Also see Walker, "Comments," 19.

46. Tommy V. Davis, telephone interview, May 22, 1987.
47. Petty, interview, May 30, 1987.
48. Walker, "Comments," 19.
49. *Ibid.,* 17.
50. *Ibid.,* 18.
51. Walker, *Texas,* 318–320.
52. Walker, "Comments," 25.
53. *Ibid.,* 19. Also see Walker, *Texas,* 320.
54. Walker, "Comments," 20. Also see Walker, *Texas,* 320.
55. Kesselring, "How," 66.
56. Operations Report, 142nd Infantry Regiment.
57. Walker, *Texas,* 321. Also see Stovall, interview, August 29, 1986.
58. Walker, "Comments," letter from Mark W. Clark to Maj. Gen. Geoffrey Keyes, January 27, 1944.
59. Walker, *Texas,* 321.
60. *Ibid.,* 320–325.
61. Roster of Graduates.
62. Walker, *Texas,* 242.
63. *Ibid.,* 322.
64. *Ibid.,* 323.

Chapter Eight: Consequences

1. U.S. Congress, *Hearings,* 43. The men were observing a longstanding tradition of ex-students from the University of Texas to meet together on March 2 no matter where they are throughout the world.
2. *Ibid.,* 43–44. Also see a copy of the resolution on page 238.
3. *Ibid.,* 44.
4. Wagner, *The Texas Army,* 227.
5. *Ibid.,* 227–232. Also Stovall, interview, September 29, 1986.
6. U.S. Congress, *Hearings.*
7. Wagner, *Texas,* 232.
8. U.S. Congress, *Hearings,* 21.
9. *Ibid.,* 25. Also see Walker, *Texas,* 374; Collier, *Freedom Road,* 80; Walker, "Great Fighting," 42.
10. U.S. Congress, *Hearings,* 27. Also see Walker, *Texas,* 406.
11. U.S. Congress, *Hearings,* 27. For a differing opinion see Fred Sheehan, *Anzio: Epic of Bravery* (Norman: University of Oklahoma Press, 1964), 46; Blumenson, *Bloody River,* 78–88, 143.
12. U.S. Congress, *Hearings,* 35. For a differing view see Robert H. Adleman and Col. George Walton, *Rome Fell Today* (Boston: Little Brown, 1968), 155. Keyes, discussing the Rapido, said the success of the 36th hinged on a successful British crossing the night before.
13. U.S. Congress, *Hearings,* 45. Also see Walker, *Texas,* 320.
14. Mehaffey, interview, August 30, 1986.
15. Clark, *Risk,* 278.

16. Wagner, *The Texas Army*, 228.

17. *Ibid.*, 229.

18. *Ibid.*

19. *Ibid.*, 230.

20. U.S. Congress, *Hearings*, n.p. See copy of letter on page 241.

21. *Ibid.*

22. Mehaffey, interview, August 30, 1986.

23. Sheehan, *Epic*, 46. "General Clark was completely exonerated by the Congressional board of inquiry, but never within the borders of Texas."

24. Adleman and Walton, *Rome Fell*, 151.

Chapter Nine: Conclusion

1. F. W. Winterbotham, *The Ultra Secret* (New York: Harper, 1974), 189. "It was Mark Clark who, in that dreary slogging march up through Italy, three times did not use the opportunities Ultra had provided, and which Alexander had planned for him: first at Anzio, then after the fall of Cassino and later north of Rome, to cut off and surround Kesselring's armies. It was Alexander who, knowing the precise distribution of German troops at Cassino, planned the surprise attack over the mountains and it was France's Juin who so brilliantly carried it out." Also see Winterbotham, *Ultra*, xii. Ultra was kept secret until spring of 1974, when the ban on releasing information was lifted. Winterbotham wrote, "The official ban on any reference to Ultra until Spring of this year 1974 has certainly had an inhibiting effect on the writing of military history in every field. I have myself made several unsuccessful attempts, on the highest levels during the past twenty years to get the ban lifted." Winterbotham, *Ultra*, 8–9. On these pages he describes other forms of codes and compares their effectiveness to Ultra. Also David Kahn, *The Codebreakers: The Story of Secret Writings* (New York: Macmillan, 1967) 612–613. "For World War II cryptology became a nation's most important source of secret intelligence."

2. Winterbotham, *Ultra*, 88–90, 189.

3. Blumenson, *Clark*, 167.

4. Winterbotham, *Ultra*, 114.

5. *Ibid.*, 114, 118. ". . . with this 'new dimension of war' not only the Commander in the field but, but also Churchill, Roosevelt, and the Allied chiefs of staff had all the cards in the pack spread out on the table face upwards." Winterbotham continued, "Some people may draw the conclusion that the Army Commanders did not understand how to play them, but that they did provide the opportunity for them to carry out Alexander's plan cannot be doubted."

6. Blumenson, *Clark*, 167. Also see Clark, *Risk*, 357.

7. Walker, *Texas*, 295–297, 300.

8. Blumenson, *Clark*, 125–126.

9. Jane Scrivener, *Inside Rome with the Germans* (New York: Macmillan, 1945) 94.

10. Stovall, interview, August 29, 1986. Also Strom, interview, August 29, 1986. Strom said, "I knew Keyes was as much to blame as Clark . . . It was only at the fourth battle of Cassino (the Rapido was really a prelude to the first battle, so you've got five battles) [that] they finally decided that you've got to send in more than one division and expect them to do anything."

11. Brig. Gen. William H. Wilbur, personal notes.

12. P. W. Wilson, "The Appian Road to Rome," *New York Times*, October 17, 1943: 34. Also see Clark, *Risk*, 2.

13. Walker, *Texas*, 372–385.

14. *Ibid.*, 392.

15. *Ibid.*, 392–408.

16. Bradley and Blair, *A General's Life*, 203–204.

17. Majdalany, *Battle*, 53.

Casualty Reports

1. Wick Fowler, "Battle Casualties: Meticulous Care Exercised In Identification Process," *The News*, October 18, 1944. Wick Fowler Collection, 36th Division Collection, Archives Division, Texas State Library, Austin, Texas.

2. Wick Fowler, "Killed in Action: Army Double Checks Reports Before Notifying Relatives," *The News*, October 19, 1944. Wick Fowler Collection, 36th Division Collection, Texas State Library.

3. Operations Report, 141st Infantry Regiment.

4. Operations Report, 143rd Infantry Regiment.

5. Operations Report, 111th Engineer Battalion.

Bibliography

Books

Adleman, Robert H., and Col. George Walton. *The Devil's Brigade*. Philadelphia: Chilton, 1966.
———. *Rome Fell Today*. Boston: Little, Brown, 1968.
Blumenson, Martin. *Anzio: The Gamble That Failed*. Philadelphia: Lippincott, 1963.
———. *United States Army in World War II/The Mediterranean Theater of Operations: Salerno to Cassino*. Washington: Office of Military History, United States Army, 1969.
———. *Bloody River: The Real Tragedy of the Rapido*. Boston: Houghton, 1970.
———. *Mark Clark*. New York: Congdon, 1984.
Bradley, Omar N. *A Soldier's Story*. New York: Henry Holt, 1951.
———, and Clay Blair. *A General's Life*. New York: Simon and Schuster, 1983.
Breuer, Alan. *Hitler: A Study in Tyranny*. 1962. Abridged. New York: Harper & Row, 1971.
Burcher, Capt. Harry C. *My Three Years with Eisenhower*. New York: Simon, 1946.
Chant, Christopher, Richard Humble, William Fowler, Jenny Shaw. Brig. Gen. Shelford Bidwell, consultant. *Hitler's Generals and their Battles*. N.p.: Leisure Books, 1984.
Churchill, Winston S. *Closing the Ring*. Vol. 5 of *The Second World War*. 6 vols. Boston: Houghton, 1951.
———. *Triumph and Tragedy*. Vol. 6 of *The Second World War*. 6 vols. Boston: Houghton, 1953.
———. *Memoirs of the Second World War*. Abrig. of *The Second World War*. 6 vols. Boston: Houghton, 1959.
———, and the editors of *Life*. *The Second World War*. 2 vols. New York: Time, 1959.
Clark, Mark. *Calculated Risk*. New York: Harper, 1950.
Clark, Maurine. *Captain's Bride, General's Lady: The Memoirs of Mrs. Mark W. Clark*. New York: McGraw-Hill, 1956.
Collier, Basil. *The Second World War: A Military History from Munich to Hiroshima In One Volume*. New York: Morrow, 1967.
Collier, Richard. *The Freedom Road: 1944–1945*. New York: Anthenum, 1984.
Davis, Kenneth S. *A Soldier of Democracy: A Biography of Dwight Eisenhower*. Garden City, NY: Doubleday, 1946.
———. *Experience of War: The United States in World War II*. Garden City, NY: Doubleday, 1965.

Eisenhower, David. *Eisenhower: At War 1943–1945.* New York: Random House, 1986.

Ellis, John. *Cassino: The Hollow Victory; The Battle for Rome January-June 1944.* New York: McGraw-Hill, 1984.

Evans, Sgt. Burtt. "Why Old Soldiers Never Die." *The Best From* Yank: *The Army Weekly.* New York: Dutton, 1945.

Feis, Herbert. *Churchill, Roosevelt, Stalin: The War They Waged and the Peace They Sought.* Princeton: Princeton UP, 1957.

Funk, Arthur Layton. *The Politics of Torch: The Allied Landings and the Algiers Putsch 1942.* Lawrence, KS: Kansas UP, 1974.

Graham, Dominick. *Cassino.* Barrie Pitt, ed. New York: Ballantine, 1971.

———, and Shelford Bidwell. *Tugs of War.* New York: St. Martin's Press, 1986.

Graves, Elinor, ed. *Life Goes to War.* Boston: Little, Brown, 1977.

Greenfield, Kent Roberts. *American Strategy in World War II: A Reconsideration.* Baltimore: Johns Hopkins Press, 1963.

Gunther, John. *Eisenhower: The Man and the Symbol.* New York: Harper, 1952.

Hapgood, David, and David Richardson. *Monte Cassino.* New York: Congdon, 1984.

Harmon, Gen. Ernest N. *Combat Commander: Autobiography of a Soldier.* Englewood Cliffs, NJ: Prentice-Hall, 1970.

Hart, B. H. Lidell. *History of the Second World War.* New York: Putman's, 1970.

———, ed. *The Rommel Papers.* Trans. Paul Findlay. New York: Harcourt, 1953.

Hastings, Max. *Overlord: D-Day, June 6, 1944.* New York: Simon, 1984.

———. *Victory in Europe.* Boston: Little, Brown, 1985.

Hatch, Allen. *General Ike: A Biography of Dwight D. Eisenhower.* New York: Henry Holt, 1944.

Heiferman, Robert. *World War II.* London: Octopus, 1973.

Higgins, Trumbull. *Hitler and Russia: The Third Reich in a Two-Front War 1937–1943.* New York: Macmillan, 1966.

Huff, S/Sgt. Richard A., ed. *The Fighting 36th: A Pictorial History of the 36th "Texas" Infantry Division.* Austin: 36th Division Association, n.d.

Humble, Richard. *Hitler's Generals.* Garden City, NY: Doubleday, 1974.

Jackson, W. G. F. *The Battle for Italy.* New York: Harper & Row, 1967.

Kahn, David. *The Codebreakers: The Story of Secret Writings.* New York: Macmillan, 1967.

Kahn, E. J., and Henry McLemore. *Fighting Divisions.* Washington, DC: Infantry Journal Press, 1946.

Kesselring, General Field Marshal A.D. *Kesselring: A Soldier's Record.* New York: Morrow, 1954.

Kurzman, Dan. *The Race for Rome.* Garden City, NY: Doubleday, 1975.

Leuchtenburg, William E., and the editors of *Life. The Life History of the United States: New Deal and Global War.* 12 vols. New York: Time, 1964.

McCullough, David G., ed. *The American Heritage Picture History of World War II.* New York: American Heritage, 1966.

McDonald, Charles B. *The Mighty Endeavor.* New York: Oxford UP, 1969.

McDonald, John. *Great Battles of World War II.* New York: Macmillan, 1986.

Majdalany, Fred. *The Battle of Cassino.* Boston: Houghton, 1957.

Marshall, Gen. George C., Gen. H. H. Arnold, and Fleet Adm. Ernest Kin. *The War Reports.* Philadelphia: Lippincott, 1947.

Marshall, S. L. A., chief consultant, and Thomas Parrish, ed. *The Simon and Schuster Encyclopedia of World War II.* New York: Simon, 1978.

Men and Women in the Armed Forces from Ellis County in World War II. Dallas: Universal, n.d.

Office of the Chief of Military History. *Command Decisions.* Ed. Kent Roberts Greenfield. New York: Harcourt, 1959.

Peek, Clifford H., Jr., ed. *Five Years, Five Countries, Five Campaigns: An Account of the One-Hundred-Forty-First Infantry in World War II.* Munich: Infantry Regiment Association, 1945.

Piekalkiewicz, Janusz. *Cassino: Anatomy of the Battle.* London: Orbis, 1980.

Pyle, Ernie. *Brave Men.* New York: Henry Holt, 1946.

Roosevelt, Elliot. *As He Saw It.* New York: Duell, 1946.

Scrivener, Jane. *Inside Rome with the Germans.* New York: Macmillan, 1945.

Sevareid, Eric. *Not So Wild a Dream.* New York: Knopf, 1946.

Sheehan, Fred. *Anzio: Epic of Bravery.* Norman: University of Oklahoma, 1964.

Shirer, William L. *The Rise and Fall of the Third Reich: A History of Nazi Germany.* Greenwich, CT: Fawcett, 1960.

Smith, E. D. *The Battle for Cassino.* New York: Scribner's, 1975.

Stanton, Shelby. *Order of Battle: U.S. Army, World War II.* Novato, CA: Presidio Press, 1984.

Storey, Robert G. *The Final Judgement: Pearl Harbor to Nuremberg.* San Antonio: Naylor, 1968.

Thompson, R. W. *Montgomery the Field Marshal.* New York: Scribner's, 1969.

Tourelett, Arthur B., ed. *Life's Picture History of World War II.* New York: Time, 1960.

Tregaskis, Richard. *Invasion Diary.* New York: Random House, 1944.

von Senger und Etterlin, Gen. Frido. *Neither Fear Nor Hope.* New York: E. P. Dutton & Co., 1964.

Wagner, Robert L. "The 36th 'T-Patch' Division." *Soldiers of Texas.* Waco: Texian Press, 1973.

———. *The Texas Army: A History of the 36th Division in the Italian Campaign.* Austin: n.p., 1972.

Walker, Fred L. *From Texas to Rome: A General's Journal.* Dallas: Taylor, 1969.

Wallace, Robert, and the editors of Time-Life. Vol. 11 of *The Italian Campaign: World War II.* 11 vols. Alexandria, VA: Time-Life, 1978.

War Department Historical Division. *Salerno: American Operations from the Beaches to the Volturno.* Washington, DC: War Department, 1944.

Winterbotham, F. W., CBE. *The Ultra Secret.* New York: Harper, 1974.

———. *The Nazi Connection.* New York: Harper, 1978.

Wolff, Luther H., M.D. *Forward Surgeon.* New York: Vantage, 1985.

Films

Cassino — A Bitter Victory. Part One. Granada Films. No other information available. Provided to author by Carl Strom.

Hearings and Investigations

United States Congressional Committee on Military Affairs, House of Representatives, on the Rapido River crossing. *Hearings.* 79th Cong., 2nd sess. H. Vol.: 1147–48. Washington, DC: GPO, 1946.

Interviews

Acosta, Mac. Personal interview, March 19, 1987. (Technical sergeant, C Company, 1st Battalion, 141st Infantry Regiment, 36th Division, at the Rapido River in January 1944.)

Adams, Gen. Paul D., Ret. Telephone conversation, February 1986. (Assigned to the 143rd just after the Rapido River crossing.)

Allen, D. H. "Blackie." Personal interview, August 15, 1986. (First sergeant, Battery B, 133rd Field Artillery, 36th Division, at the Rapido River in January 1944.)

Allen, William. Personal interview, August 28, 1986. (Technical sergeant, 1st Platoon, E Company, 2nd Battalion, 143rd Infantry Regiment, 36th Division. Crossed the river on January 21; captured and held by Germans until he escaped "the day Roosevelt died.")

Amelunke, Alvin. Telephone interview, September 14, 1987. (Second lieutenant, M Company, 3rd Battalion, 143rd Infantry Regiment, 36th Division, at the Rapido River. Crossed the river on January 21.)

Andrews, Brig. Gen. Theodore H. Telephone interview, September 9, 1987. (Major, executive officer of the 2nd Battalion, 143rd Infantry Regiment, in January 1944; crossed the river during the attack.)

————. Written interview conducted by Dr. Terry Andrews. [1986?] From the files of Col. Julian M. Quarles, Ret.

Arn, Robert M. Telephone interview, May 22, 1987. (Captain in command of D Company, 1st Battalion, 141st Infantry Regiment, at the Rapido River in January 1944.)

Arnold, Owen. Personal interview, September 4, 1987. (Technical sergeant, 1st Platoon, C Company, 1st Battalion, 141st Infantry Regiment, 36th Division, at the Rapido River in January 1944.)

Autrey, C. P. "Buddy." Telephone interview, April 27, 1987. (Technical sergeant, B Company, 1st Battalion, 141st Infantry Regiment, 36th Division, in January 1944. Crossed the Rapido River on January 20.)

Ayers, Maj. Gen. Ross Ayers, Ret. Personal interview, March 22, 1987. (Captain, assistant S-3 of the 131st Field Artillery, 36th Division, at the Rapido in January 1944.)

Bailey, George. Conversation, June 13, 1987. (Private first class, K Company, 3rd Battalion, 143rd Infantry Regiment in January 1944; bugler for K Company.)

Barnes, John. Personal interview, August 30, 1986. (Technical sergeant, fourth grade, 131st Field Artillery, 36th Division, at the Rapido River in January 1944.)

Barnett, Donald. Personal interview, September 4, 1987. (Sergeant, A Company, 111th Engineers, 36th Division, at the Rapido River in January 1944.)

Beacham, Charles M. Personal interview, March 19, 1987. (Captain, company commander, G Company, 2nd Battalion, 141st Infantry Regiment, 36th Division, when wounded at San Pietro; in the hospital at the time of the Rapido battle and did not return to the 36th until a few days after the battle.)

Bellamy, Clifton N. "Jack." Telephone interview, April 28, 1987. (Captain, 111th Engineers, 36th Division; served as the operations officer and drew up the general plan for the employment of all engineer troops subject to Major Stovall's approval.)

Blackmer, Paul. Telephone interview, July 12, 1987. (Private first class, BAR man, K Company, 3rd Battalion, 143rd Infantry Regiment, in January 1944. Crossed the Rapido River on January 21.)

Bridge, Jack. Telephone interview, May 22, 1987. (Private first class, Medical Detachment, Company L, 3rd Battalion, 143rd Infantry Regiment, 36th Division, at the Rapido River in January 1944; wounded on the night of January 20.)

Burrage, Bvt. Brig. Gen. Richard M. Telephone interview, July 27, 1987. (Captain, company commander of Headquarters 1st Battalion, 143rd Infantry Regiment, 36th Division, at the time of the Rapido crossing; also served as battalion adjutant. Crossed the river on January 20.)

Carlton, Maj. Bert D., Ret. Personal interview, June 19, 1987. (Captain, 143rd Headquarters, 36th Division; served as an assistant to the operations officer and the intelligence officer at the Rapido River in January 1944.)

Carter, James L. Telephone interview, November 1, 1986. (Private first class, 111th Medical Battalion, 36th Division, at the Rapido River in January 1944.)

Christian, Cluster. Personal interview, October 4, 1987. (T/5 (Corporal), D Company, Clearing Station, 111th Medical Battalion, 36th Division, at the Rapido River in January 1944.)

Cobb, Byrl. Personal interview, October 4, 1987. (Corporal who served as a jeep driver in the 62nd Ordnance Ammunition attached to the Fifth Army at the time of the Rapido battle; in the 36th Division until they were sent to Camp Edwards, Massachusetts.)

Cotropia, Joseph. Personal interview, September 3, 1987. (Sergeant, H Company, 2nd Battalion, 143rd Infantry Regiment, 36th Division, in January 1944. Crossed the river and was captured by the Germans; spent 500 days as a prisoner of war.)

Craft, Ross "Gus." Personal interview, June 19, 1987. (Mortar sergeant, D Company, 111th Medical Battalion, 36th Division, at the Rapido River in January 1944.)

Crawford, Wilbur. Personal interview, June 13, 1987. (Staff sergeant, K Company, 3rd Battalion, 143rd Infantry Regiment, 36th Division. Crossed the Rapido River on January 21.)

Crisman, O. Wayne. Telephone interview, May 11, 1987. (Captain, commander of B Company, 111th Engineers, 36th Division, at the time of the Rapido crossing.)

Crowther, Maj. Gen. Albert B., Ret. Personal interview, March 20, 1987. (Lieutenant colonel; served as the G-2 in the 36th Division at the Rapido River in January 1944.)

Davis, Tommy V., Jr. Telephone interview, May 22, 1987. (Private first class, D

Company, 1st Battalion, 141st Infantry Regiment, 36th Division, at the Rapido River in January 1944.)

DeFilippis, Victor. Telephone interview, November 23, 1987. (T/5 (Corporal), 3rd Battalion, 143rd Infantry Regiment, 36th Division, at the Rapido River in January 1944.)

Denholm, Maj. Gen. Charles J., Ret. Telephone interview, November 11, 1987. (Lieutenant colonel, battalion commander, 2nd Battalion, 143rd Infantry Regiment, 36th Division, in January 1944. The 2nd Battalion was sent into action for the second crossing. Lt. Col. Denholm crossed the Rapido River on January 21.)

Dietrick, Alfred "Al." Personal interview, May 30, 1987. (Platoon sergeant, B Company, 1st Battalion, 141st Infantry Regiment, 36th Division, at the Rapido River in January 1944. Injured while on patrol, January 19, and sent to the hospital.)

Dominguez, Martin. Personal interview, May, 30, 1987. (Corporal, squad leader, C Company, 1st Battalion, 141st Infantry Regiment, 36th Division, when captured by the Germans at Salerno in September 1943.)

Downey, William. Letter, September 7, 1987. (Served with K Company, 3rd Battalion, 143rd Infantry Regiment, 36th Division, in January 1944. Crossed the Rapido on January 21 and was pinned down for close to twenty-four hours before he was able to get back to the American side of the river.)

Dressel, Edward. Conversation, August 28, 1986. (With Headquarters, 141st Infantry Regiment, 36th Division, at the Rapido River in January 1944. Crossed the river during the truce.)

Drummond, Maj. Robert M. "Bulldog," Ret. Personal interview, October 4, 1987. (Technical sergeant, Medical Detachment to Special Troops, 111th Medical Battalion, at the Rapido River in January 1944. He rode in a supply plane during the Rapido battle, over the river's edge.)

Dunn, Charles F. Personal interview, August 28, 1986. (Technical sergeant, 36th Cavalry Reconnaissance Troop and Communication, 36th Division, at the Rapido River in January 1944.)

Evans, Lewis "Dude." Telephone interview, October 5, 1987. (Staff sergeant, K Company, 3rd Battalion, 143rd Infantry Regiment, 36th Division, in January 1944. In charge of a weapons platoon, he crossed the river on January 21 and swam back to the American side.)

Everett, William E. Telephone interview, July 28, 1987. (Second lieutenant, Weapons Platoon, C Company, 1st Battalion, 141st Infantry Regiment, 36th Division, in January 1944.)

Evridge, Tom E. Personal interview, May 30, 1987. (Staff sergeant, B Company, 1st Battalion, 141st Infantry Regiment, 36th Division, at the Rapido River in January 1944.)

Featherston, Ernest. Telephone interview, November 19, 1986. (Sergeant, 133rd Field Artillery Service Battery, 36th Division, at the Rapido River in January 1944.)

Fisher, Frank. Telephone interview, May 7, 1987. (First lieutenant, Headquarters, 1st Battalion, 142nd Infantry Regiment, 36th Division, in corps reserve at the time of the Rapido battle in January 1944.)

Ford, Edgar. Questionnaire, September 1987. (Captain, 141st Infantry Regiment,

36th Division, at the Rapido River in January 1944. Crossed the river on both January 20 and 21; wounded on January 21.)

Frazior, Col. David M., Ret. Telephone interview, November 25, 1986.

————. Personal interview, August 23, 1987.

————. Telephone conversation, May 1987. (Major, battalion commander, 1st Battalion, 143rd Infantry Regiment, 36th Division, in January 1944. Crossed the river twice, once on the first night and again on the second night; wounded the second night.)

German, William A. Telephone interview, July 20, 1987. (Staff sergeant, K Company, 3rd Battalion, 143rd Infantry Regiment, 36th Division, at the Rapido River in January 1944.)

Glover, Robert "Buck." Personal interview, August 28, 1986.

————. Telephone interview, February 28, 1987. (Staff sergeant, C Company, 1st Battalion, 141st Infantry Regiment, 36th Division, in January 1944. Crossed the river on January 20.)

Goad, Roy D. Telephone conversation, November 25, 1986. (In D Company, 1st Battalion, 143rd Infantry Regiment, 36th Division. He was in the hospital in Naples at the time of the Rapido River battle.)

Gomez, Lt. Col. Henry W., Ret. Personal interview, April 26, 1987. (Returned to the 36th Division from Officers Candidate School three or four days after the Rapido River battle, at which time he was a second lieutenant, Service Company Headquarters, 141st Infantry Regiment, 36th Division.)

Houston, Leroy R. Personal interview, June 19, 1987. (Staff sergeant, D Company, 1st Battalion, 143rd Infantry Regiment, 36th Division, at the Rapido River in January 1944.)

Ives, Maj. Gen. Robert, Ret. Personal interview, May 17, 1987. (Lieutenant colonel, G-1, 36th Division, at the Rapido River in January 1944.)

Jameson, Gene "Fort Worth." Personal interview, June 13, 1987.

————. Personal interview, June 19, 1987. (Staff sergeant, D Company, 1st Battalion, 143rd Infantry Regiment, 36th Division, in January 1944. Attached to another company when he crossed the Rapido River on January 20.)

Jary, William E. Personal interview, June 20, 1987. (T/4, Headquarters, 36th Division, in January 1944. Designed and produced a division newspaper that he printed weekly from September 9, 1943, to May 8, 1945.)

Jones, Manuel "Mexican." Personal interview, June 13, 1987. (First sergeant, L Company, 3rd Battalion, 143rd Infantry Regiment, 36th Division, in January 1944. Wounded in a minefield while en route to the Rapido River.)

Kendall, Dell W. Written interview (letter), September 3, 1987.

————. Telephone interview, November 11, 1987. (Gun sergeant, 3rd Squad, 3rd Platoon, Anti-tank Company, 143rd Infantry Regiment, 36th Division, at the Rapido River in January 1944.)

Killian, Col. Joseph O., Ret. Telephone interview, May 12, 1987. (Colonel in command of two battalions in the 19th Engineer Combat Corps. He and his men were attached to the 36th Division for the Rapido crossings; became the II Corps engineer in December 1944.)

Kirby, Billy E. Telephone interview, November 9, 1986.

————. Personal interview, September 4, 1987. (Staff sergeant, K Company, 3rd Battalion, 143rd Infantry Regiment, 36th Division, in January 1944. Crossed the river on January 21 and was wounded; crossed back to the American side the same night.)

Landry, Col. Milton J., Ret. Personal interview, March 20, 1987.

———. Telephone conversation, May 1988. (Major, battalion commander, 2nd Battalion, 141st Infantry Regiment, 36th Division, at the Rapido River in January 1944. He was able to get a battalion of men across the river during the second crossing; wounded four times that day.)

Lockhart, Col. Vincent M. Telephone interview, February 15, 1988. (Captain, assistant G-1, 36th Division, at the Rapido River in January 1944.)

Lord, Edward B. Personal interview, August 2, 1986. (Warrant officer, junior grade, Signal Company, 36th Division, at the Rapido River in January 1944.)

Lurie, Sidney E. Written interview (letter), October 10, 1987.

———. Telephone interview, November 22, 1987. (First lieutenant, 2nd Battalion adjutant, 141st Infantry Regiment, 36th Division, in January 1944. He got about halfway across the river on January 21; took over command of the 2nd Battalion immediately after the Rapido battle.)

Maddox, Jim C. "Bug Eyes." Personal interview, June 13, 1987.

———. Personal interview, September 3, 1987.

———. Personal interview, September 4, 1987.

———. Telephone conversation, June 14, 1988. (Technical sergeant, K Company, 3rd Battalion, 143rd Infantry Regiment, 36th Division, in January 1944. Crossed the Rapido River on January 21; served as company commander for three or four days after the battle because K Company had no officers left at the time.)

Mallory, Robert L. Personal interview, June 13, 1987.

———. Personal interview, September 4, 1987. (Private, K Company, 3rd Battalion, 143rd Infantry Regiment, 36th Division, in January 1944. Crossed the Rapido River on January 21.)

Mangum, Paul. Personal interview, October 4, 1987. (Private first class, D Company, Clearing Station, 111th Medical Battalion, 36th Division, in January 1944. Crossed the river in a pontoon boat during the truce.)

Manton, Richard M. Telephone interview, March 29, 1987.

———. Tape of military experiences, January 1988. (Second lieutenant, E Company, 141st Infantry Regiment, 36th Division, in January 1944. Crossed the Rapido River and fought until he ran out of ammunition; Germans later captured him.)

Marion, Maj. Judge, Ret. Personal interview, August 28, 1986. (First sergeant, Headquarters Company, 3rd Battalion, 141st Infantry Regiment, 36th Division, in January 1944. Crossed the Rapido River.)

McAdams, George. Personal interview, October 6, 1987. (Private first class, D Company, Clearing Station, 111th Medical Battalion, 36th Division, at the Rapido River in January 1944.)

McAfee, Gerald L. "Mac." Personal interview, June 13, 1987. (Sergeant, K Company, 3rd Battalion, 143rd Infantry Regiment, 36th Division, in January 1944. A shell hit in the middle of his pontoon boat while he was on the bank of the Rapido River.)

McClendon, Carl. Personal interview, June 13, 1987. (Corporal, M Company, 3rd

Battalion, 143rd Infantry Regiment, 36th Division, in January 1944. Shot just as he prepared to cross the Rapido River.)

McFadden, Bill C. Telephone interview, September 19, 1987. (Second lieutenant, F Company, 141st Infantry Regiment, 36th Division, in January 1944. Crossed the river during the second crossing attempt.)

McIllhaney, Albert M. Telephone interview, April 27, 1987. (Staff sergeant, B Company, 1st Battalion, 141st Infantry Regiment, 36th Division, at the Rapido River in January 1944.)

McShane, Col. Joseph W., Ret. Telephone interview, May 14, 1987. (G-3 of the 36th Division when it landed at Salerno but not with the 36th at the time of the Rapido battle; transferred to the air force after the war.)

Mehaffey, Maj. Robert E., Ret. Personal interview, August 30, 1986.

———. Telephone interview, March 24, 1988. (Major, battalion commander, 3rd Battalion, 141st Infantry Regiment, 36th Division, in January 1944. Crossed the Rapido River on both January 20 and 21. He received severe wounds just prior to his return across the river on January 22; managed to crawl across the footbridge to the American side.)

Mercer, Col. Lee, Ret. Telephone interview, May 17, 1987. (Second lieutenant when he joined B Company, 1st Battalion, 141st Infantry Regiment, 36th Division.)

Moore, Harry R. Questionnaire, September 1986. (Technical sergeant, 2nd Platoon Leader, F Company, 2nd Battalion, 143rd Infantry Regiment, 36th Division, in January 1944. Crossed the Rapido River and enemy shrapnel hit him just before his return to the American side the next night. Despite his wounds he swam across the river to get back.)

Moser, A. C. "Ace," Jr. Telephone interview, November 11, 1986. (Captain in command of Batteries A, B, and C, 155th Field Artillery, 36th Division. Ten days before the Rapido attack the army transferred him to the Rome Area Command (RAC). He was in Rome six weeks before he rejoined the 36th Division.)

Navarette, Gabriel L. Telephone interview, January 30, 1988. (Second lieutenant, E Company, 2nd Battalion, 141st Infantry Regiment, 36th Division, in January 1944. Made two patrols across the Rapido and was wounded during the second patrol. He had been the first sergeant in E Company prior to his battlefield commission shortly before the Rapido attack.)

Nelson, Rex. Telephone interview, August 29, 1987. (Private, K Company, 3rd Battalion, 143rd Infantry Regiment, 36th Division, in January 1944. Crossed the Rapido River on January 21 in a pontoon boat.)

Parks, John Bob. Personal interview, September 5, 1987. (Technical sergeant, Headquarters Platoon, Company B, 111th Engineers, 36th Division, at the Rapido River in January 1944.)

Penton, Leroy. Personal interview, October 4, 1987. (Supply sergeant, D Company, 111th Medical Battalion, 36th Division, during the Rapido battle in January 1944.)

Petree, Ernest L. Telephone interview, March 29, 1987. (Company commander, C Company, 111th Engineers, 36th Division, at the Rapido River in January 1944.)

Petty, Sammie D. Personal interview, May 30, 1987. (Technical sergeant, 1st Pla-

toon, F Company, 2nd Battalion, 141st Infantry Regiment, in January 1944.
Crossed the Rapido River in a pontoon boat on January 21 and returned to
the American side a short time later.)

Philips, Lt. Col. Julian H., Ret. Telephone interview, November 23, 1986. (First
lieutenant, 1st Platoon, G Company, 2nd Battalion, 143rd Infantry Regiment, 36th Division, in January 1944. Crossed the river during the truce.)

Puck, Brig. Gen. Armin F., Ret. Telephone interview, March 19, 1987.

———. Personal interview, April 27, 1987. (Major, provost marshal, 36th Division, in January 1944. Crossed the Rapido River late in the day on January
21; wounded while he was returning to the American side of the river on the
morning of January 22.)

Purcell, Maj. George, Ret. Personal interview, August 28, 1986. (Private, I Company, 3rd Battalion, 141st Infantry Regiment, 36th Division, in January
1944. Crossed the Rapido River on January 20 and was able to return to the
American side; attempted to cross the river again on January 21 but was unable to.)

Quarles, Col. Julian M., Ret. Written interview, June 1987.

———. Telephone conversation, June 1988. (First lieutenant, company commander, Heavy Weapons Company, 2nd Battalion, 143rd Infantry Regiment, 36th Division, at the Rapido River in January 1944. After his good
friend, Capt. Carl R. Bayne, was killed during the attack, Quarles replaced
him as S-3 of the 2nd Battalion.)

Riley, Lloyd D. Conversation, September 3, 1987. (Forward observer, Battery C,
155th Field Artillery, 36th Division, at the Rapido River in January 1944.)

Robertson, Mrs. Zerk. Telephone conversation, September 1987. (Her husband,
Maj. Zerk Robertson, was a captain, company commander, L Company, 3rd
Battalion, 143rd Infantry Regiment, 36th Division, in January 1944. He
crossed the river during the attack. Major Robertson is deceased.)

Roemer, Msgr. Bernard F. Telephone interview, August 29, 1987. (Assistant division chaplain with the 36th Division, in January 1944. He ministered to the
wounded men as they were brought into the aid and clearing stations.)

Rogers, Lt. Col. Guy L., Ret. Personal interview, June 13, 1987.

———. Questionnaire, June 1987. (Captain, company commander, M Company,
3rd Battalion, 143rd Infantry Regiment, 36th Division, at the Rapido River in
January 1944.)

Rose, Gordon. Personal interview, July 28, 1987. (Squad sergeant, K Company,
3rd Battalion, 143rd Infantry Regiment, 36th Division. Wounded at San Pietro; later recovered from his wounds and rejoined K Company but was not
with them at the time of the Rapido battle.)

Rummel, Charles R., Sr. Telephone interview, November 20, 1986. (Technical
sergeant, platoon leader, K Company, 3rd Battalion, 143rd Infantry Regiment, 36th Division, in January 1944. Crossed the Rapido River on January
21; was severely wounded and captured by the Germans.)

Sadler, Bernis W. Telephone interview, March 2, 1987. (Captain, assistant division engineer, 111th Engineers, 36th Division, at the Rapido River in January
1944.)

Saul, Kenneth. Personal interview, September 5, 1987. (Second lieutenant, G
Company, 2nd Battalion, 141st Infantry Regiment, 36th Division, in January

1944. Attempted to cross the Rapido River the second night but the current pushed his boat back to the American shore. He helped pick up the dead and wounded during the truce.)

Stallings, Fred A., Jr. Telephone interview, September 10, 1987. (Captain who served as the senior aide to General Walker on the general's personal staff at the Rapido River in January 1944.)

Stanuell, Stewart T. Personal interview, October 10, 1986.

———. Telephone interview, September 23, 1987. (Corporal, Battery C, 155th Field Artillery, 36th Division, at the Rapido River in January 1944; a forward observer.)

Steitle, Marvin. Personal interview, September 4, 1987. (Corporal, C Company, 1st Battalion, 141st Infantry Regiment, 36th Division, when he was wounded at Salerno in September 1943.)

Stem, Wiley, Jr. Telephone interview, November 20, 1986. (Captain, company commander, Cannon Company, 143rd Infantry Regiment, 36th Division, at the Rapido River in January 1944.)

Stovall, Col. Oran C., Ret. Personal interview, August 29, 1986.

———. Personal interview, September 20, 1986.

———. Telephone interview, September 4, 1986.

———. Telephone interview, September 6, 1986. (Major, division engineer, 111th Engineers, 36th Division, in January 1944. Performed reconnaissance of the Rapido area for General Walker in early January 1944; also gathered the crossing supplies and prepared the crossing area for the men.)

Streicher, Wilhelm G. Telephone interview, May 18, 1987. (First lieutenant when he joined the Cannon Company, 143rd Infantry Regiment, 36th Division, in February 1944. Later served as the company commander of both F Company and G Company, 143rd Infantry Regiments.)

Strom, Carl. Personal interview, August 29, 1986. (Second lieutenant, B Company, 1st Battalion, 141st Infantry Regiment, 36th Division, in January 1944. Crossed the Rapido River on January 20. Several days later he and Pfc Henry von Hollan met with German Captain Huffman and Sgt. Joseph Jung on the American side of the river to negotiate a truce in the C Company area.)

Sudatz, John R. Telephone interview, September 17, 1987. (Private first class, 111th Engineers, 36th Division, at the Rapido River in January 1944; helped in the attempt to erect a Bailey Bridge.)

Sumner, Lt. Col. James D., Ret. Telephone interview, September 9, 1987.

———. Telephone interview, September 10, 1987. (Major, battalion executive officer, 3rd Battalion, 143rd Infantry Regiment, 36th Division, at the Rapido River in January 1944.)

Sunday, Zeb. Personal interview, September 5, 1987. (Corporal, B Company, 1st Battalion, 143rd Infantry Regiment, 36th Division, in January 1944. Made two attempts to cross the Rapido River in a boat, one on January 20 and another on January 21.)

Taylor, Bvt. Gen. James E., Ret. Telephone interview, August 20, 1986. (Lieutenant colonel, battalion commander, 131st Field Artillery, 36th Division, at the Rapido River in January 1944.)

Terry, Enoch Harold. Telephone interview, September 29, 1987. (First sergeant of the 3rd Battalion, 143rd Infantry Regiment, 36th Division, in January 1944. Crossed the Rapido River during the truce.)

Tidwell, Riley M. Personal interview, June 13, 1987. (Private first class, B Company, 1st Battalion, 143rd Infantry Regiment, 36th Division. Crossed the river to the German side on both January 20 and 21.)

Trevino, Rudolph M. Telephone interview, November 20, 1986.

———. Personal interview, March 19, 1987.

———. Letter, April 18, 1987. (Private first class, E Company, 2nd Battalion, 141st Infantry Regiment, 36th Division, in January 1944. Crossed the Rapido River on January 21 and was captured by the Germans on January 22.)

Tully, Martin J. Telephone interview, September 6, 1987. (First lieutenant, B Company, 1st Battalion, 141st Infantry Regiment, 36th Division, at the Rapido River in 1944. He continued to organize the area after he had been wounded on the night of January 20.)

Turney, Otis P. Conversation, August 29, 1986. (With the 36th Signal Company at the Rapido River in January 1944.)

Vieregge, Carl "Banjo Eyes." Personal interview, June 13, 1987. (Sergeant, K Company, 3rd Battalion, 143rd Infantry Regiment, 36th Division, in January 1944. Crossed the river on January 21 in a pontoon boat and swam back.)

von Hollan, Henry. Questionnaire, August 1986. (Private first class, C Company, 1st Battalion, 141st Infantry Regiment, 36th Division, in January 1944. Interpreter for Carl Strom when Strom negotiated a truce with Captain Dryoff.)

Walker, Fred, L., Jr. Telephone conversation, September 4, 1986. (Lieutenant colonel, G-3, 36th Division, at the Rapido River in January 1944.)

Westbrook, Lt. Col. Joel W., Ret. Telephone interview, September 6, 1987. (Captain, assistant S-3 and liaison officer, 143rd Infantry Regiment, 36th Division, in January 1944. Became the 1st Battalion executive officer and S-3 after the 1st Battalion lost its battalion commander, executive officer, S-2, and S-3 at the Rapido River. He remained in both positions until Capt. Marion Parks Bowden came in as the executive officer in the mountains above Cassino, after which time Westbrook retained the position of S-3.)

Wethington, Ervald "Wimpy." Personal interview, September 5, 1987. (Private first class, B Company, 1st Battalion, 143rd Infantry Regiment, 36th Division, in January 1944. Crossed the Rapido River three times — twice in battle and once during the truce.)

Wheelis, John D. Personal interview, June 13, 1987. (Staff sergeant, K Company, 3rd Battalion, 143rd Infantry Regiment, 36th Division, in January 1944. Crossed the river on January 21.)

Wilbur, Richard. Telephone interview, June 15, 1988. (Private, Signal Company, 36th Division, at the Rapido River in January 1944.)

Wiley, William Greg. Personal interview, August 29, 1986. (Technical sergeant, I Company, 3rd Battalion, 141st Infantry Regiment, 36th Division, in January 1944. Crossed the river during the battle.)

Wilson, Col. Ben, Jr. Telephone interview, July 25, 1987. (Major in service at Division Headquarters at the time of the Rapido River crossings in January 1944.)

Letters

Clark, Mark W. Letter to Maj. Gen. Geoffery Keyes, January 27, 1944. From Maj. Gen. Fred L. Walker, Ret. "Comments on the Rapido River Crossing, January 1944."

Maps

Crossing Site and Division Area. Map. Italy: 36th Division, 1944. From the files of Col. Oran C. Stovall, Ret.

Military Reports

Adams, Lt. Col. John C. L., Commanding 141st Infantry. "APO #36, Memorandum: To General Walker." N.p.: Headquarters Second Battalion 141st Infantry, January 30, 1944. From the files of Lt. Col. Julian Quarles, Ret.

"APO #36, Operations in Italy January 1944." N.p.: Headquarters 111th Medical Battalion, 1944. From 36th Division Collection, Archives Division, Texas State Library, Austin, Texas.

"APO #36, U.S. Army. General Orders No. 88 Award of Silver Star, Award of Oak Leaf Cluster." N.p.: Headquarters 36th Infantry Division, March 30, 1944. From the files of Col. Julian Quarles, Ret.

"APO #36, U.S. Army. Operations in Italy January 1944, Annex #6." N.p.: 141st Infantry Regiment, February 12, 1944. From 36th Division Collection, Archives Division, Texas State Library, Austin, Texas.

"APO #36, U.S. Army. Headquarters 141st Infantry Regiment, Rifle." Statement. Pvt. Savino Manella, Medical Detachment. January 22, 1944.

"APO #36, U.S. Army. Operations in Italy January 1944, Annex No. 7." N.p.: Headquarters 142nd Infantry, February 10, 1944. From 36th Division Collection, Archives Division, Texas State Library, Austin, Texas.

Denholm, Lt. Col. Charles J., CO 2nd Battalion, 143rd Infantry Regiment. "Historical Record Second Battalion, 143rd Infantry, from 212335 Jan. 44 to 221200 Jan. 44." N.p.: Second Battalion, 143rd Infantry Regiment, January 21–22, 1944.

"Operations in Italy, February 1944, 111th Engineers Combat Battalion."

"Operations in Italy, Annex No. 8." N.p.: 143rd Infantry, February 12, 1944. From 36th Division Collection, Archives Division, Texas State Library, Austin, Texas. Also from the files of Col. Julian M. Quarles, Ret.

Roster of casualties from January 1 to 31, 1944. N.p.: 143rd Infantry, January 1944.

U.S. Army Ground Forces. Office of Technical Information. "Facts Sheet on the 36th Infantry Division." Mimeo. AFG, 1945.

Walker, Maj. Gen. [Fred L.] "Appendix 'a' FO 42." N.p.: Hq. 36th Division, 1944.

Wilbur, Brig. Gen. William H. "APO #36, U.S.A. Special Report, Operations of 141st Infantry in the Crossing of the Rapido River on January 20 to 23, 1944." N.p.: Office of the Assistant Division Commander, January 26, 1944. From the files of Lt. Col. Julian H. Philips, Ret.

Yater, Maj. Tolbert F., Commanding Medical Corps. "APO #36, Operations in Italy." N.p.: 111th Medical Battalion, March 1, 1944. From 36th Division Collection, Archives Division, Texas State Library, Austin, Texas.

Newsletters

Webb, Craig. "Veterans to Mark Rapido River Folly." *The T Patcher: Texas 36th Division Association Newsletter,* November 1984. [Reprinted] from *Washington Post,* September 25, 1985.]

Newspapers

"Army Hero Loses Life in River." (AP, Conowingo, MD) September 23, 1965. From the files of Col. Julian M. Quarles, Ret.
Bracker, Milton. "General Mark Clark Gets the Tough Jobs." *New York Times,* September 19, 1943.
Dietrick, Alfred. "Infantrymen Prepare to Invade Italy." *Express News,* n.d.
Dixon, Kenneth L. "Voice Husky, General Bids Goodby." *Washington Post,* July 23, 1944.
Fowler, Wick. "Battle Casualties: Meticulous Care Exercised In Identification Process." Wick Fowler Columns, 36th Division Collection, Archives Division, Texas State Library, Austin, Texas.
————. "Killed in Action: Army Double Checks Reports Before Notifying Relatives." Wick Fowler Columns, 36th Division Collection, Archives Division, Texas State Library, Austin, Texas.
Hill, Bob. "The Rapido: A River of Death in World War II." *Louisville Times,* January 21, 1984.
"Medal of Honor Won By Sergeant Last Seen Charging Enemy Alone." *Army Times,* April 28, 1945. From the files of Col. Julian M. Quarles, Ret.
Roddy, Roy. "Hellfire and Brimstone at Rapido." *Breckenridge American,* August 7, 1986. From the files of Maj. Robert E. Mehaffey.
Wilson, P. W. "The Appian Road to Rome." *New York Times* 6, October 17, 1943: 34.

Periodicals

"An American Abroad." *Time,* June 27, 1946: 27–30.
Blau, Gene. "The Day the Rapido Ran Red with G.I. Blood." *Cavalcade,* [October 1, 1960?].
Feder, Sid. "They'll Never Forget Mark Clark." *Saturday Evening Post* 218, May 18, 1946: 20–21, 136–139.
Fuller, Maj. Gen. J. F. C., British Army, Ret. "The Why and Wherefore of the Italian Offensive." *Newsweek* 23, June 5, 1944: 22.
Kesselring, Former Field Marshal, interview. "How Hitler Could Have Won." *U.S. News and World Report* 39, September 2, 1955: 62–66.
Mitchell, Donald W. "From Calabria to Cassino." *Current History* No. 633, May 1944: 405–409.
"Murder at the Rapido?" *Time* 47, January 28, 1946: 24.
"Sad Sack Role." *Time* 44, December 11, 1944: 29.

Sevareid, Eric. "The Price We Pay in Italy." *Nation* 159, December 9, 1944: 713–714.

[Stovall, Oran C.] "The Odyssey of a Texas Citizen Soldier." Robert L. Wagner, ed. *Southwestern Historical Quarterly* 62, no. 1, July 1968: 60–87.

von Senger und Etterlin, Frido. "Monte Cassino." *New English Review*, April 1949: 250–252.

Walker, Fred L. "The 36th Was a Great Fighting Unit." *Southwestern Historical Quarterly* 62, July 1968: 40–59.

Wharton, Don. "Escape From a Prison Train." *The Fighting 36th Historical Quarterly* 2, no. 1, Spring 1982: 13–18. [Reprinted from *Look*, March 12, 1945.] From the files of Col. Julian M. Quarles, Ret.

Unpublished Material

"History of the 143rd Infantry." N.p: n.p., [1946–47?].

Strom, Carl. "Return to Cassino 1985." N.p.: n.p., n.d.

Walker, Maj. Gen. Fred L. "My Story of the Rapido Crossing." N.p.: n.p., 1960.

———. "Comments of the Rapido River Crossing, January 1944." Alexandria, VA: n.p., 1960.

———. "Mission Impossible at Cassino." N.p.: n.p., n.d.

Wilbur, Brig. Gen. William H. Personal notes.

The 36th Infantry Division on D-Day at Salerno, Italy.
— Reproduced from holdings of the Texas State Archives

Company G, 141st Infantry, prepared for the fight, January 15, 1944.
— US Army photo

Reconnaissance Company, 636th Tank Destroyer Battalion.

143rd Infantry Message Center at the Rapido River, January 1944.
— US Army photo

36th Division review near Salerno to bid farewell to Major General Walker, who departed for reassignment as commandant at Fort Benning, Georgia.

Staff officers of the 36th Division, May 1941.
— Reproduced from holdings of the Texas State Archives

The Rapido — A River Swift and Deadly
[All photos of the Rapido River are from the files of Judge Robert Stem.
Judge Stem took the photos while on a visit to Italy in 1988. His father,
Col. Wylie W. Stem, was the company commander of the Cannon Company, 143rd Infantry Regiment, at the Rapido River.]

*The beginning of the "S" curve of the Rapido River. To the right is the side occupied
by the 36th Division. Note the swirling nature of the water.*

Photograph taken from the "S" curve in the Rapido River, with the Cassino Abbey high in the background. The building, which appears to be a corn storage warehouse, is the only new building in the plain approaching the river.

Looking downriver from the "S" curve. The buildings in the background are on the German side of the river.

Looking back toward the town of Sant' Angelo from the "S" curve.

In the background is the hill on which the 36th Division was encamped, as seen from the "S" curve of the Rapido River.

The beginning of the "S" curve as seen from Sant' Angelo.

The American side of the Rapido River, where "T-Patchers" had to carry their boats for the battle crossing.

The bridge is the site of the crossing of the Rapido River by the 141st Infantry Regiment. The left side of the area is the American side.

The prominent position of Monte Cassino overlooking the Rapido River Valley graphically portrays the German army advantage in the battle. This photo was taken from the American side.

Photograph taken from the hill on the American side, where assault boats had to be carried by the "T-Patchers." The town of Sant' Angelo is seen in the distance.

The crossing site of the 141st Infantry Regiment directly in front of Sant' Angelo. This photo was taken from the town square.

The Cassino Abbey as seen from the village of Cassino.

The blockhouse where the 143rd Infantry Regiment encamped. Approaching the building is Robert Stem, the photographer.

Group from F Company, 141st Infantry Regiment (left to right): Fred A. Ayers, mess sergeant; Herman E. Dowell, 3rd Platoon; Sammie D. Petty, 1st Platoon; Wayne Jenkins, Weapons Platoon; Robert W. Rencher, 2nd Platoon.

Boats and pontoons used for the Rapido River crossing.

*Gen. Mark Clark awarding the Silver
Star to a 36th Division soldier.*

S/Sgt. Lewis Evans with group of his men at mess.

Samuel Edgar Mallory, Frank [?], and Pvt. Robert Mallory, K Company, 143rd Infantry, shown left to right. The two brothers had this reunion in Pompeii.

Left to right, 1st Sgt. Enoch Harold Terry, 3rd Battalion, 143rd Infantry, Pvt. Albin C. Svacina, and Pvt. M. L. Hester.

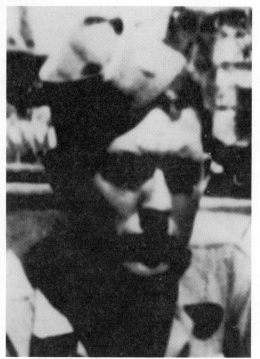

Pvt. Paul Blackmer, K Company, 143rd Infantry.

Capt. Edgar Ford, 3rd Battalion, 141st Infantry Regiment, crossed the Rapido River and was wounded on January 21.

2nd Lt. Alvin Amelunke, M Company, 3rd Battalion, 143rd Infantry, crossed the river on January 21. He received a battlefield commission two days before the Rapido River battle.

T/Sgt. Harry R. Moore, F Company, 143rd Infantry.

Pfc Ervald Wethington, B Company, 143rd Infantry.

Sgt. Joseph Cotropia, H Company, 143rd Infantry.

Maj. Milton J. Landry, 2nd Battalion commander, 141st Infantry. He crossed the river on January 21 and was wounded four times that day.

Major General Truesdale presenting the Silver Star to Maj. Milton J. Landry for action at the Rapido River on January 21–22.

Maj. David M. Frazior, commander, First Battalion, 143rd Infantry, crossed the river on January 20 and 21 and was wounded the second night.

Pvt. Robert Mallory (left) and S/Sgt. Fred D. Coe in Naples, 1944.

Willie Traxter (left) and S/Sgt. Lewis Evans, K Company, 143rd Infantry.

Maj. James D. Sumner, Jr., executive officer, 3rd Battalion, 143rd Infantry.

S/Sgt. Robert "Buck" Glover, C Company, 141st Infantry.

Gun Sgt. Dell W. Kendall, 3rd Squad, 3rd Platoon, Anti-tank Company, 143rd Infantry.

Cpl. Stewart T. Stanwell, Battery C, 155th Field Artillery.

T/Sgt. Jim C. Maddox, K Company, 143rd Infantry, crossed the Rapido River on January 21.

*Lt. Gen. Mark Wayne Clark on his
way to Salerno, September 1943.*
                    — US Army photo

*Lt. Col. Albert B. Crowther served as
the intelligence officer of the 36th Division at the crossing of the Rapido
River.*

*T/Sgt. Mac Acosta, C Company, 1st
Battalion, 141st Infantry.*

*Maj. Oran C. Stovall, 36th Division
engineer.*

2nd Lt. Kenneth Saul, G Company, 2nd Battalion, 141st Infantry.

Capt. Richard M. Burrage, company commander of Headquarters 1st Battalion, 143rd Infantry, who also served as battalion adjutant. He crossed the Rapido on January 20.

Capt. Fred A. Stallings, Jr., served on General Walker's personal staff as senior aide.

Pfc Rudolph M. Trevino, E Company, 141st Infantry, crossed the river on January 21 and was captured by the Germans.

Sgt. Alfred "Al" Dietrick, B Company, 141st Infantry, Altivila, on September 19, 1943.

T/Sgt. Sammie D. Petty, F Company, 141st Infantry in Naples, 1944.

Brig. Gen. William H. Wilbur, assistant division commander, 36th Division. — US Army photo

2nd Lt. Carl J. Strom, Company B, 141st Infantry, who negotiated a six-hour truce with Germans at the Rapido River January 25, 1944.

Hauptaman (Captain) Adam Dyroff, German army officer with whom Lieutenant Strom negotiated the truce.

Forty-one years later the two officers who negotiated truce terms at the Rapido River met in Oberhofen, Germany. Adam Dyroff was the German officer and Carl Strom the American. Shown left to right are Bob Von Tourssaint of Company C, 141st Infantry, Dryoff, Strom, and Sgt. Joseph Jung, who was with Dyroff at the truce meeting.

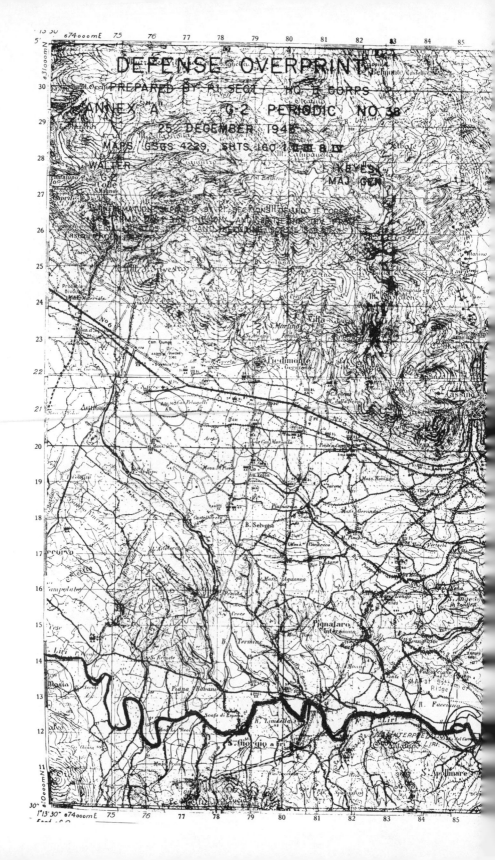

DEFENSE OVERPRINT

PREPARED BY HQ SECT   HQ II CORPS

ANNEX "A"   G-2 PERIODIC   NO. 38

25 DECEMBER 1943

MAPS GSGS 4229, SHTS 160 I, II, III & IV

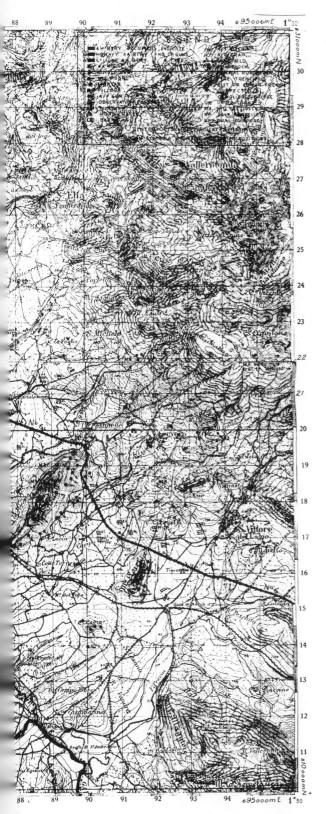

Military map of American defensive positions in the Rapido area, December 25, 1945. This copy was provided by one of the T-Patchers who took part in the battle.

Kriegsgefangenen-Offz.-Lager 64
(Oflag 64)

Datum: 22.8.1944

Ungültig   ## Ungültig

als Legitimation für den öffentlichen Verkehr.

Gültig NUR im Kriegsgefangenen-Lager.

Der Kgf. hat diese Erkennungskarte und die Erkennnungsmarke des Lagers stets bei sich zu führen. Bei Kontrolle sind beide vorzuzeigen. Verlust ist sofort zu melden.

The P. o. W. has always to carry with him this indentification card and his tag. On control both have to be presented. The loss of the card or tag has to be reported immediately.

Fingerabdruck d. r. Z. F.

Name Manton, Richard M.

Dienstgrad Leutnant

Erkennungs-Nr. 270184/IVB

Copies of an identification card and a post card issued to Lt. Richard M. Manton, who was captured during the battle of the Rapido River.

TRANSIT CAMP FOR P. O. W.

FP. Nr. 31979

Date JANUARY 27, 1944

I am prisoner - ~~slightly wounded 1)~~ - in German captivity, but in perfect health. From here I shall be transported during the next few days to another camp, the address of which I shall give you later. Only there I can get your letters and can reply to them.

Kindest regards Rich

NAME AND CHRISTIAN NAME   MANTON, RICHARD

RANK   SECOND LIEUT

UNIT   U. S. ARMY

1) STRETCH OUT IF NOT CORRECT
BESIDES NAME, RANK AND UNIT ADD NOTHING.
WRITE IN BLOCK LETTERS AND SIGN LEGIBLY.

Index

197